A Gentleman Adventurer

A GENTLEMAN ADVENTURER

THE ARCTIC DIARIES OF R.H.G. BONNYCASTLE

Edited and Compiled by
Heather Robertson
A RICHARD BONNYCASTLE BOOK 2

LESTER & ORPEN DENNYS

Canadian Cataloguing in Publication Data

  Bonnycastle, R. H. G. (Richard Henry
  Gardyne), 1903-1968.
    A gentleman adventurer

  ISBN 0-88619-074-6

  1. Bonnycastle, R. H. G. (Richard Henry
  Gardyne), 1903-1968.   2. Canada,
  Northern – Description and travel.
  * 3. Hudson's Bay Company.   I.
  Robertson, Heather, 1942-   II. Title.

  FC3963.1.B65A3 1984   917.19′042
  C84-099073-1
  F1090.5.B65A3 1984

Every reasonable effort has been made to trace
ownership of copyright materials. Information will
be welcomed which will enable the Publisher to rec-
tify any reference or credit in future printings.

Design: Catherine Wilson/Sunkisst Graphics
Maps: Geographics
Typesetting: ART-U Graphics Ltd.
Printed: T. H. Best Printing Company Ltd.

Printed and bound in Canada for
Lester & Orpen Dennys Limited
78 Sullivan Street
Toronto, Ontario
Canada M5T 1C1

The Hudson's Bay Company Archives in Winnipeg provided official reports written by R. H. G. Bonnycastle and his colleagues as well as documents relating to this period in Company history. Archivist Anne Morton made a special effort to locate material relating to R. H. G. Bonnycastle. The excerpts from the post journals of Aklavik and Coppermine quoted on pp. 106-111, 114, 124-139 are also from the Hudson's Bay Company Archives.

The excerpt from *The Beaver* and the photos indicated below are supplied by the library and photograph archives at Hudson's Bay House in Winnipeg. Information relating to Archbishop and Mrs. Isaac O. Stringer, and photographs indicated below, are from the Anglican Church Archives in Toronto.

C. H. "Punch" Dickins, retired Hudson's Bay Company post managers L. A. Learmonth and A. C. Copland, and Gerry Malahar of Winnipeg were helpful with personal recollections.

Photographs courtesy of the Hudson's Bay Company pp.13, 18, 28, 36, 40 (bottom), 59, 73, 92, 118, 120, 122-124, 128, 130, 137, 140, 147, 151, 153, 156, 161, 166, 168, 179, 197, 200; photographs courtesy of the Public Archives of Canada pp.25, 33, 51, 98 (left), 120, 126, 159 (bottom), 176-178, 189; photographs courtesy of the General Synod Archives, Anglican Church of Canada pp.99, 121.

Photographs pp. 213, 215, and 217 are by Margaret Bourke-White for LIFE Magazine © Time Inc.

Preface

For officers and servants of the Hudson's Bay Company it was a tradition and an obligation to keep a daily journal. At Hudson's Bay House, the Canadian headquarters in Winnipeg, Manitoba, clerks noted in a special ledger visitors received and memos drafted; in Indian tents and trappers' cabins, Company inspectors warmed their hands over campfires and scribbled their opinions in pocket diaries; at snowbound fur trade posts, Company managers bent over kerosene lamps and carefully recorded the temperature, the weather, the trade done, and any bits of news they had the time or imagination to include.

Until radio and airmail transformed the fur trade in the twenties, this Journal of Events, kept in duplicate and forwarded to head office at the close of every season, was the Company's main source of information about the business routine of its hundreds of isolated posts. The importance attached to the journal is reflected in the admonition pasted on the inside of every heavy cardboard cover: "Your ability to keep this book in a neat and intelligent manner will be an indication of your character and ability as a Post Manager."

The daily journals of the early Hudson's Bay Company explorers, such as Samuel Hearne's *A Journey from Prince of Wales Fort on Hudson's Bay to the Northern Ocean*, published in 1772, established the Company's claim to thousands of square miles of virgin territory and brought immortality to their authors. For modern Company men like Dick Bonnycastle, who joined the Winnipeg office as an accountant in 1925 at the age of twenty-two, a diary formed the basis of the exhaustive annual reports they were obliged to submit, often after many months' travelling between remote trading posts. A diary also had literary potential; many retired fur traders published popular novels or memoirs based on their experiences in the north. Indeed, Bonnycastle himself intended to write a book based on his diaries, but when he died suddenly in 1968 he had barely begun to work on the project.

The diaries left by Dick Bonnycastle cover a period of roughly twelve years, from 1926 to 1937, when he travelled frequently down the Mackenzie River and across the Western Arctic, first as a junior accountant and then as district manager of the Western Arctic. The diaries are fragmentary—entire months and years are missing—but it is amazing that they exist at all. Bonnycastle wrote under conditions of extreme physical discomfort, often after days on the trail and nights without sleep, scribbling in his little notebook by the light of a campfire, surrounded by chattering Indian children or bickering trappers, tucked into his deerskin sleeping-bag against the bitter Arctic cold.

Bonnycastle began these travels when he was just twenty-three, the same age Samuel Hearne had been when he started his famous journeys, and the early diaries are those of a young man—bursting with energy, obsessed with food and sleep, passionately curious about people and places, eager for adventure, innocent, trusting, judgemental, and emotional. He was also gregarious, enthusiastic, talkative. He delighted in gossip, and gossip—the moccasin telegraph that bound the isolated communities of the north together—was the lifeblood of the fur trade. But unlike most fur traders, who had neither the ability to observe carefully nor the grasp of language to express themselves, Bonnycastle had a keen ear, a sharp eye for the significant detail, and a true diarist's empathy for the strains and subtleties of human relationships. He also carried two cameras on his trips, and supplemented his journals with snapshots that have the same candid, unpretentious directness as his prose.

Although Bonnycastle used his diaries as a basis for his reports, the diaries themselves were intended for no one's eyes but his own—certainly not for the eyes of his superiors in the Company—and he kept them private until his death. Their privacy is, today, the source of their strength and charm; they give us an intimate, inside glimpse into a vanished world and into the personality of a man who helped to shape it. They are more than a travel story or a businessman's notebook; they are an anxious young man's friend and confidant, a confessional, a place to express anger and come to terms with failure, to relieve the guilt, fear, and criticism which the rigid decorum of the Hudson's Bay Company made it impossible to express openly.

In the tradition of Hearne, Bonnycastle organized his diaries into journeys. Four journeys, from 1928 to 1931, are published here. These were years of revolutionary change in the north, a period of intense culture shock, and Bonnycastle was both witness and hero—he turns up, in fact, as a character in books by people he himself is busy writing about. The enormous popular success of explorer Vilhjalmur Stefansson's *The Friendly Arctic* had created a literary chic for the north; down the Mackenzie River came a horde of naturalists and anthropologists, painters, journalists, and geographers, government inspectors, reindeer herders, and Russian refugees, missionaries, geologists, and mounted policemen, all furiously snapping photographs and scribbling, scribbling in their journals. Eskimos kept diaries in Eskimo and Indians in syllabics; the volume of published and unpublished material about this brief period in the north makes it one of the best documented in Canadian history. Bonnycastle made *Life* magazine in the summer of 1937, when the famous American photographer Margaret Bourke-White accompanied the Governor-General, Lord Tweedsmuir, down the Mackenzie River; Bonnycastle published his own account of that trip, "Lord Tweedsmuir as a Mountaineer", in *The*

Canadian Alpine Journal. Indeed there are as many photographs *of* Dick Bonny-castle as *by* Dick Bonnycastle; tall, blond, and handsome in his caribou parka or *artigi*, he was the perfect image of the romantic adventurer.

The diary entries presented here have been shortened, trimmed of repetition and redundancy, and edited for clarity and coherence. But the voice and style are Bonnycastle's own; they reflect the attitudes of his time as much as his own opinions and observations.

Dick Bonnycastle discovered no new lands or lost tribes; his geography was the bleak bureaucracy of the Hudson's Bay Company at a time when it was struggling for survival in the face of technological evolution, economic collapse, and social upheaval. He is in the thick of the action, and lucky enough to encounter all the danger and disaster the most intrepid explorer could wish for. Yet his four journeys also provide the framework for an inner voyage, the transformation of an impressionable young accountant into a seasoned, expe-rienced executive who is able to face frustration and hardship with patience, courage and good humour.

The Bonnycastle diaries are an adventure story, an autobiography, and a unique, unprecedented glimpse into the secret workings of one of the world's greatest commercial empires. Diaries record the present for the future; the Bonnycastle diaries capture a brief moment with a clarity and authenticity that increase as the moment recedes in time.

Introduction

In the 1920s, the Company of Adventurers of England Trading into Hudson Bay was doing things in much the same way as it had since being granted a royal charter in 1670. The basic barter of the fur trade had not changed. The Company continued to count with its own money, the skin. Beads and calico, tea, tobacco, lard, and ammunition still formed the staple trade goods, and both goods and furs still travelled by ship, steamboat, barge, canoe, dogsled, wagon, and on foot. The Company even measured time by its own calendar: the Company year, or "outfit", started in June when the first boats began to ply the rivers and lakes, bringing in a fresh supply of trade goods and taking out the winter's catch of fur. Year One was 1670, the year of the first shipment of trade goods to Canada; Dick Bonnycastle joined during Outfit 255.

After two centuries of monopoly and another fifty years of dominance, the Hudson's Bay Company had become weighty with tradition, encrusted with ritual, burdened by its own fame. Although it had relinquished control of the Canadian north-west to Ottawa in 1870, the Company remained as imperious and autocratic in its attitudes as it had been when its governors ruled half a continent. It was less a commercial enterprise than an austere religious order modelled on the lines of the Royal Navy. Obedience was demanded above all else; Company "officers" were distinct from "servants", and the officers themselves were ranked by the amount of brass on their caps, from the district manager's "badge with flag and gold leaves, gold cord and braid on peak" down to the post manager's simple flag. Indians and Eskimos were hired as Company guides, interpreters, and handymen but they occupied a lower social order; post managers were forbidden to entertain natives in their homes even when they were married to native women.

HBC trading posts were laid out in military-style compounds with the warehouse, manager's house, and storehouse forming three sides of a square surrounded by a picket fence. The buildings were uniformly painted white with red roofs, red doors, and green trim. The Company was even more precise about the sign, specifying length, breadth, thickness of the board, and style of lettering: "The Company's signboard must be lettered in Old English style to conform with the standard signboard as authorized," stated the post manager's manual. "At inland and other isolated posts the lettering will be white on a black background; at 'line' posts the lettering will be gold on a dark green background."

The governors demanded from all Company employees, officers or servants, a level of performance and devotion to duty all but beyond the capabilities of the most brilliant and dedicated; when they failed, they were verbally abused, arbitrarily transferred, or dismissed without pension. The governor in London ruled with the power and the terror of a Sun King; the humble post manager was little more than a slave. He was to keep the compound clean, the grass short, and the store scrupulously tidy; he was not to gamble, make homebrew, trap or trade for his personal benefit. He could vote but he could not take part in politics or public affairs, make a charitable donation, employ a relative, accept a present, enter into a contract, institute a legal proceeding or marry without permission from the district manager. He was not to discuss Company affairs with anyone outside the Company. He could be transferred or dismissed without notice or appeal. In return, he received a house, a small amount of furniture, and a ration of food which he was expected to supplement by hunting and fishing. Young men apprenticed as clerks for five years at $250 a year; even after a lifetime in Company service, few post managers made more than $1,000 a year. The Company's parsimony matched its passion for profit.

A detailed assessment of each employee's abilities was kept on record at the Winnipeg office. Emphasis was on moral character, self-discipline, and ambition. Loyalty stood at the head of the list, salesmanship towards the bottom; a man could be forgiven much if he was considered a good "Company man". Anyone who deserted to the opposition—there were many—was blacklisted as a renegade. Post managers were inspected regularly by district managers and district inspectors and were subject to flying visits by the fur trade inspector, the fur trade commissioner and, once every hundred years or so, the governor himself. Otherwise post managers were left to their own devices, with only the stern instruction of the manual to fall back on:

> To be successful a manager must possess initiative; he must be constantly seeking ways and means of profitably increasing the volume of his business. He must have a thorough knowledge of his customers and be able to direct their energies, particularly of natives, for their own advancement as well as for the advancement of the interests of the company. Every activity of the unit should be carefully examined and controlled at all times and the care of the property of the company should be kept constantly in mind.

For its servants, the Company had traditionally relied on Highland Scots, Ulstermen, and Orkney Islanders—people accustomed to isolation; the governors were English. It was also traditional for Company men to work their way up from apprentice clerk to manager to inspector and commissioner through long, patient years of service at trading posts. The few Canadians in the Company service were almost all the mixed-blood sons of Scots factors who had married Indian wives—and their prospects for advancement were small.

Dick Bonnycastle broke that tradition. Even though he was Canadian he came in, as one post manager put it, "through the front door". He was hired as an accountant at the Winnipeg office for $1,200 a year. Within four years he would be appointed district manager of the Western Arctic without having spent a single year as a post trader. His rapid advancement put some noses out of joint: he symbolized change, youth, modernization, efficiency, boldness. However much these qualities would have endeared Bonnycastle to Prince Rupert and the original Adventurers, they were not highly valued in 1925. Yet Bonnycastle's methods and personality would do a good deal to push the Company, with much anguish and upheaval, into the twentieth century; by the time of his death it would be both urban and essentially Canadian.

Richard Henry Gardyne Bonnycastle was born on a homestead near Dauphin, Manitoba on August 25, 1903, the eldest of the six children of the local magistrate, Judge A.L. Bonnycastle, and Ellen Boulton. His mother's father was Major Charles A. Boulton,* who had led Boulton's Scouts against Louis Riel and the Métis in the North-west Rebellion of 1885. Major Boulton was as renowned in the west as Riel himself: during the first Riel Rebellion in 1869 he had led a group of homesteaders in unsuccessful opposition to the Métis government. Captured by Riel, imprisoned at Fort Garry, and sentenced to death, Boulton was reprieved only when Riel's attention was diverted to another prisoner—the irascible Orangeman, Thomas Scott, was shot instead. Major Boulton published an account of his adventures, *Reminiscences of the North West Rebellions*, one of the best true stories in Canadian literature, and was appointed to the Senate by Sir John A. Macdonald.

Richard himself was named for his ancestor Sir Richard Bonnycastle, a captain in the Royal Engineers who was posted to Canada following the Rebellion of 1837 to strengthen Kingston's defences against possible American invasion, and laid out much of old Toronto. Knighted for his efforts, Sir Richard retired to a farm near Belleville, Ontario, and published a series of lively accounts of his travels throughout his adopted country: *The Canadas in 1841; Newfoundland in 1842; Canada and the Canadians*, and *Canada As It Is, Was and May Be*.

Like most of the settlers who came west from Ontario before the railroad, the Boultons and Bonnycastles were stoutly British, Anglican, and Conservative. Young Richard's grandmother, Augusta, Major Boulton's widow—known affectionately to the family as "the Duchess"—was adamant that the refinements of civilization should be preserved on the very edge of the great, lone land and her daughter Ellen, a strong-minded woman who wrote poetry and founded her hometown newspaper, supported the family traditions. The Bonnycastle children hunted rabbits and hoed potatoes like other prairie

---

* The Grange, an elegant Toronto home now preserved as part of the Art Gallery of Ontario, was built in 1817 for one of the Boultons.

"The Duchess" presides over tea. Richard stands in back row centre

children, but they also came home for afternoon tea, dressed for dinner, studied the piano, and played tennis on the lawn.

Dick was sent to school at St. John's College in Winnipeg, then Trinity College, Toronto. He entered Wadham College, Oxford, in 1922 and in 1923 he played centre on the undefeated Oxford hockey team which won the world championship; a future prime minister, Lester Pearson, played defence and a future governor-general, Roland Michener, was spare. After taking his BA and his law degree in 1924, Bonnycastle was called to the bar in Manitoba and started practice with the prestigious Winnipeg firm of Aikens, Macauley. He hated it.

Bonnycastle (second from right) at Wadham College, 1924

10

The Oxford hockey team goes to Belgium. Bonnycastle on left at back; front, from left, Roland Michener, Lester Pearson

When a family friend, British consul A.N. Wiseman, suggested a job with the Hudson's Bay Company, Bonnycastle jumped at it. It offered him everything law did not: challenge, excitement, physical activity, the risk of the unknown, and the possibility of a brilliant business career. The Hudson's Bay Company was a legend; the Arctic was a mystery. The North-west Passage had been conquered less than twenty years before by Norwegian explorer Roald Amundsen, and Vilhjalmur Stefansson's voyages across the ice pack had created a sensation in the early 1920s. The Arctic was Canada's new—and last—frontier. Its appeal was irresistible. Sir Richard Bonnycastle had stood at the brink of Niagara Falls; Major Boulton had reached the North Saskatchewan River; Dick Bonnycastle would go farther—to the edge of the known world, to the frozen Arctic sea where Sir John Franklin and his ships, the *Erebus* and *Terror*, had vanished only eighty years before.

He would go, and he would find everything he was looking for; he would also find terrible poverty and disease, jealousy, backbiting, snobbery, incompetence, corruption, and the decay of a great feudal empire. By 1928, trading posts which had once boasted libraries and billiard tables had fallen into shabby ruin; post managers were often drunk, illiterate, and irresponsible. The new fashion for Arctic white fox had brought white trappers and traders pouring down the Mackenzie River after the First World War, and these had undermined the native economy and destroyed the once absolute authority of the Company.

They had also brought tuberculosis, venereal disease, influenza, and booze; by the end of the 1920s the native population of the Mackenzie River had dwindled from about 15,000 to some 2,000. Free traders were undercutting Company prices and offering fancier merchandise—typewriters, gramophones, sewing machines, watches, lipstick, silk underwear and pyjamas. The economy was changing from feudalism to *laissez-faire*; the natives were becoming more independent and outspoken, less willing to trust that the trader was giving them a fair deal. And very often he wasn't—prices paid for furs were kept as low as possible, the price of goods marked as high as possible, and native trappers usually had only the trader's word for financial records. Company policy fluctuated between extreme generosity—a grubstake of $5,000 to $10,000—and extreme punishment when the trapper failed to pay it off. Reports of unscrupulous trading, starvation, and epidemics reached Ottawa's ears; as a result a rush of missionaries, nurses, mounted police, and civil servants came to clean up the mess.

The newcomers built their own houses in their own compounds and formed tiny, tight colonies knit together by rigid social pecking orders, cliques, gossip, feuds, fears, and endless games of bridge. The Company did not particularly welcome the "outsiders" but it learned to tolerate them—much of Dick Bonnycastle's time would be spent in an endless round of ritual social calls. The old

Inside a Hudson's Bay post (Fort Simpson) and outside (Fort Chipewyan)

autocratic Company style was going out of fashion: Mackenzie District Inspector Philip Godsell was dismissed for arrogant and "bumptious" behaviour; in 1926 his wife Jean created a scandal when she beat up the wife of the RCMP corporal in full view of the assembled population of Fort Fitzgerald:

> Blinded by a curtain of flaming red, I reached out, caught her by the coat-collar and smashed my fist into her face. For the next few minutes I thrashed the trembling, snivelling creature within an inch of her life, and sent her crawling, and moaning back to the barracks with the warning that if, on any future occasion, she as much as dared mention my name this would be but a infinitesimal sample of what she would get the next time.

Despite the influx of money and new residents, though, Arctic self-government was non-existent; indeed, government of any kind was minimal. The Commissioner of the Northwest Territories lived in a log Government House at Fort Smith and governed his vast domain with the help of a council, composed largely of Ottawa civil servants, that met infrequently in Ottawa. The Department of Indian Affairs took responsibility for the treaty Indians; the Anglican and Roman Catholic churches shepherded their flocks, and the RCMP tried to maintain law and order. The north was still a dangerous place—missionaries were murdered, mounted police froze to death, explorers starved, trappers drowned, traders' wives were mauled by dogs—yet the arrival of wireless, radio, and, before long, the airplane were gradually reducing the danger and creating a clamour for more of the amenities of civilization: for more doctors—one doctor in Aklavik, Dr. Urquhart, had been serving the entire Western Arctic—better schools, economic development, self-government, and government regulation of the fur trade.

In the summer of 1928, responding to a petition demanding responsible government for the Northwest Territories, the Department of Indian Affairs despatched C.C. Parker to investigate the grievances of the Indians; the Department of the Interior commissioned Major L.A. "Locky" Burwash to explore the Arctic coast and check on the reports of starvation among the Eskimos; and J.F. Moran was assigned to hold a public inquiry into complaints about trapping regulations, liquor and game laws, taxes, social services, the fur trade, and whatever problems the residents cared to raise. All three men were to travel north on the Hudson's Bay Company supply boat, the *Distributor*. Dick Bonnycastle was to be on the same boat with his superior, Fur Trade Inspector Hugh Conn, an irascible little Ulsterman whose terrible temper was matched only by his absolute devotion to Company interests.

Their assignment was to conduct an exhaustive investigation of every fur trade post along the Mackenzie River, and throughout the Western Arctic, to discover the source of the Hudson's Bay Company's failing fortunes. For the Company had lost control in the north. The economy was changing: Imperial Oil was developing the oil field at Norman Wells; prospectors were searching for gold and silver; fly-by-night free traders had introduced a cash economy among the natives. The Company's political base, the Indians—once the proud

Philip Godsell, inspector for the Hudson's Bay Company, who later wrote popular books about the Arctic

wives and children of famous post factors, the loyal "family" of a mighty patron—had been reduced to patients and pupils, cooks and choreboys; and the great factors themselves, the "Gitchie Okemows" once feared as demi-gods, were more often than not the objects of laughter and ridicule for their pompous manners and foolish brass hats. The unthinkable was happening—the Hudson's Bay Company was losing money. In spite of wholesale dismissals, transfers, and a new district manager, Louis Romanet, a genial Frenchman recruited from the opposition Reveillon Frères, the Mackenzie District had lost $40,000 in 1927.

As Hugh Conn's accountant and junior partner, Bonnycastle was to examine the post accounts and make himself familiar with the region and its people. He and Conn would not always be welcome visitors, and his tasks would be exhausting and difficult. It might have been his British qualities—good family, good looks, and good morals—which initially attracted the Hudson's Bay Company to Dick Bonnycastle, but it would be his skills as a prairie boy which enabled him to survive: his ability to run thirty miles a day behind a dog-team, his love of hunting and camping, his acceptance of hard work and spartan conditions, his politeness and tact with strangers and generosity towards companions, the imagination to get himself out of a tight spot, and the honesty to measure others by the same yardstick he used on himself.

Native post manager and his wife

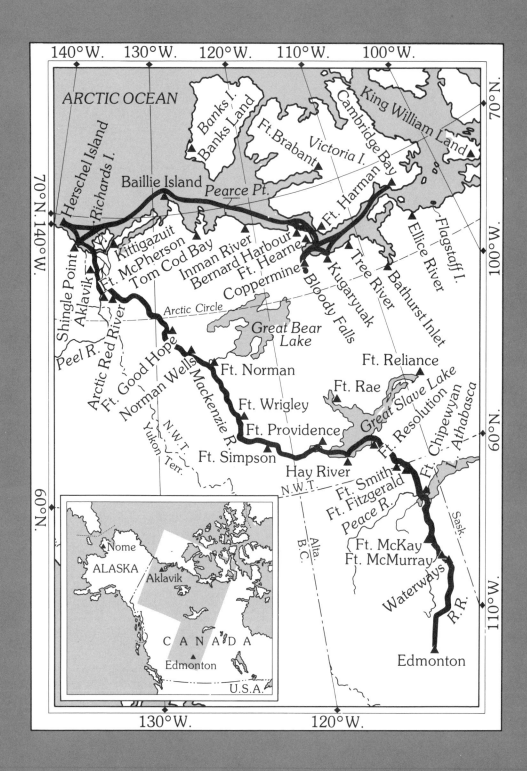

ARCTIC OCEAN

140°W.   130°W.   120°W.   110°W.   100°W.

70°N.

Banks I.
Banks Land

Ft. Brabant

Victoria I.

Cambridge Bay

King William Land

100°W.

Herschel Island
Richards I.

Baillie Island

Pearce Pt.

Ft. Harman

70°N. 140°W.

Flagstaff I.

Ellice River

Shingle Point
Aklavik
Ft. McPherson
Kittigazuit
Tom Cod Bay
Inman River
Bernard Harbour
Ft. Hearne
Coppermine
Bloody Falls
Kugaryuak
Tree River
Bathurst Inlet

Arctic Red River
Peel R.

Arctic Circle

Great Bear
Lake

Ft. Good Hope
Norman Wells

Ft. Norman

Ft. Reliance

Ft. Rae

Ft. Wrigley

Mackenzie R.

Ft. Providence

Great Slave Lake

Ft. Resolution

Ft. Chipewyan
L. Athabasca

60°N.

Yukon Terr.
N.W.T.

Ft. Simpson

Hay River

N.W.T.

Ft. Smith
Ft. Fitzgerald
Peace R.

Sask.

110°W.

60°N.

Nome

ALASKA

Aklavik

C A N A D A

Edmonton

U.S.A.

Alta.
B.C.

Ft. McKay
Ft. McMurray

Waterways

R.R.

Edmonton

130°W.   120°W.

Down the Mackenzie River to the Arctic Coast and Back to Fort Good Hope, in the Summer of 1928

1

Edmonton; June 19: Mr. Conn and I paid a courtesy call at the Fur Trade office, and left what clothing we would not need on the trip to go into cold storage.

At the railway station we met several friends and our fellow passengers. Most of the passengers are going north of Fort Smith, and this is the first trainload that will make the connection with the northbound riverboats at Fort Smith. There was a feeling of suppressed excitement, newcomers going north for the first time, curious and full of questions, nostalgic old-timers wishing they were going north again. There is a spirit of camaraderie in this crowd which is bred of the north.

At last we had the "all-aboard" signal and the train pulled out on its halting 300-mile journey to Waterways. There are three or four passenger coaches, including two sleeping cars, one combination sleeping and dining car, and one day-coach. After much jolting, coupling, and uncoupling, the train picked up a mixed freight of twenty-five to thirty cars, including five cars of buffalo on their way to the Wood Buffalo Park on the Slave River.

The first part of this 24-hour journey is through the beautiful, fertile Bon Accord Valley, but this soon gives way to miles and miles of muskeg, lakes, timber, and *brûlé*—most uninteresting. We made several stops at small sidings. At Lac la Biche there was a stop of 1½ hours, and all of the passengers with the exception of myself disembarked to see the town and lake and to stretch their limbs. I remained and wrote letters.

Hugh Conn and I were fortunate to have a drawing room, so we had a small party in the evening and entertained some of our fellow passengers including a Captain Perfilieff, a Russian-born artist from the Academy of Natural Sciences in Philadelphia.

Waterways, Alberta; June 20: We didn't get up until around 9:30 this morning, but managed to get breakfast before we arrived at Waterways at 10:30, where we found the river vessel *Athabasca River* and swarms of mosquitoes.

"The 'Muskeg Limited', a conglomeration of dirty red box-cars, flat-cars, and one very rickety old-fashioned coach with caboose tacked on to the rear, at length backed protestingly into the station. Everyone immediately made a wild dash for the nearest car, threw on his bed-roll and grub boxes, clambered aboard and used his baggage in place of a seat.

"The lucky ones got hard plush-covered berths in the coach but the majority were forced to make the best of the open flat-cars. As the engine gave her last wheezy whistle the nondescript train, with much bumping and a good deal of noise and ostentation, commenced her swaying journey through prairie land and muskeg.

"Twice a day there would be a brief stop for meals, then the passengers would all pile out onto the track with frying pans and tea kettles in their hands, build hurried campfires, sling on the kettles, warm up a tin of pork and beans and snatch a hasty meal.

"After the first fire everyone knew everybody else and the artificial barriers which civilization imposes were very soon let down. There were four white ladies aboard; a missionary's wife bound for Aklavic near the shore of the Polar Sea, a very practical Scotch woman who arose to every emergency; a Mounty's wife, all paint and lipstick, silk stockings and smiles, who proved a positive thrill for the mosquitoes who demonstrated their appreciation, much to the girl's discomfort and disgust; Mrs. Doyle, a recent bride, on her way to join her husband at Fort McPherson, as pretty as she was sensible, and Mrs.

Harris who was to winter with her trader husband at Fort Good Hope, six miles from the Arctic Circle.

"A truly remarkable railroad was the A. & G. W., as the rotting box-cars, which had fallen from the crazy track into the ditch, so amply testified. Straight ahead it went, up hill, down dale, through the woods and into the deepest muskegs where, for hours at a time, the rails would be invisible beneath the watery slime. Once or twice, after frenzied efforts to reach the top of some ridge, the engine would stop with a loud despairing snort, then the conductor would apologetically ask all the passengers to please jump off and walk in order to reduce the load.

"After backing up a couple of miles the engine would come swaying along, puffing and wheezing mightily, and finally top the hill. 'All aboard' some overalled trainman would yell and we would jump on once again. Ere long the train would come to another stop—a clay-cut—and each passenger would have to take hold of the business end of a

shovel and help remove a few tons of clay and earth which had fallen in upon the track.

"When on the second night we arrived at Lac La Biche we received the discouraging news that it would be a week or more ere we could proceed, some of the track ahead having been washed out by the rain. A few days later the same thing happened behind us and for two weeks we were literally marooned in this smelly oasis, surrounded by an ocean of swamp and mud on every side."

Philip Godsell

"Despite her renown the *Distributor* was simply a flat-bottomed wooden scow with two superimposed upper decks that looked very much like the verandahs of early Canadian and American houses. Stacked around the locomotive steam boiler were lengths of wood: the fuel for the furnace. Every eight hours during the entire journey we stopped to take on a new supply. The location of the new supply was marked by a 'lopstick', which was usually a tall spruce tree near the bank that had been shorn of all its branches except those within a few feet from the top. There the cords had been stacked by the wood-cutters during the winter. Day after day, with the steam engine puffing and the paddle wheel chugging, we slid north on the brown oily waters that flowed sluggishly between ever-curving shores.

"Attached to each side of the *Distributor* was a huge flat barge and two more were pushed ahead. These were loaded with freight. The towing and pushing of these barges seemed an amazing feat in view of the fact that neither the steamer nor the barges drew more than four feet of water while floating over one thousand tons of supplies.

"As we approached each little settlement, the entire population swarmed the riverbank, for this was the biggest event of the year. It made a gay scene in the summer sunshine with most of the men in colored shirts or in uniform; the white women with their light summer frocks; while the vivid cotton dresses and shawls of the Indian women added a bright accent."

Archdeacon Fleming

The *Athabasca River*

We boarded and got our cabins. Hugh Conn got the general manager's cabin, and I am sharing with a Mr. McMillan from Montreal who seems a pretty good scout. I sat at the captain's table. The food was pretty good but rather cold by the time it got to the table.

On board the "Athabasca River"; June 21: Breakfast is served from 7:00 to 8:00, and I barely made it! We saw the train off at 10:30, where I met Bishop and Mrs. Stringer, who were going out en route to the Yukon Territory. This will be the last train I see for some time.

Hugh Conn and I then drove over to Fort McMurray, in a taxi, as there are some staff changes in the making—changes that seem rather sweeping. We had lunch there, and afterwards spent an hour in conversation with a man called Sigidur, who was working on nets for the Lake Athabasca Fishing Company. He has fished a lot in the north and he and Hugh Conn have a great deal of mutual acquaintances. We shopped at McMurray for about an hour and then returned to Waterways. The Athabasca River is high, it rose three feet yesterday, and is full of driftwood.

We left Waterways at 6 p.m. The *Northland Echo* pulled out right after us and passed us while we were taking on firewood. Later we caught up and passed her above Fort McKay. By this time it was pretty dark and the two steamers, all lit up, rushing down the swollen river, the dark masses of the trees on the banks standing out against the faint light of the sky, made an impressive sight.

We spent the evening playing bridge, joined by Captain Thomas Smellie, late master of the famous Company ship *Nascopie* of the Eastern Arctic, who is on his way to do a survey at the mouth of the Mackenzie River. After a late snack of tea and pie provided by the night watchman I stayed on deck alone for a while. Everything was so peaceful, the little light remaining in the northern sky beautifully reflected on the dark water of the river.

June 22: A beautiful day, but I felt tired. After lunch I had an hour or two nap in the pilot-house. At Jackfish quite a number of Indians got on board bound for Chipewyan. This was the first group we had met and cameras were clicking. To me it looked very amusing and would have made a great cartoon. We had a fine run across the end of Lake Athabasca to Chipewyan, where we arrived at 5 p.m. We found Gaston Herodier there, Roach the clerk, and John James Loutitt, who is going south to take over Fort McMurray. I don't know why but I don't feel well, both in my stomach and in my head. I tried to walk ashore. I scarcely ate any supper, but felt worse and went to my cabin. Was driven out by the heat. I felt better outside and retired at 10:30, but couldn't get to sleep for a noisy party next door.

Fort Fitzgerald, N.W.T.; June 23: Feeling much better. We arrived at Fitzgerald around 7:30 a.m. on a perfect morning. A wonderful forest fire on the other side of the river a couple of miles back. It was only on a small front but it would blaze up occasionally, flames shooting way up, and the roar of it could be heard distinctly.

We crossed the portage to Fort Smith in the Ryan brothers' new Dodge and found the *Distributor* ready to receive passengers. Everything was nicely

The steamer *Distributor* and Captain Gardner

painted and a ventilating grille had been put into the cabin doors. A lot of bulldog flies around but they don't seem to bother us too much. Up at the Hudson's Bay office we met Mrs. P.H. Godsell, wife of the Mackenzie District inspector. She certainly is different from what I imagined, quite attractive in fact. Rumour has it that she and her husband are the cause of the dissatisfaction amongst the Hudson's Bay people here. Hugh Conn certainly believes they are.

Fort Smith, N.W.T.; June 24: Walked upstream through the bush to view the rapids, which weren't that impressive, although there is a lot of water coming down. There are quite a number of pelicans in the rapids. After dinner the government people took Hal Woolison, purser on the *Distributor*, Conn, and myself to play tennis on their board court. Woolison and I won three games so we are the champions.

The District Office set-up here at Smith is quite nice. District Manager Louis Romanet has his own office and stenographer, Inspector Philip Godsell has a lovely office in the store, nothing like it in the Winnipeg office.

The post at Fort Smith

Squarebriggs, the relief manager for Fort Simpson, is a queer bird. He seems to be drunk most of the time. Hal Woolison advised him to square up before he met the district manager and was warmly thanked for his advice which indicates what a weak sort of person Squarebriggs is. I can't understand Commissioner French's taste in engaging a man like this.

Passengers on the *Distributor*; note Hugh Conn in front of smokestack

On board the "Distributor"; June 25: Went ashore for a game of tennis around 5 p.m. Bill Champagne and I were trimmed 6-2 by the government people. They gave us a cocktail and we took them down to the *Distributor* for supper, then returned for two more sets. Sailed at 10:30 p.m.

June 26: Stayed in bed until noon, had lunch, read some of "Lawrence and the Arabs", then played a hand of bridge and reached Fort Resolution around 8:00 p.m. We stayed there for three hours and then started to cross the lake to Hay River.

June 27: Decided to do some work so I started at 2 a.m. and continued until we arrived at Hay River at 6 a.m. It was a lovely morning so we went up to say "How do you do" to the Anglican Mission people. We ran across a Mr. Moran, chief inspector for the District of Mackenzie, who is conducting a government inquiry to get the views of the residents on the laws of the country. After breakfast I went to bed until 11 a.m. and then had a darned good bath in nice clean water. I had another sleep after lunch and then went in for a swim. I must have stayed in too long because I felt rotten after. Feeling better after supper, I went ashore with the crowd and played football with the Indians, who beat our team 4-2. Captain Perfilieff is turning out to be quite a versatile person. He organized games ashore and makes a great cocktail. Had another swim before the *Distributor* pulled out. We took a bit of tossing at first and several people were sick.

Mounties horsing around

June 28: The *Distributor* arrived at Providence at 6:45 a.m. The Company men, Bill Garbutt and Fred McLeod, met us. Mrs. McLeod had a specially large pair of moccasins for me. They are a nice fit, and although she wanted six dollars for them I didn't like to refuse, but I doubt they will ever be much use to me. Captain Perfilieff is buying a lot of old beadwork. He gets along well with the people because of his jolly manner. I would like to buy some curios myself but I don't want to spend any more money than I can possibly help. In any case the best time to buy is during winter, in the off-tourist season.

At Providence Mr. Moran held a mock outdoor inquiry for the benefit of photographers. An old man named Jones who hasn't been out of the country since 1898 was there. Jones's tirade against the traders displeased Hugh Conn very much. He lit into the old man and was quite insulting, I thought. I did my best to smooth things over with the old man after Conn left and found him very interesting.

When a man in Hugh Conn's position loses his temper so easily he plays directly into the hands of anyone who has a legitimate beef against the traders. Osgoode, one of our fellow passengers, tells me that what old man Jones says is true. He says the average traveller in the country resents the cheeky attitude of the Company clerks and other employees who think they are the salt of the earth. Nothing puts the backs of the white population up more than this because they are powerless to do anything against the Company. It is easy for Company employees, safe in the fold, to take such an attitude.

Be that as it may, a man in a senior position like Hugh Conn should learn to control his temper and not act like an ignorant and bumptious young apprentice clerk. He cannot tolerate for a moment anyone who has views contrary to his own.

A court enquiry in Fort Providence; Bishop Breynat gives evidence, while Bonnycastle and Hugh Conn stand behind Chief Inspector Moran's table

PA-45020/PUBLIC ARCHIVES CANADA

It looks as if Jack Hornby, the explorer, is lost. He went into the Barrens by the north-east end of Great Slave Lake; I recall their departure in an eighteen-foot canoe. He had with him a young Englishman about twenty-five years old, a graduate of Cambridge, I understand, and a young English public school boy, a relative of his own. They had a very small outfit and intended to support themselves by hunting. Old man Jones says there are rumours around that they have all perished, the usual Indian stories of finding rifles and ammunition and not seeing any signs of the party. I have never heard that these rumours are being investigated, probably because the RCMP had some trouble with Hornby before.

We left Providence at 2 p.m., en route to Simpson.

Fort Simpson

Fort Simpson; June 29: We arrived here between 6:30 and 7 a.m. Harry Yelland came into my cabin and woke me up, but I gave him a drink and sent him away, and went back to sleep until 11 a.m. Then I dished out some more drinks to Yelland and Crooks and took Yelland in to dinner. He was pretty tight by this time. After dinner I visited the company people and shook hands with Dave Hooker and Fred Camsell. Garbutt and Skinner both borrowed a bottle of whisky off me. Skinner is to leave a replacement with the father at Simpson for us on our return.

On board the "Distributor"; June 30: Pulled out from Simpson at 9:15 a.m. I got up when the whistle blew, intending to say goodbye to the people, but there wasn't a soul down to see the boat off. I suppose everybody was tired after yesterday. We have a few new passengers. Flynn Harris, the Indian Agent, is going as far as Aklavik paying treaty. Dr. Truesdell, the resident government medical officer, is going as far as Fort Norman. Dr. Agnew, a dentist, is going as far as Cambridge Bay and then out to Vancouver. Harris and Truesdell are very keen bridge players and play for half a cent a point, which is pretty steep.

The Northern Traders post at Fort Norman

Son of a wealthy English factory owner, Jack Hornby had drifted around the north for twenty years—disappearing into the Barren Lands with barely enough food for a few months, appearing a year or two later half-starved and boasting of his ability to live off the land, becoming more aloof and eccentric as the years passed. In June of 1926 Hornby headed towards the Thelon River with two companions, Harold Adlard and Hornby's cousin Edgar Christian, seventeen and just out of school. When they had not reappeared by the spring of 1928, the RCMP began making inquiries of trappers and prospectors in the area. In July, a group of geologists found the bodies of the three men in a cabin on the Thelon River: they had starved to death the year before. The pathetic story of their lingering deaths was recorded by Edgar Christian in his diary, which he placed in the stove for safekeeping before he died.

May 20—June 1st.
have existed by Walking and Crawling in and out of house finding plenty of food in fact more than I could Eat but owing to its quality did not keep me going sufficiently to get Rid of it as I ate it being insufficient in grease I think. On 22nd I found Lots of meat under snow and 4 good big meaty bones covered in fat and grease. These put me on my Legs for 3 days Cutting wood Etc and I cooked up Enough fish for 4 days and then Rested thinking I could Lay to and Strenthend when the weather might be warmer and I would find more grub thawing out and even shoot Ptarmigan if I could walk. Alas I got weaker and weather was blowing Snowstorm for 4 days after that and not Even thawing in day time. Now June 1st I have grub on hand but weaker than have Ever been in my Life and no Migration north of birds and Animals since 19th (Swan).

    Yesterday I was out Crawling having cut last piece of wood in house to cook me food I had which is a very fat piece of Caribou hide but while out I found fish and meat in plenty and greasy gut fat on in sides of foxes and 2 Wolverine containing Liver and hearts and Kidneys and Lights 1 fox Carcacass. All this I cooked up leaving the hide as a Cache. I ate all I could and got Rid of much fould food from my system, apparently been stopping me walking. At 2 am went to bed feeling Content and bowl full of fish by me to Eat in Morning.

    9 *am.* Weaker than Ever have Eaten all I can have food on hand but heart peatering? Sunshine is bright now see if that does any good to me if I get out and bring in wood to make fire to night.

    Make *preparations* now.

Got out too weak and all in now. Left Things Late.

The *Distributor*

It was hot today, but tempered by a cool breeze, so it was fine sitting out of the heat of the sun. Simpson to Wrigley is as lovely as any part of the river, with the Nahanni and Mackenzie mountains to view. After lunch Hooker and I took $4 out of Harris and Osgoode at bridge.

Fort Norman; July 1: Arrived at Wrigley about 1 a.m. Tim Gaudet, the post manager, was there to welcome us. I called on Mrs. Gaudet and family. Their two strapping daughters should have been married by now but Tim will not let them marry Indians and he is pretty particular about white men. They will probably never marry, and heaven knows to marry an Indian would be better than that.

I gave Tim a drink and got the dentist to extract a tooth for one of the girls. She screamed like hell, but he got the tooth out. We left Wrigley at 3 a.m. and an amusing game of bridge followed. Went to bed at 5 a.m. and slept until noon. When I got up I learned that Archdeacon Fleming had held a service at 9 a.m. but neither Hugh Conn nor I was there.

Arrived at Norman about 3:30 p.m. There are lots of Indians and the American tourists are having a great time with their cameras. I also met one of the Porsild brothers, the botanists who are involved in the movement of reindeer from Alaska.*

Archdeacon
(later Bishop) Fleming

* A.E. and R.T. Porsild had investigated the Mackenzie River district for the suitability of reindeer herding in 1926, to supplement the erratic caribou; in the summer of 1928 they were exploring the Great Bear Lake area. Reindeer were imported into the Arctic on their recommendation in the 1930s, and remain there today.

Fort Good Hope; July 2: We left Norman at 1:30 a.m. Hugh Conn, that hot-tempered Irishman, had a hell of a row with Archdeacon Fleming over Fleming taking moving pictures in which Hugh Conn appears. They were most impolite to each other, I am told!

Arrived Good Hope at 4 p.m. Curiously enough, we found the interpreter to be Japanese. He really looks like an Indian and has been in the country twenty years. He also does the cooking. Gaston Herodier and William Skinner are taking over here for the HBC, and as the Syrians are firing their trader here it looks like an entire switchover in all the companies. George Ray, the new Northern Traders' manager, is an ex-Hudson's Bay Company manager of the James Bay District. Quite a comedown for him. Flynn Harris, the Indian Agent, said when he asked the sub-chief from Good Hope how things were going the chief replied, "Fine, we have the trading companies exactly where we want them," which shows the Indians aren't such fools.

It is from Good Hope that we hope to start out with dogs this coming winter. Herodier is to get toboggans and snowshoes ready for us and Hugh Conn's twelve dogs will be coming downriver on the second trip of the *Distributor*. I don't know what the travelling will be like, all running or all riding, but I am looking forward to it very much. I hope I feel better than I have done on this trip. I feel completely spineless with not an ounce of pep. I suppose it is the heat and lack of exercise. I shall have to work myself into better shape when I get off the ship.

District Manager Romanet keeps referring to me as his successor next year. He says to me, "Well, you can have the job, you are welcome to it. You will get grey. They can fire me, I've done my best." I believe he is scared but trying to make a joke about it. He says it is easy to criticize, and asks us to bear in mind the difficulties he has had to contend with. He is really worried. I am sure he has reason to be, but I believe he has done his best and is rapidly improving. I told him there was nothing to worry about in the fact that Mr. Conn had been sent to inspect his district. I said, "Why, he has inspected James Bay, Lake Superior, and Saskatchewan," and Romanet drily remarked, "Yes, and the district manager has been fired in each case." I realized I was taking the wrong course there. He thinks Hugh Conn is the Company hatchet man.

Romanet admitted the district staff were hopelessly out of date and had not changed with conditions. He also showed me a report on the future of transport, which included a decent steamer with a tourist trade down the Mackenzie. It occurred to me there might be a great future in the tourist and transport business, and there might also be a considerable trade, even at the expense of lower profits. It seems to me a closer study should be made. More accurate business methods and accounting might bring about better results.

"It was immediately obvious that [Flynn] Harris was a personage of more than usual importance, and that he expected to be treated with becoming deference." *Jean Godsell*

The harbour at Fort Norman. For Bonny-castle's later ascent of Bear Mountain (in background) see Epilogue

Arctic Red River

Arctic Red River; July 3: Arrived at 7 p.m. It has turned out to be a very hot evening, and I have a splitting headache—partly Scotch and sun, I suppose. Captain Perfilieff gave us an excellent cocktail made from alcohol, Old Buck rum, milk, eggs, vanilla, and sugar. He is a splendid bartender and I must get his recipes.

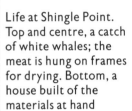

Life at Shingle Point.
Top and centre, a catch
of white whales; the
meat is hung on frames
for drying. Bottom, a
house built of the
materials at hand

Eskimo breakfast at
Shingle Point

Aklavik; July 5: We arrived at Aklavik about 1 a.m. and found the entire population on hand to greet us. We landed first down by the Northern Traders' store, which I didn't like very much, just for appearances' sake. I was the first one ashore.

I woke about 11 a.m. and there wasn't a sound in the place. Every single soul was asleep all over Aklavik and on the steamer. I carted my things to the store; Hugh Conn bought some fur from Karl Peterson, 26 white foxes at an average of $48.30 and 38 at $50. I thought this was high but Conn says Northern Traders paid $52.50 average for a lot of 41 and $55 each for 20 picked skins. Played some bridge and lost to Flynn Harris again, he is the luckiest man I ever knew. We had breakfast at Mrs. Lyman's hotel around 3 a.m. and I turned in two hours later, sort of running two days into one with the long hours of daylight.

Aklavik; July 6: There was some unpleasantness over liquor permits today. Inspector Vernon Kemp wanted to take them all to the police barracks. Max Finkelstein of Northern Traders told him not to touch their permits or he would take it up with Ottawa. So I don't think Kemp took their permits, although he did ours. The Northern Traders certainly order permits indiscriminately. They seem to use anybody's name, without permission.

The *Distributor* pulled out about 10 p.m. It felt a little bit queer seeing her go off. As soon as she had gone, we repaired to Mrs. Lyman's for a snack. After that we saw about our grub which is being put up for our departure for Herschel Island tomorrow—Amos will be taking us in his schooner. We have agreed to take Captain Perfilieff and the Americans to Herschel for $100, so we will be a party of seven, including Brecklin, the engineer for the *Aklavik.*

Before we bedded down in our loft Hugh Conn made a fuss over getting away in the morning, and told Amos to get us up for an 8 a.m. departure. I told Amos we should get a good sleep.

Hugh Conn

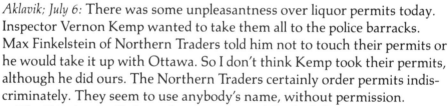
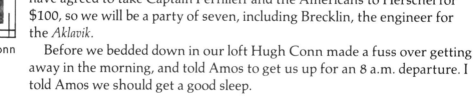

At sea; July 7: We both had a wonderful sleep. I had Captain Smellie's and my own eiderdown under me and slept in my four-point blankets. It was cool and with a nice soft bed it was wonderful. In spite of Conn's anxiety about getting off early, it was between 11 a.m. and noon when we were having breakfast. Next we loaded up, a hell of a business because everything had to be packed down the riverbank, then up a narrow gangplank to the schooner, and there always seems to be about ten times as much stuff as you imagined there was.

We loaded steadily for two hours—all our baggage, Conn's big hampers of samples, two barrels of gasoline, all our grub, cooking utensils, firewood, and ice for water because the river there isn't too clean. Then Amos moved downriver to his tent to load his family and dogs. This is always exciting. The dogs howl like hell and are so terribly keen to get on board that they almost drag their owners after them. This always starts the other dogs in the settlement howling, a sure sign that somebody is arriving or departing.

There was a stiff breeze blowing when we cast off. Amos's schooner is a good one with a very old Wisconsin engine which knocks out about eight miles an hour. Captain Perfilieff offered to cook our first meal. He mixed up four cans of pork and beans, one of Irish stew, one of Canadian boiled dinner, and one of tomatoes. We also scrambled twenty eggs, with bread, butter, rolls baked by Mrs. Lyman, and tea, of course. Conn refused to eat the mixture. He made rude remarks and gave some advice to the cook. I

"Found Bell river. Ripped canoe in rapids. Reached LaPierre House. Deserted. Broke in. Obtained food. Five days later reached Indian settlement on Porcupine River. Having heard of Mackenzie epidemic refused to let us land. Reached Alaska border on 31st. Found mounted police who brought us to Yukon by boat. Toe of one member frozen. Trip not recommended to tourists."
Captain Vladimir Perfilieff

don't really think he means what he says but he does make the most venomous remarks in such a way that I fairly boil and other people don't know what to do. He never tries it on me. I wouldn't stand for it.

We ran out to sea before midnight.

Shingle Point; July 8: We found the sea calm so Amos stopped the engine to clean the plugs, which took about an hour. Then, with about 45 miles to go, the engine started to give trouble on account of dirty gasoline. The breeze freshened and later we ran into fog and drizzle. We were very nearly lost at one time and found ourselves going in the wrong direction. The shore was hard to see since it was snow-covered and in a fog haze. We had a little rough sea which made some of the dogs sick.

We made Shingle Point by 7 a.m. The first thing we had to do was thaw out and make breakfast. Conn and the boys went to the mission house to sleep and I used post manager Pat Carroll's bed. I was awakened at 3 p.m. by the police boys with a bottle of whisky, they had just arrived from Aklavik. We had a meal together and they pulled out for Herschel Island. I started to work on the post books. It turned out to be a miserable evening, quite dark, and we had to light the lamp.

Shingle Point; July 9: Inventory is in a mess. I worked on the post books while the others played bridge. We were interrupted by the return of the police boat—they had a close shave with some impenetrable ice and had to turn back. After we'd had a meal we all turned to and had a grand clean-up in the summer kitchen, which was in a hell of a mess. We are quite a crowd now in one small room, four HBC men, five RCMP, and four Americans.

July 10: After midnight we tried to make ice-cream. We all took our turns at the freezer but it came to nothing. An amusing half hour with a lot of fun over our efforts. Wrote up my diary before going to bed around 5:30 a.m. We are a bit crowded on the floor, occupying such a small area. I have been working on inventory. We are taking a lot of depreciation because we are closing down Shingle Point. The others are amusing themselves, two tables of bridge going practically all day. Perfilieff whipped up some fried egg sandwiches and toasted sardine sandwiches for supper, and we had another bottle of Scotch. There is still a lot of ice out there and it doesn't look as if we can get away for several days.

July 11: I slept on the table last night as I find the floor too crowded. Hugh Conn cooked a very meagre breakfast of porridge, bread, and jam. Some of the boys went looking for caribou. They sighted a band of about 40 to 50. They didn't shoot any, which is just as well because Inspector and Mrs. Kemp arrived. With the arrival of the Inspector the police boys pulled out without any further delay. If they don't come back tomorrow we will try to make the crossing.

July 12: We had the famous Conn breakfast again this morning. He got quite annoyed because the Kemps didn't come right away when summoned to eat, which was in bad taste and quite unnecessary. It was blowing a little but we got off by 4:00 p.m., and stopped at an Eskimo camp to let two men off. While shoving off Griswold was a bit careless with the pole, and fell overboard and went under. I grabbed him when he came up and hauled him out none the worse.

Around 9:00 p.m. we ran into the ice and were forced closer to the shore. Finally we sighted the police boat at Stokes' Point, and followed them, but after a bit of manoeuvring we found ourselves being forced back towards the land. After numerous attempts, with me hoisted to the masthead in a bucket as ice-master, Amos decided to go back and find a harbour, although we were only four miles from Herschel Island. We could see the police had made the same decision. We tied up at the entrance to a lake with a sandbar across it. The police arrived, short of gasoline, so we gave them twenty-five gallons and some oil and they took off again.

July 13: It has been a beautiful night. The sun doesn't set at all. The ice moved in against us and pushed our stern around, so we are now broadside to the shore and threatened with the possibility of being shoved up on the beach. We seem to be hemmed in completely by ice, as far as the eye can see. The police are tied up some two miles along the coast.

The American boys set up tents on the shore and cooked breakfast outside. Hugh Conn refused to eat it. Later he decided to have a cup of tea and a hardtack biscuit. Spent a tolerable day sitting around the campfire.

About 4:00 p.m. we saw two men coming along the beach. It turned out to be Constable "Frenchy" Chartrand and an Eskimo. They had crossed from Herschel Island that morning and landed six miles along the coast from where we are stranded. Chartrand wanted to know if any of us wanted to go back to the island with him. He gave us the astounding news that Fred Wolki, who had the Kemps with him in his boat, had taken a northern course from Kay Point and managed to get around the ice. It is discouraging to think we might have made it if we had got farther north, galling to think we have been beaten so easily. However, Conn simply refuses to leave the schooner and seemed unwilling to let me go with Chartrand, who got some food and started back. In the evening a thick, wet fog descended on us which turned into a cold, miserable rain. The ice around hasn't moved but it appears to be melting considerably.

Herschel Island; July 14: Hugh Conn got up at 8 a.m. and reported that the ice had shifted and there was open water a couple of hundred yards offshore. We struck the tents and shoved off. The first 200 yards were tough going. I was in the bow, Conn at the wheel, and Amos in the engine-room. We turned, backed up, wriggled about before getting into open water. Amos's wife gave her quiet husband an earful when she thought we were taking undue risks, but he never said a word. I was hoisted up to the masthead in the bucket again. There was a freezing wind but I was warm in my duffel parka and snowshirt. There appeared to be loose ice all the way to the island, but we managed to follow a tortuous route through. Finally we hit a narrow channel running to the settlement some eight miles distant. We made it in four hours, and found the police had got there around 8:30 a.m.

Bill Murray, our manager, and Mrs. Murray had a splendid meal ready for us. The house is very comfortably fixed up, a woman certainly does make a great difference to a place. It is great to be here, good meals and a comfortable bed at last. In the evening we visited the police barracks and I got a much-needed haircut, and then we paid a visit to the Kemps.

July 15: A perfect day, warm but with masses of ice drifting slowly past all day. They think it is going to be a bad year for shipping. There is so much ice it isn't likely we'll see any schooners for some time.

Mrs. Murray is due to have a baby within the year. She wants to go outside with the second *Distributor* from Aklavik. This means she will be cooking for us for some time. She is quite willing to wait until the third *Distributor* so as not to leave us in the lurch, but we would not hear of that. If the company had more people like the Murrays everything would be fine. They work like Trojans and both deserve well of the company.

"Herschel Island . . . has cliffs around it and two good sand spits, and the interior rolls away to hills on which are small blue glaciers. There are several small streams running in summertime, and the usual ponds and tundra and fossil trees and boulders." *Charlie Klengenberg*

July 16: Invited to dinner by Captain Perfilieff and the boys. The captain cooked an excellent meal and then we all went to the Kemps' to play progressive bridge. I won the prize, a hundred cigarettes. After supper Perfilieff entertained us with an exhibition of circus and strongman acts. He is excellent at telling stories which had us in fits of laughter.

Mrs. Murray has decided to remain until the third *Distributor,* which is fortunate for us. She is a peach.

July 19: We are told that there is a bit of influenza around among the native people and that Philip Naryak's family is all down with it. They give up easily when illness strikes them, which makes recovery more difficult. Stanley's wife is also said to be in the last stages of consumption.

Having a stove is a great comfort and makes working in the office very pleasant. I got quite a good day's work done except that around 9 p.m. Perfilieff came and asked Hugh Conn and me to join them at bridge since this was their last night on the island—Amos is taking them to the mainland tomorrow. I didn't feel we could refuse under the circumstances.

This is the third day of strong easterly winds and prospects for the ships should be excellent. I expect the company supply ship *Baychimo* next Wednesday, July 25. There are a few grounded bergs with heavy seas breaking over them, the biggest surf I have ever seen, a great sight.

July 20: This morning I discussed the possibility of buying sealskins with Bill Murray, who thinks we might get up to eight hundred or a thousand. The only fly in the ointment seems to be that the Eskimo prefer to keep the seal intact to save the blubber, so would not want to skin them for $2 each.

Hunting caribou at Bathurst Inlet

I put in a good day's work and am pretty well caught up and ready to take a look at the Herschel Island books. It is still blowing hard with no sign of ice. Strange that there are no schooners arriving. It would be a joke if the supply ship arrived and no natives here.

Stanley's wife died last night. Murray had been pleading with him for months to take her to Aklavik but he wouldn't go. The other family is still down with the flu and all we can give them is simple remedies and plenty of opening medicine. I expect that since this flu can come downriver it will go through the whole country.

July 21: The only arrival today was Thomas Oomak, the Anglican Church catechist, from his camp at Nunalook. The heavy swell from the east persists but the wind is moderating. There must be something wrong around Aklavik since ice and weather conditions wouldn't have held up the schooners this long.

I was pleased today when Mr. Conn agreed to my suggestion that we charge the whisky used for entertainment to expenses. He said that if Commissioner French said anything he would speak to him about it.

Bill Murray has a bad cold now and the Eskimo patients do not seem much improved.

July 22: There was another death here today, Peter, a small boy who either belonged to or was being looked after by Johnny One Arm. The Inspector also informed Stanley that he must bury his wife Laura today.

Mr. Conn and I discussed the affairs of the Western Arctic district for several hours before retiring. He feels that Commissioner French is not

Bonnycastle with friends

doing the right thing in neglecting to appoint a district manager who would stay in the district. Conn thinks this is very important but he can't think of anyone who would take the job. They are going to give Paddy Gibson a shot at it. His only experience with the company since he came to us from the RCMP is three years at King William Land. He is the only man in the district I haven't met so I don't know much about him, except that he knows very little about books and can't keep his own post accounts. But he would probably soon learn.

Personally I don't see why the district manager, if he has one or more good inspectors, should winter in more than once during his term of office. I really think he would be more valuable outside. There is a vast amount of organizational work to do: requisitions, transport, hiring, and negotiations with the government. It seems to me that the jackpot the district has been put into is the direct result of not having anyone outside who knew anything of the district's requirements besides, of course, not having anyone in the district who is worth a damn either.

I do agree that a district manager should be appointed immediately. It is demoralizing for the staff to be dealing with a new supervisor every year, each of whom has new plans and ideas and doesn't in the slightest degree appreciate their efforts, good or bad, during the past year. It really is a shame. Scarcely any progress is being made in the Western Arctic at all. Commissioner Brabant sets up Fort Harman, Fort Hearne, Ellice River, Perry River, and practically closes Cambridge Bay; Mr. Conn comes along determined to close Harman, Hearne, Ellice and Perry River, opens Pearce Point, Coppermine, and Kugaryuk, moves Bathurst, King William Land and Fort Brabant. He also orders new buildings for these posts without any assurance from the government that we will not be forced out next year. Next year someone else will come along and decide on new locations and abandon old ones. There is nothing stable, no continuity of policy, tremendous overhead, everything done on the spur of the moment without any thought for the future or consideration of the past.

July 23: This has been a perfect day but not a single arrival. Really it is becoming mysterious. What has happened?

After lunch the police inspector asked us to come and help bury Laura, who has been dead for several days. We all went along. Murray and I carried the coffin out of the Eskimo house where it was lying, pushed it down the beach on a buggy, then carried it out to a dory. Corporal Chitty and Constable Pearson rowed the dory over to the bottom of the bay, to the cemetery, where a shallow grave had been dug. Thomas Oomak, the Anglican deacon, read a few prayers in Eskimo. Then we shoved the coffin in the grave and I helped shovel dirt on it. The grave was less than three feet deep. We all turned out for the burial, whites and Eskimos alike, except the woman's husband who was sick. The native population at Herschel at this moment numbers five families, twenty-one souls. We seldom see any of them as they are sick. Bill Murray does what he can for them, mostly seeing that their bowels move, and Mrs. Murray and Mrs. Kemp carry food to them every now and again.

July 23: Just as we had finished breakfast we sighted a boat. It turned out to be Blake of Arctic Red River, with the police boat following. They had bad news for us. There had been a terrible epidemic down the river and right out to the coast, a kind of flu followed by pneumonia, the natives dying off like flies. No white people have died. There are thirty-five dead at Simpson, twenty-three at Fort McPherson, thirteen at Aklavik, seven at Shingle Point and Whitefish Station. The dead include Topsy from the island here, Laughing Joe and Peter Cheechuk, the island's best hunter. Topsy had a small baby, no more than a week old.

Things are terrible at Aklavik, we are told. Everybody who can get about is busy carrying soup to the sick and feeding dogs. At Aklavik they couldn't bury them fast enough, some corpses lying for five days before being finally buried. Evidently the white population isn't altogether exempt. Parsons and his family had it, also Belcher of the RCMP, and one of the sisters at the mission isn't expected to live.

Laughing Joe, right

"At about this time an outburst of influenza followed by lobar pneumonia attacked the passengers on the *Distributor*. Nurse McCabe, who was traveling with me on her way to All Saints Hospital, Aklavik, was kept busy tending those who were stricken. At each settlement after the steamer departed, the people succumbed and the epidemic raged up and down the river, taking a final toll of more than three hundred Indians.

"As we continued toward Aklavik, influenza continued to strike down first one and then another of the passengers on the *Distributor*. Nurse McCabe was by now much overtired so she went off to her cabin hoping to snatch some sleep despite the heat, humidity, and mosquitoes. We came in sight of Aklavik in broad daylight almost exactly at midnight on July fifth. The bright sunshine, the soaring temperatures, the tall grasses, and the trees forty or more feet in height made it difficult to believe that we were now one hundred and twenty miles north of the Arctic Circle."

Archdeacon Fleming

"Fortunately Mr. Murray, the Hudson's Bay Company manager, had had pre-medical training at a Scottish university. He and his wife, Nance and myself, and other Mounted Police personnel, went to work immediately to treat these unfortunates. Their surprising lack of resistance against what was, to a white man, a minor condition, was alarming. In very short order every Eskimo on Herschel Island was ill.

"Displaying in some instances a form of panic, they resorted to the strange practice of endeavouring to cool the body in order to regain health. It seemed impossible to make them realize that it was the illness which caused the raised temperature, not the reverse. One man, who customarily wore his hair at considerable length, cropped his head completely, leaving almost a bare scalp. Most of them threw aside their deerskin robes, even their clothing. While we were with them they would do what we bade them, but the minute we left the clothes would come off and they would sit naked in a draught to reduce their temperatures!

"To maintain any form of control in a dozen separate houses was an impossibility with so few persons available to impose proper care. Only one recourse was possible—hospital treatment. But there was no such institution, nor was there a doctor, and there were no nurses. From the empty Anglican building we improvised a hospital. We put to bed the worst cases, using blankets obtained from the Hudson's Bay Company. Each patient was provided with nightwear—full-length combinations of heavy wool. From these, escape was impossible. Mrs. Murray and Nance bathed the bodies of the women and their report of the disagreeable task was as distasteful as our own experience in performing a similar office for the men. But we put them to bed and kept them there."

Inspector Vernon A. Kemp, RCMP

Diary of Rev. C.H. Clarke, Fort Simpson

July 6, 1928: Very warm and sultry. Unpacking and storing away supplies. Number of Indians ill. Called this evening on Cholo, Joe Hope, Little Doctor, Jas. Horasi, Kli, and Betthe. Many whites also sick with cold, "grippe" I think.

July 7, 1928: Very warm and dry. Made round of tents visiting sick. People nearly all laid out, not a tent where there was not someone sick, generally the whole family. Gave them "grippe" tablets. Dr. Truesdell went down river with steamer.

July 8, 1928: Very warm. Thunder shower in p.m. Small congregation. Most people laid up with "grippe". Called on some. They seem a little better, also at hospital.

July 9, 1928: Indians in and out for medicine. Visited people down trail. Cholo and Katthe very weak. Harry Camsell called for medicine for his father. Very weak. Grippe. Shower this evening.

July 10, 1928: Josephine got us up this morning at 6 a.m. "Harriet is dead! Harriet is dead!" A shock to us both. I saw her Saturday. Did not seem seriously ill. Jennie gave her a sheet. I went up later and had prayers with them. Took gruel to Cholo and Katthe. Arranged with Inspector Moorhead re Harriet's burial. Corpse brought to church porch. Spent day visiting sick. Cholo and Katthe, I am afraid, will not live. Several others are very ill. Mr. Camsell, Harry, and Mary down in bed. I went with Sister to several camps after putting mustard plaster on Cholo. Had to go to Inspector again re coffin.

July 11, 1928: Buried Harriet this a.m. Cholo boys came just after funeral to get me to go down and see their father. I went. He had breathed his last. We rolled him in his blanket and in a sheet and the boys carried him on the stretcher to the porch.

July 12, 1928: Went to bed last night with grippe. Took quinine etc. Got up about 10 a.m. Very weak. Buried Cholo today. Modest Mo dead, body brought to porch, Noga (RC) and two RC children dead. Visited sick. Took more quinine. Went to bed early.

"As we progressed downstream the disease became more and more serious, whole settlements with only two or three able to move about, a chorus of hacking, racking coughs with no other sign of life but hungry dogs howling to be fed.

"At Norman on a sunny day following the payment of Treaty I was fascinated by the frenzied, almost maniacal gambler's song on the lower level where the Indians were camped. Someone had commenced a blanket game early in the afternoon and as the day progressed the song was taken up one after the other gradually increasing in force of passion into the evening and then gradually dying out with exhaustion and the oncoming grip of influenza. It was like a swan song followed by sudden sickness and an ugly death."

C.C. Parker, Dept. of Indian Affairs

"I improvised quarantine regulations of an exceptional nature. With the backing of all whites, directions were issued completely forbidding any interchange of visits between those who had come from the infected areas to the south and those from either the east or the west, as yet free from the scourge. The Roman Catholic church had sent in a new schooner with clergy and lay workers. They agreed, as did the Anglican missionaries when they arrived, to conduct their religious ministrations under a strict form of segregation, open-air services replacing those customarily held indoors. Store hours were speedily agreed to by all trading concerns so that customers from the south carried out their barter at different hours from their friends who came from the east or west.

"Mindful of the pending arrival of the three deep-sea ships from the Pacific, we constructed quarantine flags using cut-up sheets dyed yellow. These we flew from our several flagstaffs. It was the period of the midnight sun—twenty-four hours of daylight—and these vessels might arrive at any hour of the twenty-four. Both the *St. Roch* and the *Baychimo* would be heading into the waters of the Coronation Gulf, the habitat of the Kogmolliks and other Eskimos as yet untouched by the epidemic. We could not take a chance of any seamen becoming affected and carrying the germs into those remote parts.

"Certain personnel from both ships had of necessity to come ashore. Moreover, a few of us who had been working at Herschel were due to travel with the vessels into the far eastern waters. I was scheduled to voyage on the *St. Roch* as far east as Cambridge Bay, twelve hundred miles away on Victoria Land. The *Baychimo* was to take Mr. J.F. Moran, representing the Department of the Interior, on his visits to outlying posts. Mr. Hugh Conn and Mr. R.H.G. Bonnycastle of the Hudson's Bay Company had likewise arrived to meet the *Baychimo* and journey with her to the Company's far-flung outposts. Archdeacon Fleming of the Anglican church was to be another passenger.

"Coming as we did in close touch with the disease, in our capacities as hospital orderlies, undertakers, and pall-bearers, the clothing we had worn at those grim tasks must be left behind. All who were journeying into the non-infected regions would wear only such garments as had not come in contact with the sick."

Inspector Vernon A. Kemp, RCMP

Bonnycastle (left) with
Pat Carroll

When the police got to Shingle Point they found things in a terrible condition. Carroll, the post manager, had pulled out for Aklavik taking Brecklin the engineer with him. He had absolutely no business to go there under the circumstances and must have left the natives when they were at their worst. The police found five bodies at Shingle Point, with not a person in camp able to stir. The dogs were so weak with hunger they could hardly stand. The bodies were decomposing and the police buried them in one grave. Only Peter Cheechuk had a coffin. The others were wrapped in blankets.

Constable Millen said our house at Shingle Point was just as Carroll and Brecklin had left it, beds slept in and dishes dirty. I can't understand Carroll doing this, it is unlike him. It is a disgrace to desert the native people that way. He may have gone to Aklavik for help, but surely he would have left a note to that effect.

Amos and his wife have apparently adopted Topsy's baby. I can't understand how the infant managed to survive. The natives are simply hopeless when it comes to handling sickness. We give them medicine and ask them to stay in bed. As soon as they begin to sweat they go outside to cool off, which is suicide. As soon as our backs are turned they disobey instructions. Those who stay in the house keep it absolutely airtight and don't let in a breath of fresh air. As soon as they get sick they immediately think they are going to die, and just lie around and moan. However, our two deaths to date are not due to flu, and I think the sick ones are improving.

The *Baychimo* is in the ice 10 miles east of Point Barrow. Although we are hoping she will get through, it is quite possible things may go badly with her. Inspector Kemp is already arranging protective measures to prevent the flu from travelling east with the *Baychimo*. No one is to be allowed off and no one is to board the vessel except those going east who will board at the last minute. Constable Millen will travel on the ship and see that there is no mixing between people on board and those ashore.

This morning Hugh Conn would not hear of Moran, the government inspector, or Archdeacon Fleming, who are now both on the island, coming near the Company house. Moran will probably have to sleep on the beach, which is all right with Hugh Conn. I find this giving everybody the cold shoulder very uncomfortable. When we first arrived here Conn appropriated the living-room and closed the door in case we might discover that there was one. There is a cosy sitting-room but he will not invite anyone in because they might make a habit of it.

July 25: What a day! Just as we were having breakfast Mrs. Murray announced that Stanley was on his back outside his tent. With one accord we all said "Dead?" and Inspector Kemp, who had just arrived, replied, "Stone dead." We just looked at each other. Kemp said his men were taking the body to a house where there was already a corpse. I went with Kemp to see Corporal Chitty and Constable Kennedy pick the body up.

So I saw my first corpse. It was not a pretty sight. His head lolled back, mouth wide open and eyes staring. The arms were pretty stiff and stuck out partly from his sides. They had difficulty in getting the body through the doorway so I squeezed the arms to his sides. His flesh was horrid and cold. He was clothed in an ordinary *artigi,* khaki pants, and deerskin boots. We tied the arms to his sides, closed the eyelids, and propped him straight so we could get him into a coffin easily. We covered the face with brown paper and left him there.

I had a natural aversion to touching the corpse, feeling I might catch something. The most disagreeable feature was the ghastly yellow colour of his face. I didn't like the horrible smell that hung around, which turned out to be the eucalyptus with which Kennedy had doused himself. I shall probably always connect this smell with that occasion.

Inspector Kemp asked Murray and me to help him with the burials. We started on the coffin while the two constables dug graves for two in the cemetery close to the water's edge. We took the coffin to the morgue and inserted Stanley as he was. It was a perfect fit. Then we went over and took spells at grave digging, but only got down to eighteen inches, where we encountered the permafrost and let it go at that.

At the barracks I was handed two wireless messages for Hugh Conn. One read, "Arrived safely. Pat Carroll died peacefully of pneumonia between Shingle and Aklavik." I was thunderstruck. So that was why Brecklin and Carroll had left Shingle Point. Brecklin had evidently tried to get him to hospital at Aklavik and not made it in time. I apologized mentally for the remarks I had made about them leaving the natives. This is a terrible shock to everyone—it brought things home to us and gave everybody a bit of a fright. We knew Carroll hadn't been in the best of health, but he was a nice chap and this completed his thirty-second year since he first paddled down the river from Athabasca Landing to Herschel Island. We wired Winnipeg about his death and the epidemic amongst the native people, assuring them we were all right. There was nothing else we could do, but the air felt morbid.

RCMP Inspector Kemp with daughter Daphne

Shortly afterwards the inspector suddenly rushed out of his house saying that the police boat, four miles out and bound for Shingle Point, seemed to be in trouble. Chitty and Millen were desperately waving flags out there. We returned the waves and I went on the roof with a smudge in hope they would see the smoke. Everybody got into a panic because we thought the boat must be sinking. Kemp asked me to row him out to the boat and I rushed around getting oars. At the height of the panic we suddenly realized we had overlooked Blake's schooner, but by the time we had got a hundred fathoms of chain in, Constable Gourley got one of the whale boats going and started out of the cove at an agonizingly slow speed. The odd look through the glasses convinced us that the boat was getting lower in the water. We could hear them shouting and expected to see them jump overboard at any moment. The rescue boat eventually reached them and, to our astonishment, started to tow the police boat in! It was only a broken crankshaft, but they were afraid of being blown north into the ice.

I returned rather weakly and had some tea. After supper the burial party was called out. We loaded both coffins on a skiff and Corporal Chitty rowed them to the bottom of the bay. Some of us walked around the shore, others crossed in boats. We carried the bodies, four men to a coffin, to the shallow graves near where the old whalers buried their dead. There were nine white men and one Eskimo present when Archdeacon Fleming read the prayers. We piled sod on the graves and felt much better now that it was over with.

I went to work in the office. Didn't do a great deal. The police released a case of whisky which had been in their care all winter. We donated three bottles to them for medicinal purposes and had a good drink of whisky, honey, and hot water before turning in. I felt splendid.

July 26: I have been able to spend the entire day in the office and have got a lot of work done. I had the office to myself since Bill Murray stayed in bed to try to clear up his cold. Thomas Oomak the deacon is down sick and doesn't seem to be making much progress. Philip Naryak is also sick. Kemp found he had cut off all his hair because he felt hot! He got a bawling out and a wool toque from the inspector, who told him to wear it. Of course the next time Philip was seen by the inspector, he wasn't wearing the toque.

Blake

Blake, the white trapper, has around $10,000 worth of fur with him. He came three times to see Conn, who ignored him and carried on a conversation with Moran about damn all. On the third visit I interrupted the senseless conversation and asked Conn for a price on Blake's furs. We had a wired bid. It was low but I gave it to Blake. He came in the evening and sold us 10 marten. If Conn keeps up this foolishness we are going to lose this fur. Bill Murray is furious at Conn.

July 27: Alveira, wife of Philip Naryak, died in the night and was buried this morning. She leaves around six kids. Philip is quite sick and may also die. His latest symptom is that he appears blind and says he can't see his house, although he is inside it. He seems to have the wind up, which makes things worse.

Blake's schooner got back from Shingle Point and reported ten deaths there to date.

We drew up a sweepstake today on the hour of arrival of the *Baychimo.* My time is 1:30 to 3:30 a.m. any day. Gourley heard the *Baychimo* today but

The *Baychimo*'s launch

said she seemed far away. She was sending CQ which means "all stations stand by", next thing to an SOS, so we don't know what to think.

We managed to do a heavy business deal with Blake tonight and as a result he is going to buy his outfit from us. The other half of his fur is going to go to Captain Pedersen of the Canalaska Company to pay off his debt. Conn gave him a good price on the 10 marten so everything is now satisfactory. We had a small celebration over the deal.

July 29: Things have got into a terrible state here. Conn acts like an absolute boor with Inspector Kemp and the two churchmen, Archdeacon Fleming and Bishop Geddes. Geddes and Kemp are taking the sickness among the natives very seriously and arranging four-hour shifts for the white people to look after them. Conn's reaction was that there would be no four-hour shifts for him or any of the Hudson's Bay men if he had anything to say about it. Mrs. Kemp and Mrs. Murray are working their heads off for the sick. When Inspector Kemp mentioned this Conn flared up and said the women shouldn't go near the sick and why couldn't the police do this work, they were doing nothing anyhow. Kemp asked me what was wrong with Conn, he was making things so difficult for everybody. He is unbearably rude to them and in what he says about them.

In business matters Conn is also impossible. Murray and I have worked like hell to get a promise from Blake that we would get half his fur, around $9,000. Conn will not give us a price and says Blake and his fur can go to hell for all he cares. Another incident—Murray said he had arranged to help Inspector Kemp dose the natives since he had some experience of this.

Conn said he should leave that alone and get on with his work, so Murray said, "We get our living from the natives, you know." Conn was wild! He shouted out that he had done "far more for Indians than you ever have." Murray replied politely, "I know you have, Mr. Conn." At this Conn left the office. Murray was white with anger. I really thought he was going to cry.

If I had been in Bill Murray's shoes I would have resigned on the spot. I consider this the culmination of a long line of provocation. Conn even tries to run the house, shuts the door in visitors' faces and asks Mrs. Murray not to invite her friends here. We are so ashamed of him we can hardly hold our heads up. Surely when the native people are in trouble we should do all we can for them. We are not here only to buy their fur and sell their merchandise. Here is such a splendid opportunity to show we have their welfare at heart, especially these days when the company is being criticized so much by people who claim we are exploiting the natives. If we run after them when they are well and able to hunt, then, by God, we should not throw them down when they are sick.

My nerves are so strained I can't work properly. I have to keep my feelings bottled up. I feel like a dog having to keep silent because at all costs I must preserve the peace between Conn and myself for this year. This is my big opportunity and I must stick it out with Conn if I possibly can. Never again will I go on a trip with Conn if I can help it. I am doing my best to preserve relationships and drop in nearly every day for a word with the Kemps and the bishop's people.

Blake came again today, looking for a drink. Then he gave me a box and asked me to open it; it contained 140 ermine skins. He opened another box with 11 marten in it. He suggested we divide his fur up now and take what we wanted. It was late at night but we would have been foolish to turn down this unexpected offer, so we divided the fur and selected our share, making sure we had the best. We ended up with all the ermine, 75% of the marten, 60% of the lynx, and 300 muskrat. Blake said he wanted to celebrate so I went to Conn and got a bottle of whisky which I gave to Blake. He got half tight before going to bed.

As we were washing up the dinner dishes the *Baychimo* came in and anchored, having observed our yellow quarantine flag. The flag, which was Inspector Kemp's idea, has been misinterpreted by Conn who says it's being flown as an insult to the Hudson's Bay Company, the inference being that we have a yellow streak. The arguments between the inspector and Conn just go on and on.

July 30: It was nice getting mail. I was up so late I am a wreck this morning. Captain Pedersen's Canalaska ship, *Patterson,* got in an hour behind the *Bay-chimo.* Hugh Conn and I went down to see Captain Pedersen and were cor-

dially invited on board. We bought some boots and ivory carvings. We had coffee and sandwiches with the Kemps in the evening, and peace is now evidently cemented. Mrs. Pedersen presented little Daphne Kemp with a doll and scads of clothes for it.

Working hard today to clean up some of the work before we leave the island.

August 1: We left Herschel Island at 10:30 a.m. on the *Baychimo*. I felt rotten most of the day. We got up dead tired, then there was a fresh easterly breeze which made the ship move a great deal. I swore all day I would never again come into this horrible country. I really hope I don't come back, although I am feeling a little better now.

Conn and I share a cabin, the same cabin as we had before, and it is really comfortable. We do our office work in the chart room. The meals are good. Pat the steward does the cooking in addition to his regular work and I don't know how he gets through. I am in the first sitting at the captain's table with Conn, Mr. Moran, Purser Patmore, Mate Shorty Somers, and the dentist, Dr. Agnew. Our new man, Donald Watt, has joined us now.

August 7: I am fed up with this trip and I hate it. It is just a case of work all the time. I seldom get on deck to see what is going on. The novelty has worn off and I haven't much interest in the work because Conn's ideas are so extraordinary. His business ability seems to be almost nil, and even Donald Watt is beginning to see that. So let's hope Conn continues on to King William Land on the schooner and leaves us alone so that at least we can do our work properly. It gets on my nerves when there is a disagreement, but I have to keep my mouth shut and always appear cheery and bright, even when I'm shy of sleep and the work isn't going well and I feel as cheerful as a funeral. However, by God, I'll see this excursion through if it is the last thing I do.

Coppermine; August 8: Slept until 7 a.m. when we arrived off Coppermine and dropped the hook. I went ashore in the ship's launch. This certainly is a lovely place. We seem to be in a huge bay, almost landlocked, with hills all around it, beautiful clear water, and a touch of green to the hills. They have a store erected here, also four or five tents so that each man has a tent and there is also a mess tent. They have an Eskimo woman in a cotton dress doing the dishwashing with a cigarette dangling from her lips. There are a few natives here but apparently all quarantine regulations have been forgotten. It should be an excellent location for a trading post if there is any fur to be got here.

First Mate Coe paraded all the crew this morning. They are complaining that they are required to work too long hours and don't get enough sleep. This morning at 2 a.m. they refused to work any longer and had to be given four hours sleep before they finished loading at Bernard Harbour. I understand the captain has now fixed the hour of midnight as when work must cease for the day.

Ikey Bolt

Soon after lunch we started on an excursion upriver to Bloody Falls, a journey of about twelve miles. Mr. Conn thought this might be a nice break for everyone, and it certainly is a peach of a day. There were around a dozen white men in the party, mostly passengers, and three Eskimos, Patsy Klengenberg, his brother-in-law Ikey Bolt, and a young boy. We managed to get the schooner *Polar Bear* ten miles upriver until it got too shoal. We took to the bank and scrambled along the river until we came to a native fishing camp near the falls. The natives were getting white fish and Arctic char by net and spear. The people in the two tents were very hospitable and interested in us. We went on to see the falls, which aren't really falls at all but very fast rapids running through a rock gorge with steep cliffs on either side. They are picturesque and we took several pictures. They are named Bloody Falls after the massacre of the entire Eskimo camp by Samuel Hearne's party of Indians.

We started back to the boat at 7 p.m., Patsy Klengenberg and I walking together yarning about the country; we had some food which the steward had put up for us; bread and butter, tongue, pig's feet, hardboiled eggs, doughnuts, and some oranges. We were about the last to return. The *Polar Bear* started downstream and all of a sudden hit bottom. We were high and dry and it looked as if the boat was going to capsize. There was nothing for it but to have most of the people walk downriver to Coppermine. A few of us, including the captain and Ikey Bolt, took the jolly boat and started off downriver—six miles—to get help.

When we arrived at the *Baychimo* it was broad daylight. We awakened the

Spear-fishing at Bloody Falls

chief engineer, got the ship's launch, and set out to tow the *Polar Bear* off. A lot of talking took place, but finally the engineer decided to sink a deadman on the riverbank. We buried a couple of timbers—I nearly died digging the hole for them—then came the heart-breaking work of fixing up tackles. More than a ton of chain had to be taken out on the skiff. Then, with the launch moving off and taking the slack, the schooner jerked forward a couple of feet. This was repeated time and time again, and with the sails up, and all of us pulling on the shorelines, we got her off. We then had the backbreaking work of recovering the chains and anchors and digging up the deadman. With the help of a bottle of rum the captain had brought we accomplished it, but there was one very sleepy man—me!

We started downstream, the launch going ahead and taking soundings. It was now a very beautiful morning, the sun high and quite hot. We sat on deck, had a snack, and dozed off—Patsy even fell asleep once at the wheel! We made the *Baychimo* at 8 a.m., a very sorry-looking lot. I had the good sense to be wearing overalls but the others were plastered with mud from head to foot. My sealskin boots kept my feet dry but they were now so much pulp. All the squabbling and bickering that took place when we were pulling the boat off was forgotten. Everyone had decided—no more excursions!

While we lay in ambufh, the Indians performed the laft
ceremonies which were thought neceffary before the engagement. Thefe chiefly confifted in painting their faces;
fome all black, fome all red, and others with a mixture of
the two; and to prevent their hair from blowing into their
eyes, it was either tied before and behind, and on both
fides, or elfe cut fhort all round. The next thing they
confidered was to make themfelves as light as poffible for
running; which they did, by pulling off their ftockings,
and either cutting off the fleeves of their jackets, or rolling them up clofe to their arm-pits; and though the muf-
kettoes at that time were fo numerous as to furpafs all cre-
bibility, yet fome of the Indians actually pulled off their
jackets and entered the lifts quite naked, except their
breech-cloths and fhoes. Fearing I might have occafion
to run with the reft, I thought it alfo advifable to pull
off my ftockings and cap, and to tie my hair as clofe up as
poffible.

By the time the Indians had made themfelves thus
completely frightful, it was near one o'clock in the morning of the feventeenth; when finding all the Efquimaux
quiet in their tents, they rufhed forth from their ambuf-
cade, and fell on the poor unfufpecting creatures, unper-
ceived till clofe at the very eves of their tents, when
they foon began the bloody maffacre, while I ftood neuter
in the rear.

In a few feconds the horrible fcene commenced; it was
fhocking beyond defcription; the poor unhappy victims
were furprifed in the midft of their fleep, and had neither
time nor power to make any refiftance; men, women, and
children, in all upward of twenty, ran out of their tents
ftark naked, and endeavoured to make their efcape; but
the Indians having poffeffion of all the land-fide, to no
place could they fly for fhelter. One alternative only remained, that of jumping into the river; but, as none of them
attempted it, they all fell a facrifice to Indian barbarity!

The fhrieks and groans of the poor expiring wretches

were truly dreadful; and my horror was much increafed at feeing a young girl, feemingly about eighteen years of age, killed fo near me, that when the firft fpear was ftuck into her fide fhe fell down at my feet, and twifted round my legs, fo that it was with difficulty that I could difengage myfelf from her dying grafps. As two Indian men pur-fued this unfortunate victim, I folicited very hard for her life; but the murderers made no reply till they had ftuck both their fpears through her body, and transfixed her to the ground. They then looked me fternly in the face, and began to ridicule me, by afking if I wanted an Efquimaux wife; and paid not the fmalleft regard to the fhrieks and agony of the poor wretch, who was twining round their fpears like an eel! Indeed, after receiving much abufive language from them on the occafion, I was at length obliged to defire that they would be more expe-ditious in difpatching their victim out of her mifery, other-wife I fhould be obliged, out of pity, to affift in the friendly office of putting an end to the exiftence of a fel-low-creature who was fo cruelly wounded. On this re-queft being made, one of the Indians haftily drew his fpear from the place where it was firft lodged, and pierced it through her breaft near the heart. The love of life, however, even in this moft miferable ftate, was fo predo-minant, that though this might juftly be called the moft merciful act that could be done for the poor creature, it feemed to be unwelcome, for though much exhaufted by pain and lofs of blood, fhe made feveral efforts to ward off the friendly blow. My fituation and the terror of my mind at beholding this butchery, cannot eafily be con-ceived, much lefs defcribed; though I fummed up all the fortitude I was mafter of on the occafion, it was with difficulty that I could refrain from tears; and I am con-fident that my features muft have feelingly expreffed how fincerely I was affected at the barbarous fcene I then wit-neffed; even at this hour I cannot reflect on the tranf-actions of that horrid day without fhedding tears.

SAMUEL HEARNE

August 9: I slept until 12:30 and then got up feeling stiff and sore, and still sleepy. I got to work, however, and did the Fort Hearne accounts, which seem okay. In the evening Donald Watt and I went paddling in a twelve-foot canoe—it's very cranky and one of the new clerks fell out of it yesterday. We are enjoying our stop-over here and even Hugh Conn is in good humour. It looks as if the discharging will not be over before tomorrow night. We are still ahead of schedule.

Donald Watt and Coppermine manager F. A. Barnes with Bonnycastle (right)

August 10: Finished up the Fort Hearne and outpost accounts by the time the cargo was finally discharged at 9 p.m. but the captain decided not to pull out until tomorrow morning. This has been a good day. By lunch time I had forgotten all the hard work up the river. I am beginning to get more enjoyment out of the voyage, probably on account of Mr. Conn's improved disposition!

August 12: We got to Tree River about 9 a.m. Ray Ross certainly has his house, store, and warehouse in splendid shape. I can safely say these buildings are the neatest we have yet seen in the Arctic. Unfortunately, however, they have the smallest fur collection anywhere, a complete washout.

We left Tree River at 5:45 p.m. for Wilmot Island, where we will leave the trapper-traders Patsy Klengenberg and Ikey Bolt with their outfit. Then we go on to Bathurst Inlet, Cambridge Bay, and Flagstaff Island. It looks as if we're going to be pretty late getting back to Shingle Point. So it may be nip and tuck to catch the *Distributor.*

Ray Ross

Cambridge Bay; August 15: Awakened this morning to find we are anchored just off Cambridge Bay in a fog with drizzling rain, thoroughly miserable in fact. Soon after breakfast Mr. Conn left on the launch for Cambridge Bay some 16 miles away. He sent Paddy Gibson back with the launch with all his books so that I could go over them and let him close them off himself. He is going to be made inspector by degrees, I think, but he is very weak on accounts and needs some instructing from me. Gibson seems a thoroughly nice chap, about thirty, an Irishman and a Freemason which no doubt appeals to Hugh Conn. He seems to have his head screwed on right. He will be okay, I think.

Paddy Gibson (left) and Constable Frenchy Chartrand

There was an amusing incident during supper. Someone started a most annoying whistle and kept it up. The captain became furious and made for the pantry to tear a strip off the steward. He nosed around and at last found it was Archdeacon Fleming who was the cause of our annoyance. The captain looked quite sheepish on his return.

August 16: We are still anchored outside Cambridge Bay. A gale blowing with very wet weather into the bargain. I had a splendid day and finished up Perry River where John Livingstone is manager. His books were in fair shape but the results are terrible. They have to give out presents and enormous credit advances to the natives to get a share of the fur. This debt and gratuity situation should be given serious thought.

August 18: Arrived in Cambridge Bay at 6 a.m. Mr. Moran has told me he is very sore with Hugh Conn's insinuations that the Company is not getting a square deal from the government. Conn is thinking of wiring the governor in London about it, and Moran told him to go ahead and wire. Moran says if he were ashore he would never stand for Conn's insults but since he is a guest on the Company ship he must take it smilingly. Conn even asked Moran to refuse the Canalaska Company, our opposition, a permit unless

Fleming (right) at the Anglican mission at Cambridge Bay

they put their buildings alongside ours. He is afraid they may build some-where down the bay and intercept the Eskimos coming in to trade. Conn told me we may have to move our post if Clarke, the opposition manager, builds somewhere else. This after we have erected our buildings on the best site in Cambridge Bay, built a nice house, warehouse, store, Eskimo visitors' house, and wharf!

Moran called me aside today with another complaint. He had been in our house with Conn when Dr. Agnew came in and, in fun, said to Moran, "Are you a native here?" Conn immediately spoke up and said, "No, not a native, but a damned nuisance." Moran is considering informing Conn he will deal only through me on government and Company business. He feels his department is being insulted. After all, he is Chief Inspector for the whole of the Northwest Territories.

Donald Watt and I have had a hard day on the Cambridge Bay post and depot mess. I am tired and overworked and I sincerely hope I never visit this country again. The game isn't worth the candle.

August 23: Awakened to find we had been on the move since 4 a.m. but the captain is uncertain of our position. The compass is useless. He couldn't take a latitude and couldn't see land except faintly at intervals. However he kept on going, keeping land when he could see it on the port bow, thinking it was Melbourne Island. We kept going like this for hours, then began to realize that something was wrong because there was apparently no end to Melbourne Island! Then land appeared on the starboard bow as well. It was decided we were proceeding east along Victoria Land and the land appear-ing on the starboard side must be Jenny Lind Island. We were going in the wrong direction! So we put about and went in the other direction.

We put our Eskimo passengers aboard their schooner with their gear. There was quite a choppy sea and they immediately got seasick over everything.

August 24: We were just about 10 miles past Wilmot Island when the cap-tain sighted what appeared to be a signal flag flying on an island about 8 miles on our port beam. He blew the whistle and sent up a distress signal to let whoever it was know they had been seen; then he stopped the ship and the chief engineer, Hugh Conn, and myself set out for shore in the launch. The sea was choppy and we got quite a dusting. We could make out three people, a tent, and what looked like the remains of a boat. As we arrived at the beach it was evident that this was Patsy Klengenberg, Ikey Bolt, and the young boy, the same three we had dropped off at Wilmot Island on our way east. They had started off for Bernard Harbour in their boat, the *Dr. Rymer*. When the storm which had delayed us at Cambridge Bay hit them they sought shelter behind the island. While they were at anchor the wind changed to the opposite direction, they dragged anchor, then the

chain broke and they were driven ashore. They saved practically everything, including the engine, but the boat was a total loss. It had been very
flimsily built, the ribs looking as if they were for a canoe.

The island on which the survivors had landed had only one small pool of
drinking water which would soon have dried up. They planned to build
some kind of boat from the wreck but fortunately we came along. It's an ill
wind that blows nobody good—perhaps they will now want to buy the
Nauya from the company!

August 25: My birthday—twenty-five years old today! A rather distasteful
incident just took place. I was in the saloon and Archdeacon Fleming asked
me if I could throw any light on a question he had to ask: "What does Mr.
Conn mean by all the insults he is passing my way?" He then went over all
the incidents, one by one, too numerous to relate here. They ranged from
odious comparisons between the Anglican nurses and the sisters of the
Roman Catholic mission at Aklavik to insulting remarks about the archdeacon's friends. District manager Ralph Parsons might be "an ignorant
fish-eating Newfoundlander", as Conn had said, but at least he was a gentleman, said Fleming. Fleming even mentioned the fact that he had great
difficulty in getting permission to hold services on board ship.

I have never seen a man so wild as the archdeacon was. He was trem-
bling like a leaf and could hardly speak at times. I told him I tried to mind
my own business and found my position very difficult but my hands were
tied and I had to keep my mouth shut. The archdeacon wanted to know
where I stood in case this came to a showdown. I frankly said I had felt like
quitting but I had to see this job through, otherwise I might as well quit the
Hudson's Bay Company service. I must admit that Conn is nice to me, so

long as I don't say a word in protest, so I feel like a hypocrite in a way. But I think my policy is the right one.

We arrived at Bernard Harbour at 10:45 p.m., and anchored 5 miles off-shore in a perfectly calm sea. Some of us went ashore in the launch, and we met Major "Locky" Burwash, the government explorer-type, who reported that there had been a tremendous gale all along the coast. The storm caused high water at Baillie Island and the whole place was flooded, with such things as barrels of gasoline washed away—they even had a schooner tied up at the back door in case the waters rose higher. Several schooners had been lost. It is fortunate that our schooner, the *Nauya*, is here, since we

have been able to sell her to Patsy Klengenberg and Ikey Bolt for $8,500, half cash.

Gasoline isn't too plentiful here. We have to replace some borrowed from the police, which we had forgotten about, and Patsy must have fuel for the *Nauya*. Major Burwash also wanted some gasoline but Conn told him, in a rather nasty way, he couldn't have any, here or at Cambridge Bay. I boiled inwardly but couldn't say a word.

Aklavik; September 2: We entered the mouth of the Mackenzie and arrived at Aklavik at 10:30 p.m. There was quite a crowd on the riverbank to greet us. We had all the village gossip and were pleased to hear that the *Distributor* was held up by wind at Fort Resolution—this means we have at least ten days to work on the Western Arctic books before she arrives. A godsend.

We have taken up residence in the loft of the warehouse again. I have two caribou skins for a mattress and my eiderdown robe so I'm going to be quite comfortable. I am glad to be back in Aklavik after all the misery we went through on the coast, sleeping on a very narrow settee, nowhere to

The Company post at
Aklavik

hang your clothes, no sleep except when Conn chooses to sleep, nowhere
to entertain friends. Above all we felt the lack of adequate office space, two
planks nailed together and propped up by a drawer in the chart room, and
Donald Watt and myself sitting on two boxes. I still wonder how we
accomplished so much.

September 3: We slept in until around 12:30 p.m. and then had a late breakfast over at Mrs. Lyman's hotel, an excellent meal of bacon and eggs. We
then got hold of Amos and got him to bring the schooner nearer the Company buildings for loading. It took us all afternoon to unload the two
schooners and get all the fur into the warehouse, our dried fish into the
icehouse, and all the baggage off. It was hard work packing everything up
the steep riverbank.

Constable Millen had a nasty experience coming up on the schooner—
he was sleeping in the engine room and got a touch of carbon monoxide
poisoning. The Eskimos noticed him and dragged him onto the deck, and
he collapsed and was not conscious for a few minutes. The Eskimos around
here have an idea this is what caused Carroll's death on the schooner from
Shingle Point to Aklavik. There must be an exhaust leak.

September 13: We started on the Aklavik post this morning, Conn taking
stock with Jack Parsons, the manager, calling it out. I started in by checking
the cash which was $500 over. Parsons says this is his cash sales since the
first of the month, of which no record is kept! Next I added up the Indian
blotter for sales to date this month and posted them in the daybook.

It has been absolutely miserable, snowing and sleeting. We had beefsteak
for lunch and roast beef for dinner. Mrs. Lyman has very few customers
now.

Most of the Eskimos have pulled out. A few were in the store today and
Parsons took in $100 in cash sales. I think more of him now than I did—
when he wants he can be very nice.

Winter seems to be coming on although we should still get some good
weather. It's going to be great when the *Liard River* pulls out and we are
really cut off from civilization.

September 14: A perfect day, air like a tonic, clear sky, beautiful sunshine, the
mountains in a snowy mantle. It feels good to be alive.

We are having our meals at Mrs. Lyman's. She is a terrible talker. She gave us an earful of gossip tonight, all about Northern Traders and the amount of liquor being consumed there. It must have been a fright after the *Distributor* pulled out, Campbell apparently didn't draw a sober breath for days and the natives are allowed to take anything they want. I don't understand how they hold things together at all. Surely Finkelstein can't know about it.

September 15: Another perfect day, the air almost balmy but with a hint of crispness in it. I did not sleep well. I tried out my deerskin bag but it isn't long enough. It is soft and warm except at the shoulders which it doesn't cover completely. There is an opening halfway down which lets in the cold unless you fold it tight around you and lie on the folds, which isn't comfortable. Sleeping in a deerskin bag is quite an art, it seems.

I make a practice of splitting wood at Mrs. Lyman's before meals. It is excellent exercise. Stock taking and auditing continued today. We are doing fine and should be away from here by the middle of next week.

September 17: Mrs. Lyman gave us fish twice today. An excellent salmon for dinner. She is doing our laundry and making a snowshirt for Mr. Conn. She certainly is a woman of many parts but seldom stops talking.

Campbell of Northern Traders is down to drinking extracts now. He bought a couple of bottles from Parsons. Campbell says he hasn't been able to do anything this summer and is to go to Arctic Red River. Northern Traders must be in a bad way.

September 18: There was ice in the water pail this morning so I put on a fire. The same old grind today. I worked by candlelight until 10 p.m. in the office and then went back to my shack to write personal letters. It is nice in there with a stove and gas lantern and all our kit hanging up around us and even a bunch of foxes hanging in one corner. My sleeping bag is ready to crawl into. It is most cozy. I'm really fond of this old shack.

Bonnycastle's "shack" behind the Aklavik post

September 19: We are on a fish diet now. We have had fish for two meals every day for a week. Mrs. Lyman cooks it very well in different ways and it is not hard to take. Potatoes are gone so I guess it's time to pull out. Hugh Conn is in good form tonight and told a lot of stories after supper. I worked until 10:30 p.m. A good display of northern lights after dark.

September 20: We are to leave tomorrow. I had a very busy day and finally decided I wouldn't go to bed at all. This is the last chance to get mail out and we will have to post it here before we leave. After dinner Conn gave Parsons verbal instructions. Parsons says he is gaining the Eskimo trade and that figures will prove it. But he has given out $16,000 of credit although Romanet, his district manager, has only authorized $6,000.

After dinner I went to say goodbye to a number of people, and paid our account with Mrs. Lyman. She certainly is reasonable in her charges—$1 a meal, $8 for laundry, $5 for Mr. Conn's snowshirt, and six loaves of bread for $2. Of course she is very ambitious and wants to build a restaurant and boardinghouse—no doubt she wants to merit Conn's approval as the Company could help her considerably.

September 21: The day broke clear and frosty. We had breakfast at 7 a.m. and packed our stuff. The canoe is a 24-footer and there is tons of room. We put three reindeer skins on the bottom and one across the thwart, sitting on it like the Governor-General driving in an open car with bearskin robes over the seats. We took Conn's eiderdown robe for a cover and were as comfortable as could be.

We left Aklavik at 9 a.m. in perfect weather. We waved goodbye, the Evinrude motor purred, and we were on our way. It was an entirely new experience for me and I thoroughly enjoyed it. I could even laze a little. As we curved around the winding streams of the delta we occasionally caught a glimpse of the mountains, the snow-covered slopes blending beautifully with the blue sky and the trees in their autumn colours. Alternately sleeping stretched out in the bottom of the canoe, reading, or simply chatting, the time passed pleasantly and we made good progress upriver. At 2 p.m. we boiled a kettle and had an excellent lunch of corned beef, beans, bread and butter, cheese, ham, and tea. Washed our dishes and then on our way again.

Everything went well until darkness began to fall and the boys had some difficulty finding the channel. Several times we ran onto sandbars. As it became darker it also turned colder, and I went to sleep covered by an eiderdown robe. At 10:30 p.m. I was awakened by a crash—we had run into a number of canoes and a whale boat tied up to the riverbank. It turned out to be an Indian camp about 18 miles from Fort McPherson. James Greenland, the father of one of the guides, was camped there with his family so naturally the boy took us to his father's tent in the bush. It was a large tent, 20 feet by 20, and well lit by a couple of candles burning on sticks driven into the ground. The floor was carpeted with spruce boughs, and all across one side was carpeted in addition with blankets, eiderdowns, and quilts of all colours. All very comfortable. They had a stove burning and two Indian women were cooking as we sat around a tabletop laid on the ground. Then our host got up, spread an oilcloth over the table, and set out some dishes with what looked like a plate of delicious fried fish. It turned out to be rabbit. Tasted fine.

After that excellent meal, which also included coffee, doughnuts, and jam, we got up and made our excuses. The old man apologized for not being able to put us up for there were nine of his children all asleep there. It was a nice clear night so we returned to the canoe and went to sleep under the stars.

Fort McPherson; September 22: Got up at 7 a.m. after sleeping fully clothed— even to my moccasins, since my feet stuck out the bottom of Hugh Conn's sleeping robe. It was a beautiful clear morning but cold, and the water was ice-cold for washing in. We went to James Greenland's tent for breakfast. He cleared his family out. It was funny to see some of the Indian children coming out of the tents for their morning exercise with only little night-gowns on and nothing on their feet. The chill air and frost on the ground didn't bother them one bit.

We had porridge and fried eggs, and sat and chatted for a while with James Greenland. He said he had always traded with the Hudson's Bay Company, and last year he and his boys trapped $6,000 worth of fur. We were off again by 9 a.m. A lovely run, perfect Indian-summer weather, a

Left, Hugh Conn and John Firth; right, William Firth

hint of frost in the air but a warm sun and everything so still and quiet. We had a view of mountains covered with trees a few miles back from the river while, beyond, another range poked snow-covered pinnacles into view here and there, beautifully white against the blue sky.

We arrived at Fort McPherson at noon. We took our despatch cases and walked up the hill where we met William Firth coming down. He took us to a small house at the rear of the dwelling where he had fixed up a nice large room for us, furnished with a camp stove, beds, tables, and a washstand. There was new linoleum on the floor and the walls were freshly done up with beaverboard and oilcloth. It really is nice and a change from Aklavik where nothing was done for us.

Four of us sat down to lunch at 1 p.m.—William Firth, his clerk Murchison, Conn, and I. We weren't bothered with any womenfolk; Mrs. Firth keeps out of sight. Conn then started taking inventory and I began checking the books with Murchison. He is a nice chap to work with—big, competent-looking, and self-reliant, also apparently well educated—but he is casual and careless with the books. He likes to use a method of his own which is the quickest way to the end, without much regard for detail or accuracy.

We had dinner at 7 p.m. and I stayed and chatted with William Firth and Murchison. Both are very intelligent and we had a pleasant evening. Before turning in I made some notes of the inaccuracies I had found and the methods used, but I made no criticism to the two staff members. I crawled into my deerskin sleeping bag, which is now comfortable since it was lengthened by Taylor Pokiak's wife.

September 23: We had a pretty poor lunch but an excellent beef dinner. William Firth killed his steer two days ago. Just before dinner old John Firth came in to see us—he is pretty old but still gets around with the aid of a stick. When he first arrived it had taken him two years to reach Fort McPherson from York Factory on Hudson's Bay. William Firth says there are still some old Indians who give him half their fur; the other half must be traded with old John Firth, and they declare they will continue trading with him until he dies. A fine tribute to a grand old man and a faithful company employee for most of his lifetime.

William Firth is a smart chap and a good talker who knows the natives and their country like a book. After dinner there was some pretty strong criticism of the Company, its officials and methods. What I liked was that they finished up by saying there was no better company to work for. William Firth said he would take a job as interpreter rather than quit.

September 25: William Firth told me some scandalous stories of how he had done the opposition in, and sometimes the Indians too. He certainly hasn't any scruples. I would sooner have him for me than against me. His knowledge of the Indians and his command of their language are invaluable assets. If a good man were put in charge here and William made assistant and interpreter, which I don't think he would mind (being thus relieved of his responsibilities), we would have the advantage of his capabilities and be relieved of his shortcomings.

September 26: James Greenland came in to see Mr. Conn to complain that William Firth had only paid his boy Robert $35 for fetching us from Aklavik and the hire of the large canoe and engine, although we paid for the gasoline. Greenland said he liked William Firth, but he was always trying to do him down, and he wanted something for the hire of canoe and motor. Conn agreed and asked what he wanted; on being told he demurred a bit but finally gave him $40, and he was satisfied.

At 10:00 p.m. we finishing checking inventory extensions, seven hours of it. The chief drawback to this inspecting business is working every day, Sundays included, and every night except when you are travelling. Life at the trading posts is fine—after a good day's work you can draw up a chair to the stove, have a pipe and a book—but going back to work, night after night, is no good.

September 27: Quite a snowfall, and some people had their dogs and toboggans out hauling wood. The snow transforms this country and is a welcome change. I shall be glad when freeze-up comes.

September 28: I think a good looseleaf manual is needed as regards post accounting. We find post after post using different methods, some lax, some quite accurate, but nothing is laid down in black and white. Things are done or not done just because this has been the way since time immemorial.

Arctic Red River; September 29: Packed our dunnage bags and bedrolls, towed them on a tobaggan down to the RCMP *Regina,* and loaded up. The boat is small and heavily loaded. They have a tiny camp stove inside which kept us nice and warm. We arrived at Arctic Red River at about 10 p.m. and immediately carried our bedding up to the Company house on the hill. Verbille, a free trader, and his wife were there playing the gramophone to a number of white trappers. We were met by Dodman, the Company manager, halfway up the hill; his Indian wife gave us ham and eggs and coffee. The carpenter here is putting up a new house for us. Accommodation is limited so we spread our bedrolls on the floor.

September 30: The most appalling situation prevails. The books are in a terrible mess. Angus Hooker is a very untidy bookkeeper and there has been little done all summer. Cash is loosely handled and was $500 over. I don't think much of Dodman—he is breezy and pleasant but there isn't much to him. Staff and organization in this district are both, I am afraid, very weak.

Wilson and Johnson of the RCMP were in a couple of times and Dodman, Angus Hooker, and I paid a short visit to the barracks this evening. Hutchison and Cummings of the Good Hope detachment are here as well.

Angus Hooker

October 1: All dogs have to be tied up from today on, according to police orders. It is quite cold, down to 12 or 15°F. There is a good covering of snow and the small lake here is almost covered with ice. Winter seems to have arrived. The air is great and I feel a different man from what I did in the summer. As soon as we get to Fort Good Hope I shall take regular exercise to get into shape for the trail.

I got in a fairly good day's work and got everything posted up for July. Hugh is taking stock, a rotten job. The store is as cold as mischief, much colder than outside. I don't know how he goes on with it the way he does, year after year—it must be monotonous and tiresome.

Johnson of the RCMP dropped in during the evening so we knocked off work and had a rubber of bridge and then turned in. I sleep out in the porch, which is pretty cool, but the deerskin sleeping-robe is the clear rig.

October 2: No one has any idea of how the debts stand at all. The fact that Dodman doesn't even balance the cashbook is a good indication of his qualities. Of course his native marriage is against him, and he is weak. I am afraid he is not really fit to take charge of a post. The house is a filthy mess, the kitchen is terrible and the office is very untidy. I consider these little details to be a fairly good evidence of a man's character and efficiency.

Angus Hooker, I am sure, will never amount to anything. He is willing but lazy. He can spend more time over nothing than anyone I ever saw. The old carpenter is as slow as molasses in January. Since we arrived he has put only half a dozen rows of shingles on two sides of the roof. I am sure a good worker could have shingled the whole roof in that time.

Campbell of Northern Traders is here now. Northern Traders go to awful expense in connection with the natives. At Easter they had the house full of them; some stayed for a week and were fed on canned meats. I am sure all these things will tell against Northern Traders in the end. They surely can't make both ends meet that way and they are bound to go under unless they change their ways. If we keep operating on a sane basis, improving slowly but surely, I think we will come out on top in the end.

Conn thinks this must be the worst district the company has now. These lower posts certainly are bad. We hope to find better conditions upriver. They should have more time to get things up to date before we arrive there. This would be an interesting district to work for, I hope I get the chance.

October 3: We work under rather odd conditions here, Dodman's half-breed babies squalling, Indian women laughing in the kitchen, Mrs. Dodman suckling her baby about six feet from me. Walter Jamieson and Jimmy

Ancoin, two woodcutters, came in tonight from about 60 miles upstream. Jimmy had to have a tooth pulled. The operation was successfully performed with no trouble at all, and they stayed for supper. They are both sleeping on the floor.

October 4: I didn't sleep well last night. I was warm enough, really, but the floor seems awfully flat. It shouldn't, as I have slept on one long enough.

Today I was trying to get Johnston's interpretation of the new trapping laws. Conn butted in, flushed red, flew off the handle, and laid down the law flat—as if nobody's interpretation but his counted. Johnston admitted that some of Conn's remarks were news to him, but he will no doubt administer the law as he sees it.

Dodman's father works in the Company wholesale department in Montreal. He is a fine old man, I understand. It was a dreadful shock to him when his son married an Indian. This fact has been kept from his mother, although Dodman went outside himself last summer. I can't work when the kids are squalling and the house is in an uproar.

I discovered an entry crediting certain Indians with a bonus, as it was called, last outfit. It seemed to me a cleaning up of certain accounts and looked bad. Mr. Dodman has an awful ride coming to him and will be lucky to survive. Conn jumped him today for not teaching the Indians respect. They march into the house without knocking and sit down and smoke. It's a crime, all right, but Dodman says the Northern Traders take whole families into their house. Of course, having a native wife makes a difference. But I don't know what a man like Dodman would do if he lost his job. He will have to buck up.

The Red River is frozen over pretty solidly but nobody has walked over it yet. They have been working on the *Bluefish* getting her ready for our trip to Fort Good Hope.

October 6: We are trying to leave tomorrow at noon. They say a little ice is running on the Mackenzie now, which looks bad. The thermometer is almost down to zero tonight.

I dropped in to see MacLeod, the Northern Traders' man here, tonight. He is a very nice chap, a bit rough and ready but good-hearted to a degree and honest. He keeps his house like a new pin in spite of being married to a native woman. He says he hates keeping books, and I don't suppose bothers with them very much. He doesn't seem to me to be the type of man we want but I wonder if our ideals aren't too high. Can we attain them? What kind of a man do we want anyhow? It's hard to ask the kind of man we want to stay in this country, and we can't get the type we want at our price. Salary is a sticker. We don't pay enough.

On board the "Bluefish"; October 8: Got up about 5 a.m. Pitch dark and cold. Packed the last of our stuff and our bedrolls and took them down to the boat. We had a little engine trouble in getting away and the steering tackle broke but we soon mended it. Angus took us up a wrong channel about 10 a.m. and we ran into shoal water. We had to pole back for about a mile. Then one of the engines developed an awful grind and had to be stopped. Nothing for it but for Angus and Fred Cardinal to take the engine down. It took until after 7 p.m., long after dark, to put it together again. We waited with bated breath when they started it. It ran fine for half a minute, then the same knock. We have wasted a whole day and made only 15 miles. Our patience is being sorely tried but the boys only said, "Well, we'll take her down again while you sleep." I admire their patience and industry. It means practically an all-night job and they have already had a long day of it.

The boat has two Universal 12-15 hp engines. The cargo space is only four feet from floor to deck and this is where we sleep. I spread out my deerskin, my eiderdown robe, and then my deerskin bag, so I am comfortable enough.

October 9: After grinding the valves by hand the boys had the engine fixed by 5 a.m. We turned to at daylight and pulled out at 8:30 a.m. up the right channel. I washed up and then took the wheel from Mr. Conn. We are steering largely by the official department map. It is a fine day, not too cold, and I have plenty of time for meditation while looking after the boat.

We make very poor time. There is something faulty about the boat's design; two engines of this power should shift a boat of this size quite fast. I was visited by Roy Wright, a white trapper, who rowed alongside, made fast, and came aboard while we were moving. He had been visiting some fish-nets upstream. He stayed awhile and woke Angus and Fred up.

Conn relieved me at the wheel while I cooked dinner on our tiny stove.

Conn at the wheel. Left, Fred Cardinal; right, Angus Hooker

After washing up I relieved him again and kept at it until 7 p.m. I had volunteered to keep going in the dark but Fred took over, ran the boat too close to shore, and she was aground. This was rank carelessness on his part because the shore could be seen quite plainly even though it was dark. We started again and found that only one engine was driving. We made the shore in circles and found we had a broken coupling. This meant another all-night job for the boys. They drilled a hole in the shaft and put a bolt through while Conn and I slept. We are getting worried. Two days have got us only 60 miles upstream and the season is pretty well advanced—Conn even talks of turning back as we might not be able to get through.

October 10: Started just before daybreak but made rotten time with the strong current against us. Conn insists on keeping in midstream when everybody knows the only way to make time upstream is to creep along the bank out of the current. We reached Travaillard River where Bill Clark, an oldtimer, runs the outfit for Northern Traders, and stopped there to try to borrow a new coupling. There is a lot of ice along the river and it certainly looks like freezing up.

I took the wheel while Conn had a sleep. I got into very fast water where I barely made half a mile in half an hour, but finally got through it and made good time along a willow cut-back. Conn got up about 8 p.m. It was pitch black and cold. He couldn't see in the dark so I said I would steer all night. Angus and Fred took turns on the engine.

It was a strain on the eyes working in the dark. At times I couldn't tell if we were moving at all, and all I could see was the dim outline of the shore. I had to keep a lookout for sandbars and judge by twists in the river where to cross over. Angus brought me a cup of tea now and again. Once I did run bang into a sandbar. We stopped dead but floated off again. It was 5 a.m. when we put a rope ashore.

The ground was frozen and snow-covered, with ice all along the water's edge. We drove a stake into a sand beach and tied up at that. I was so dead tired that while holding a flashlight as Angus did something to the carburetor I fell asleep three times, sitting up, and dropped the flashlight each time.

October 11: Conn took the wheel all day and with his idea of keeping well out into the stream we had a poor run of 30 miles. I slept until 10:30 a.m., cooked a salmon for breakfast, and went back to bed until 4:30 p.m. I cooked dinner for the others and took the wheel for the night run. We had a few stops during the night, one to fix the steering gear. Hugh Conn got annoyed—he even accused us of running into fish-nets. We ran into ice around midnight and decided to tie up until daylight, as it was very dark and a strong breeze was getting up.

October 12: I got up at 6 a.m. and climbed a hill to see where we were. We started off, Fred at the engine while Angus and Conn slept. We crossed the river, got into shallow water, and ran aground; after we poled off we found the pump wouldn't work, being plugged with sand. I got tired of poling against the stream and pitched the anchor overboard. Conn made irritating remarks about sandbars, adding that if we had been running all night this wouldn't have happened. This is nonsense because we got onto the sandbar in broad daylight.

They got the engine running at last but we got into several nasty situations with slush ice and had to toss the anchor out to prevent us drifting. The boat swung and jerked at the anchor and when we got the engine going again it was hard to get the anchor inboard at the right moment. Conn lost his head and swore at us. I nearly came back at him but managed to hold off. There was nothing to panic about. Conn is so impractical, like an old woman learning to drive an automobile, jerking the wheel this way and that.

We struggled for hours against wind and current along a limestone cliff, then ran into shallow water for several hours between sandbars and islands. When it was almost dark a snowstorm hit us. We continued on because the dim outline of one bank could be seen. Then we got into the stream and lost sight of both banks. With nothing to guide us, I kept the storm on my left cheek, but I am convinced we turned at least one complete circle. We came to shallow water but kept going until we had the riverbank in sight.

We had a nasty incident today. We'd lost a gasket doing engine repairs. This caused a gas leak and we kept the engine-room windows wide open, but when the snowstorm came someone closed the windows. Conn sat in the engine-room doorway while I was outside in the storm. He had given us a tot of rum which was most acceptable. I noticed his head was lolling against the doorway but I assumed he was tired. Then Angus came along, tapped him on the shoulder, and asked if he was going to turn in. Conn didn't move or answer, even when we shook him. When he came around he looked ghastly, pale and perspiring, and asked in a strange voice if he had fallen asleep. He knew that the gas had got him. He got up shakily and told us his heart had almost stopped. It was still very irregular and fluttering. I think we nearly lost him.

There was nothing to do but keep plugging along upstream in the driving snow. The heavy snow started to coagulate on the water and drifted into patches that got bigger and heavier—we cut through these as we couldn't avoid them in the darkness. If this slush thickens and starts to freeze we will be in a dangerous position. We tied up while it was still snowing heavily. The water is fast.

Got up at noon and the snow had stopped. Conn was asleep too close to the engines. I asked him to move but he said he was too weak. I offered to drag him out on the tarpaulin but he wouldn't hear of that. By the time he had crawled ten feet he was fagged out. He just gasped and couldn't speak. His heart is pretty nearly finished, I am afraid. I covered him up and he muttered he was all right so I returned to the wheel. It is a queer sensation, this race against freeze-up, and for all we know there may be a dying man on the boat.

October 13: The slush is thick and the current swift so we are making very slow progress. We stopped twice for pump trouble, and I had to hold the boat close to the shore so we didn't get into the slush.

Around 8 a.m. we sighted a motor boat which appeared to be at anchor. Then we realized that it was imprisoned in about an acre of drifting slush. It was the fine new RCMP *Battleford*—she had dragged anchor and was being carried along by the heavy slush. We decided this would be a terrible loss to the Fort Good Hope detachment and resolved to salvage her even if we had to take a grave risk. We worked our way in to her and Angus and I jumped on board, hauled up the anchor, and got a towline on her. I woke Conn up, gave him a cup of tea, and informed him of our prize. He was feeling better and went on board the police boat where there was a lovely stove.

Our craft now moved painfully slowly with this double load. We sighted Fort Good Hope miles ahead on the left bank of the river. There seemed to be a lot of ice drifting past over there so I decided we should get above the

settlement before attempting to cross over, then drift down as we crossed the river. We could see people lining the bank and watching us. I didn't go far enough past the place. It's strange, but there is always a tendency to be impatient and pull over without knowing why you are doing it. Anyhow, we were halfway across the river when we were level with the settlement.

I kept edging over, looking for an opening through the slush where I could make for the shore. I made for an opening and headed full speed for the riverbank. A border of slush extended fifty feet offshore, the outer edge perfectly even, and along this edge rushed the current and the moving slush. We couldn't possibly get through that barrier. In some places it was three feet thick. The population was now running along the shore carrying ropes to throw to us but we were too far out for them to reach us.

We heaved out two navy-type hundred-pound anchors but they never checked us for a moment. We continued to drift downstream. Conn, of course, bellowed and roared but no one paid any attention. I chopped a step off our gangplank with an axe, split it, and got a nail out which I nailed to a pole with part of it protruding. This would give us something to reach with if we got anywhere near one of the lines they were throwing to us.

Then George Cummings from the settlement ran down, pushed a toboggan a few feet out into the slush, and with a mighty heave threw a line with a piece of ice attached to it almost to the edge of the floe. Very gingerly I managed to get the nail under the line and pull it in. This was fastened to a heavy rope the people had struggled along the shore with. We made fast our end; the other end was anchored to a rock. We pulled our bow tightly against the shorefast ice and managed to get out of the fast current. Using our small canoe as a ferry and pulling ourselves along by the thick mooring rope, we managed to drag everything over the ice to the shore.

We got Conn safely ashore—by this time they had toboggans and dogs waiting for us on shore. Angus and I were the last to leave the boats, and while they were loading the toboggans we walked to the settlement.

"This uniform hat business, worn with civvies, is an absurd idea of the Governors. The one with the badge looks all right but the gold-braided and corded ones are ridiculous."

The rescue party was the company crowd, assisted by the priest. The police took us straight to the barracks and gave us an excellent meal. I feel pretty well all in, only three restless hours of sleep each day for the past four days. Exposure to snow, sun, and wind has burned my face the colour of a cooked lobster and my lips are cracked and dried up.

We only got here by the skin of our teeth. I was agreeably surprised by the good nature and patience of Angus Hooker and Fred Cardinal with the engine and everything else. Conn is a poor man in a boat. Were it not for his unfortunate experience with the carbon monoxide gas, which turned everybody's sympathy towards him, we should very likely have had words before the end. I don't like to have anyone swear at me, as he did once, though I think he did regret it afterwards. Peace at any price!

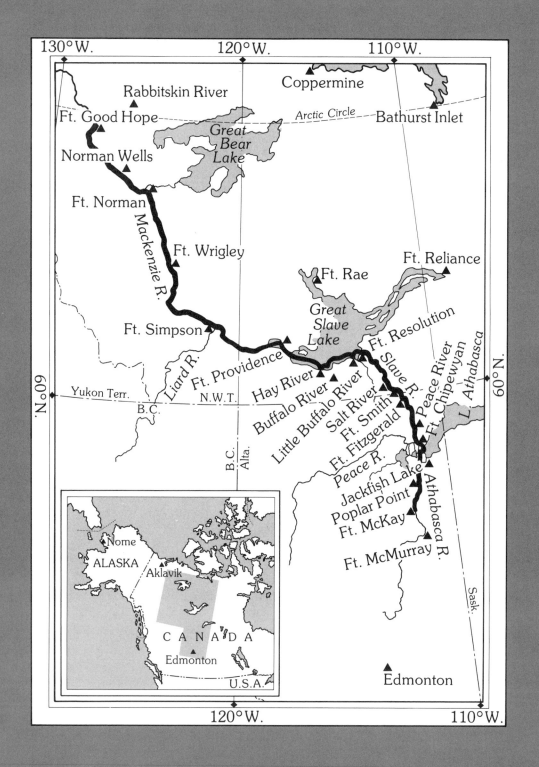

130°W.   120°W.   110°W.

Coppermine

Rabbitskin River

Arctic Circle

Ft. Good Hope   Bathurst Inlet

Great Bear Lake

Norman Wells

Ft. Norman

Mackenzie R.

Ft. Wrigley

Ft. Rae   Ft. Reliance

Great Slave Lake

Ft. Simpson

Liard R.

Ft. Providence   Ft. Resolution

L. Athabasca

Yukon Terr.

B.C.   N.W.T.   Hay River

60°N.

Buffalo River

Little Buffalo River

Salt River

Slave R.

Peace River

Ft. Chipewyan

B.C.
Alta.

Ft. Smith

Ft. Fitzgerald

Peace R.

Jackfish Lake

Poplar Point

Ft. McKay

Athabasca R.

Ft. McMurray

Sask.

Nome

ALASKA

Aklavik

C A N A D A

Edmonton

U.S.A.

Edmonton

120°W.   110°W.

A Winter Journey on Foot from Fort Good Hope to Fort McKay: October 1928 to March 1929

2

At Fort Good Hope, Bonnycastle and Conn were the guests of the new post manager, Gaston Herodier—a French martinet, famous for his omelettes and calisthenics, who had been demoted that year from his position as district manager of the Western Arctic. The post affairs were in a mess, thanks to the incompetence and laziness of the staff before Herodier took over. Herodier compensated by cooking splendid feasts of roast beef, corn on the cob, stewed pears, and omelettes, but the food did not improve Hugh Conn's sour temper.

Even when they'd finished the books, they were forced to stay on. They could not proceed upriver by dogteam until the river ice was thick enough to carry their weight—and until they had learned to drive a dogsled.

October 21: After breakfast Conn said we would hitch up a team of dogs and go to have a look at the big barge in the Rabbitskin River, so we got a toboggan, harness, and five dogs. We tied the toboggan to some bushes and, taking one dog at a time, put them into harness. This was my first experience. Some job, too: we had tandem harness, and the dogs had never worked before in anything other than Eskimo-style harness.

As soon as they were harnessed Conn sat on the box we had lashed to the toboggan, and I slipped the rope from the bushes and jumped on. All the dogs started off except the leader—there was a terrible mix-up and an awful fight. We went through the routine again and the same thing happened. Then we changed the lead dog and things went better. The dogs trotted along at about four miles an hour, Conn on the box shouting at them while I ran behind with the trailing-rope or rode on the back of the toboggan when the going permitted. We had several more mix-ups and got into terrible tangles with the traces, but on the whole we managed all right and I enjoyed it enormously.

It was a lovely day. We took a narrow trail through the bush and all the dogs had to do was follow it. No geeing or hawing. I ran a great deal. It was about 4 miles each way to the barge and back so I was a bit tired, and

Company warehouses
at Fort Good Hope

awfully hot—I had to change my clothes when I got back. I suppose that in winter three or four times that distance will be a good day's run. I'm sure I will enjoy the travelling. It was great riding on the toboggan with all five dogs trotting along, one behind the other, each with its tail curled over its back. When we get seven dogs in a string we shall have quite a handful.

We came back to a good lunch of eggs and sausages. Afterwards I sat down to read *The Cloister and the Hearth*, which I have been reading for ages. I read right through until suppertime, dozing off once in a while, so I had a perfectly lazy afternoon. I have enjoyed today more, I think, than any day since leaving civilization. I have had a real rest from work. It is the first day I have done no work since arriving in the Western Arctic last summer, not counting the days we were travelling.

October 22: Overcast but mild. I dropped in at the police barracks and they prevailed on me to stay for supper; we had cow liver, rabbit, and lemon pie. The priest has been checking up on the liver. I am told it is the custom that when a steer is butchered anywhere on the river the liver must be shared by all the white people. A second steer was slaughtered today so Bill Skinner went with the liver on a platter and gave some to the priest and George Ray of Northern Traders. There is absolutely no game to be had here and even the fishing is poor. There are very few white people here and what there are aren't up to much. I would hate to be stationed anywhere in this district.

October 24: A lovely day but colder. Victor Lafferty and Chinah were both telling me they think the river will soon freeze over. It is rising a bit, which they take as a sign it is blocking up downstream. I hope they are right. It can't freeze too quickly for me.

October 25: Chinah is making me an Eskimo-style harness and Victor Lafferty is making a toboggan and my snowshoes. The trail shoes they use in the country seem ridiculously small to me but mine are to be larger. I took a run to the pond on the Rabbitskin River trail for exercise. I am getting into better condition all the time.

October 27: The frames of my snowshoes are finished and have gone to Mrs. Chinah to have the *babiche* laced in. The women do a lot of work—all the muskrat skinning—and they are said to catch a lot of marten. The new beef we are eating is full of sinew and we are having a lot of fun over this *babiche*, as we call it.

Last night the bread was mixed. They bake about a dozen loaves at one time and freeze them right away. Each loaf is thawed out as it is required and is as fresh as if it came right from the oven. This is the first baking since we arrived two weeks ago yet we have had the best bread we could eat. Herodier worked in the kitchen from 7 a.m. until noon, cooking pies, which Conn likes. The only remark from Conn was, "Why didn't you put crust on top of the pie?" Then he passed me a whole pie and said, "This is your share." As he left the table he addressed me sarcastically with, "Are you not going to have another course?" Tempers flared and the whole meal was spoiled for everyone.

October 28: While we were at breakfast Victor Lafferty came in and announced that one of our dogs had been killed during the night, and sure enough we found the big black pup dead. Several dogs had got loose and piled on him. We lost a good dog but I think we have too many anyhow. Conn was a bit sore and inclined to blame other loose dogs rather than ours. Police orders are that all dogs are to be tied up, and as Conn lets several of ours run around he can't criticize others for doing the same.

Conn and I hitched up seven dogs Eskimo-style and went for an 8 to 10 mile run. Mutt, one of our dogs, managed to escape twice and we had to give him a good hiding, but then we put him in the lead and he was fine there. I had a hard time holding on to the trailing-lead going downhill at the Rabbitskin but I didn't let go. We went up the Rabbitskin and came back following the Mackenzie. We were tipped off several times but always managed to right ourselves. It was good going on the frozen slush a few yards out from the riverbank, but here the dogs nearly got away. Conn got left behind and I was dragged on the glare ice nearly half a mile until I snubbed the rope around a log. It was terribly funny. I arrived home all bruises. Feeling splendid.

October 30: The coldest morning so far; not having a thermometer, I can only guess it is about ten below. Four dogteams arrived tonight—two came here, two to Northern Traders. They are said to have come 80 miles in only one sleep, which is good going. There are others to come in for the All Saints' festival November 1. They brought no fur yet since trapping only begins legally November 1. No doubt they have some fur but are afraid to bring it in since the police are here.

October 31: A lot of Indians arrived today and now the place is alive with dogs. They have been trading this morning. Herodier is having a hard time instilling the doctrine of "nothing for nothing"—they don't like it a bit. The Indians are dissatisfied because we have only oak toboggan boards instead of the hickory they like. Conn declared that the Indians didn't know the difference between oak and hickory, that Herodier could paint "hickory" on the boards and they wouldn't know better.

Paul Louchioux, the Northern Traders' interpreter, says it is dangerous travelling immediately after freeze-up. The water drops at once but not the ice, which is hung up. Should one go through there is a dangerous current which would sweep one away. I guess I shall hang onto a rope when we cross. Paul also told us of a lake where there are man-eating fish. The priest told him he had blessed the lake so it is okay now! But the priest also told him of another lake that hasn't been blessed and is still dangerous!

November 1: Today all the Indians went to church. Also Herodier—he was dressed in his city clothes for the occasion, but he is always neatly dressed. Three sleds arrived while everyone was in church so I sent them to Chinah's house. Herodier, Skinner, and Victor Lafferty have been trading all day. Apparently the Indians have made pretty good hunts already. The police searched some sleds but found nothing. Today is the first day of the trapping season. Some Indians wanted to know if Herodier would accept their marten but he advised them not until Christmas, so they are going to leave parcels in his care which will be returned to them at Christmas.

Chinah may quit. He is taking time off to set snares; he told Victor Lafferty he is starving because now he is not allowed "country food" along with his rations. He gets a good ration but the Indians are awful eaters. He is an old man but a good worker and a strong HBC propagandist. It will be too bad if he does quit.

At 4 p.m. I came from the office and found Conn and Hooker hitching up the dogs by the river so I joined them. Mutt was in the lead. He made a dash for the water, came to a stop right at the brink, then headed up the beach the wrong way. Conn was left behind and I tripped and fell, still hanging on to the trailing-rope. I was dragged a bit before it was pulled out of my hands and the dogs careered up the beach dragging the empty toboggan. I caught them after a half-mile run. Angus arrived, we turned them around and came back at a tremendous pace. We tried to stop them near Conn: I stuck out my leg and almost got it twisted out of joint. It is impossible to hold back seven dogs with an empty toboggan when they want to go. The joints of my fingers were nearly pulled out from hanging on to the rope. The dogs will not go like that all winter, I'm afraid.

November 2: Old Chinah pulled out early this morning for the bush, where he is to hunt. Herodier had intended to give him some meat and frozen fish but the old man took off without knowing this. He never mentioned his departure to anyone. Chinah was jealous of Victor Lafferty, according to Conn, because Victor "gets everything he wants from the store and helps himself at any time." Both Herodier and Skinner vouch for Victor's honesty. He is white, or a very white halfbreed, well-educated, and an efficient interpreter. His ration is $50 per month on which he has to feed a wife and five children, which means he must buy extra food from the store. Chinah is a straight Indian, speaks no English, does the post chores, and gets a ration of $35 per month.

Old Chinah

The remaining Indians pulled out today—ten sleds from the HBC, many heavily loaded, and others from the Northern Traders.

November 5: Chinah returned and was interviewed by Herodier. Apparently he doesn't want to quit after all. He is like all Indians, you never know what they want to do. Chinah says he is old and only thinks about "his belly", and wants more grub. Herodier made it plain that he is the boss and if Chinah comes for his rations today it means he still wants to work. If he doesn't come for his rations he is to get the sack.

This afternoon I had my first experience of dog-driving. I took John, Rover, and Elowtuk on a small toboggan. I suppose they knew I was new on the job. I had a hard time to get them going. They started fighting and trying to beat it into the bush. We went a mile or two but it was heavy going so I turned them around and in doing so dropped the whip. I tied the toboggan to a tree stump while I retrieved my whip. When my back was turned they jumped and the rope came off the stump and they were away. I tore after them all the way home but couldn't overtake them. I got another whip, had a rest, then drove them back to the same place, retrieved the lost whip, and came home in fine style. I think the thing to do is let them know at the start who is boss and beat them properly so they respect you.

"Let them know at the start who is boss. . . ."

November 7: Our exhibitions of dog-driving around this post have certainly made us the laughing-stock of the place. Conn is poor at training dogs, changes them every minute so that no dog knows his place in the team. They fight and tangle and run the wrong way. He uses different systems of harness—the Nome style is our third. He hasn't definitely picked out our two teams yet. Yesterday when he was disentangling dogs and altering their positions he was flat on his back several times. It is too bad that the general inspector of Fur Trade should become the laughing-stock of Fort Good Hope.

November 11: Armistice Day. It doesn't seem like ten years since the war ended and yet a lot has happened, to me anyway. This next year should bring forth a lot too. I wonder what everyone at home is doing today?

November 12: Conn showed me his report on the four lower Mackenzie River posts. We had quite a discussion about the district. His reports seem to lack something: I should say they are good statements of the present situation, but there aren't any tangible suggestions for changing the state of affairs. He agrees with me that the Company has no prestige whatsoever in the country and that Northern Traders probably has more. We have lost our grip completely. One can't say it is the post managers' fault and let it go at that. They do leave much to be desired but I should say the district manager is at fault. Either he is not the man for the job or else he has too much on his hands. His inspectors on the lower river have been worse than useless. I blame Romanet for this loss of prestige. Conn says he would hate to be in his shoes. So would I.

It pleased me to be shown his reports. I was beginning to wonder if he was keeping them from me for some reason.

November 14: Twenty degrees below zero. Busy all day getting ready to leave. We are to have three teams. Victor Lafferty will be guide with a load of 400 pounds of dried fish. Angus Hooker will take the grub and part of the baggage. Hugh Conn and I will take the balance.

We should have enough grub. We have 69 meatballs, 70 slices of bacon, beans cooked and frozen, bannocks and doughnuts. I have cut down my stuff but Hugh Conn has an awful pile of junk.

We bid adieu to the police, the priest, and George Ray. We intend to get up at 5 a.m. when it begins to get light. I'm afraid this will be a hard trip.

On the trail; November 15: We did get up at 5 a.m. Dark, clear, and cold. By daylight we were ready and had the dogs hitched. We have terrible loads. Victor Lafferty has six dogs with fancy harness and sleigh bells, Angus Hooker has six dogs hitched tandem style, Conn and I have seven dogs— Mutt, Otto, John, Peart, Gaston, and two we borrowed—an awful mess. Victor led off—his dogs pull like Trojans—and we followed with Angus last. Chinah came as guide. We got out of the settlement okay except that our dogs got away. We caught them halfway down the hill. We took the portage on the eastern side of the Ramparts. This took us 8 miles through the bush on a very tough, crooked trail.

I trotted along practically all morning. The sunrise was glorious. It was a beautiful day, sun shining and frost on the trees. At noon we stopped and boiled the kettle. We cut spruce boughs to stand on around the fire and cooked beans. After lunch Chinah returned to Good Hope. Then we had to unhitch the dogs and take the toboggans down a very steep gully in the walls of the Ramparts. We crossed the river, which was pretty rough, and climbed the far bank for another mile-long portage.

We camped at the end of this portage. The procedure is as follows: while Conn unties the dogs, Victor, Angus, and I cut firewood and spruce boughs. We spread the spruce boughs as thickly as possible over an area to fit the tent. Then we pitch the 10′ x 12′ x 5′ wall tent. Hard work altogether. Then we set up the stove, light it, and start a fire outside. We fill the kettles with snow and put them on. While Conn cooks we feed the dogs. Then into the tent, have supper, wash up, and turn in. Mitts, duffels, parkas, moccasins, and socks all have to be hung up to dry, wood and kindling readied for morning, sore limbs and blisters attended to, and a hundred and one other things.

All this was new to me the first night. We camped about 4 p.m. and it got dark almost immediately. I was tired and turned in by 9 p.m. We spread Conn's canvas on the brush, then his eiderdown, our deerskin bags, and my eiderdown over the lot. This made a very warm bed. Conn and I stripped but Victor and Angus rolled up in their eiderdowns with most of their clothing on.

For supper we had fried meatballs and bacon, bannock and jam, followed by tea. I find myself very thirsty and drink a lot of tea. We have covered about 12 miles.

November 16: Conn's alarm went off at 6 a.m. It was pitch dark and cold in the tent. I slept very poorly, stiff and sore and not very comfortable. It sure was cold getting dressed but it didn't take long. There was no thought of washing. Lit the fire and the one outside, melted snow, boiled water, made porridge, cooked bacon, and made tea. Conn did the cooking while I rolled our bedrolls. Then we ate, washed up, struck the tent, hitched the dogs, and started off while it was still dark and snowing a bit. We followed the riverbank, crossed the mouth of some river, then followed the edge of the Mackenzie River upstream. We crossed to an island on smooth, snow-covered ice. It was pretty thin. Victor went ahead of his dogs and tested the ice with an axe. The dogs were very obedient, stopping or following him as they were called. Between the island and the other shore it was very rough, but where the ice is rough it is dead safe.

After that it was fair going. We made camp on a point about 4:30 p.m. We had to fetch firewood and brush from away up the riverbank. A terribly hard job. I was tired and sore. We have covered only 13 miles with scarcely any riding for me. Tried the snowshoes and immediately got a blister.

November 17: A long day. Good going all morning but I had to foot it. A cold wind and a miserable lunch as Conn was in a rotten temper. After lunch another long river crossing which was very rough. We had to stick to the rough ice because the smooth is unsafe. Then open water forced us along the bottom of a high bank, miserable, heart-breaking work and a gale of wind. Darkness forced us to camp in a rotten place with a high bank to climb to get into the bush. I don't know how we got everything up but we made a fair camp. Everyone was all in. Even the dogs were tired. Travelled about 22 miles.

November 18: Off before daylight. Good glare ice made it possible for me to ride. Passed Ed Rosen's shack in the morning and caught up to him on his trapline about noon. He had a lynx in one of his traps so we went to see it, and took a picture of it. Made camp after dark on an island. Angus was so far behind we had to build a fire as a beacon for him. The usual slavery making camp, with the usual rotten remarks from Hugh Conn. I am very stiff and sore tonight. A long day, 35 to 40 miles.

November 19: Delayed by open water and thin ice. Conn got so miserable I let him go ahead and walked the last five miles into camp after dark. Conn was sullen and silent. I thought things were coming to a showdown. He ate nothing and then became ill. We all turned in early. I was very tired after

Ed Rosen

walking for most of the day. My legs and feet are practically ruined. Distance—about 25 miles.

November 20: Conn says if he feels no better he will stop at the Norman oil well and rest there. I know he is pretty sick and I try to look after him all I can. Everyone is sympathetic and willing to help.

Quite early we met George Hurst going over his trapline. We had lunch at Hurst's cabin, a comfortable, bright, tiny shack. It is glorious to get under a roof and sit on a chair! Hurst's Indian wife and children were there. She was putting a fine cross fox on the stretching board. George said he also had a nice silver fox. Conn thought he was lying because he didn't show it to us.

We made Mundy's cabin before dark. He is seventy-seven years old. He was wrecked here when his scow was caught by freeze-up—he took out the 850-pound engine, took the scow apart, and built a cabin from the material right on the side of a creek. The cabin is actually built into the bank. It's small but it was lovely not to have to make camp. The old man was glad to see us and we talked to him until it was time to turn in. A pretty tight squeeze but we managed. We made about 30 miles today. My feet are in agony!

Fort Norman; November 21: By daylight we had been travelling three hours. Conn is in good form and we had a bit of fun at the last fire camp taking snaps. Then we crossed the river, passed by Bear Rock and Bear River, crossed again opposite the fort, climbed the bank, and we were in Fort Norman. What a relief to arrive here. My feet are in absolute agony. Distance today about 31 miles.

In the next six weeks, as Bonnycastle and Hugh Conn continued to leapfrog upriver from Fort Norman to Fort Wrigley, Fort Simpson, and Fort Providence, Bonnycastle's illusions about the romance of travelling by dogteam evaporated into the hard reality of running thirty miles a day over rough ice, making camp at 40°F below zero, and the incessant strain of Hugh Conn's savage, unpredictable temper. Arriving at a post footsore and exhausted, he was put to work almost immediately on the books, while Conn started taking inventory with barely a pause for a cup of tea.

Fort Providence

At these upriver posts they found the same poor results, slovenly management, petty jealousies and bickering between white and native employees that had distressed them downriver. With all his fatigue and frustration, Bonnycastle's self-control never faltered; his "peace at any price" philosophy paid off on January 3, 1929 at Fort Providence when Hugh Conn promised to make him district manager of the Western Arctic the following summer.

"I was very pleased he would be so friendly after all our little encounters," Bonnycastle wrote. "I think things will turn out okay."

Conn's approval was a signal that Bonnycastle had passed his apprenticeship. He had demonstrated his ability to endure physical hardship and psychological stress without breaking—the diary shows how close he came—and had displayed unusual qualities of resourcefulness, courage, and endurance. As a Company employee he had proven to be intelligent, obedient, and honest, a hard-working, clean-living Christian gentleman in the very highest Company tradition. He had also come to understand and appreciate the north and its people; the slower rhythm of life, the social rituals, the unforgiving terrain and implacable climate, the special skills of survival. His new maturity is reflected in the diary. The tone becomes more confident and composed, less critical and self-centred. By January 15, 1929—as the dogteams near Hay River—he is able to accept his lot calmly and even cheerfully:

"I had to foot it pretty nearly all the way to Hay River. The going was either glare ice or snowdrifts. My feet were awfully sore but the pain of running on snowshoes was better than the exhaustion resulting from plunging through the deep snow without them. I was last and lost sight of the others. Mutt lost the trail once in the dark but I soon found it again. I had a job keeping my nose and chin from freezing as there was a slight breeze which was very cold.

"The others far outdistanced me with my heavy load but I kept on plugging over the last 13 miles, running most of the way. The dogs' feet were sore and bleeding a bit. I hit a used trail for the last couple of miles and was able to ride. I was half an hour behind the others in arriving in Hay River.

"We had a cold trip. The thermometer hasn't risen above 40°F below since we left Providence. My feet are sore, blisters under the soles and skin off the knuckles of my toes. The blood came through my socks, but not as bad as in Hugh Conn's youth when, according to *him*, his moccasins were 'dyed red with blood'. Conn started in on the stock-taking right away. It seemed a bit unreasonable to me since we had been up since 2 a.m. and travelled over 30 miles. However, *c'est la guerre*."

Bonnycastle had now been initiated into the elite fraternity of "old northern hands". He was no longer a tenderfoot.

This turning point in his own life occurred simultaneously with an event which would utterly and irrevocably transform the culture and economy of the north, an event which, ironically, rendered immediately obsolete all the lessons in traditional bushcraft Bonnycastle had learned with so much painful effort—

Garbutt "said our mail had been sent back to Winnipeg. That just about broke my heart. Conn went out and came back with two large envelopes, one mine and one his. It had been a hoax arranged in the interval between his arrival and mine. I was completely taken in. . . ."

the arrival of the airplane. As with many revolutionary breakthroughs, its significance was not immediately apparent, and it is noted as a curiosity amid the daily gossip of the Hay River settlement, where the mission provided a focal point for a busy social round of teas, dinners, and games.

Hay River; January 19: Garbutt made a count of the muskrat yesterday, 5,345, which is 100-odd short. Conn counted them again today and got 5,360. I shall have to count them now, I suppose.

This afternoon I checked most of the inventory. After supper I went to the Singletons, the Anglican people, and got some September copies of the *Winnipeg Tribune.* Old, but interesting. Salkaeld of the RCMP came in and we had a game of bridge. About midnight we went around to Cameron of Northern Traders to listen to the news; the King is better and there is an aeroplane en route to Fort Simpson. That was about all the news but we heard some good music.

January 23: Busy all day finishing up the work. It dropped to 51° below last night. Cold but no wind.

Dropped around to Singletons' to say goodbye to everyone. The mission people and the police were there for a social evening. Cameron of Northern Traders dropped in and I went with him at midnight to hear the news. We heard that the aeroplane had made Fort Smith okay and is due at Fort Simpson tomorrow. It is to bring trapper Rags Wilson and the Northern Traders' fur.

On the trail; January 24: Up soon after 5 a.m. and off in two hours. Mrs. Storkerson, Charlie Klengenberg's daughter, who is at the mission here, made me a pair of boots. Our loads are small as we are not carrying a tent, stove, or dog food.

It has been very cold, nearly 50° below. I rode a bit in my eiderdown robe and we made Buffalo River at 1 p.m. After eating we loaded 20 big "conies", a sort of freshwater ling, and pulled out over a 9-mile portage. A good trail had been broken. I ran most of the way, on snowshoes which again took the skin off my toes. We camped at the end of the portage, my first open camp. With a big fire and lots of brush and bedding we had a fine night, warm as toast although we let the fire go out in the night. A lot of rime collected on our blankets from our breath.

January 25: Wind terrible. I had a lot of trouble with my nose and chin and they froze slightly in spite of me.

At noon an aeroplane passed overhead. The dogs heard it first and were going for it when it came in sight! On account of the ground drift I only saw her for a couple of minutes, flying low.

Soon after that I lost the others but kept on going along the lakeshore. Then I realized I must have passed them, or they had gone out to Bitch

Island, at any rate they were not ahead of me. I searched for their tracks without avail. I pushed on along the shore intending to make Little Buffalo River, or camp in the bush as I had no idea where Little Buffalo River was. I had an axe and matches, fish for the dogs, but no grub or bedding. I figured I was okay if the worst came to the worst. I wasn't sure I could find a good place with lots of dry wood. It was cold.

After the sun went down I made about 10 miles, running sometimes ahead, sometimes behind the dogs, watching the bush for a suitable camping place with heavy woods and good shelter. As I came around a point I saw the smoke from the houses at Little Buffalo River. I was glad. It was very cold.

I drove up to the houses and tried three before I could find anyone who spoke English. I finally found one woman and went to her house, where I unhitched the dogs, put my sled away, and brought in my blankets. She fed me moose stew and tea and borrowed some honey from another house for me. All the men from the settlement were away at Fort Resolution. In civilization it would be considered not the thing to sleep in a house when the woman's husband was away. This country is different.

The husband arrived home about 8 p.m., just as I was turning in, and soon after him came my lost partners, much relieved to find me. Conn said it was their fault and I had done quite right. There was much pow-wowing about how we had missed each other. It turned out they had gone north of an island instead of south as they had told me to do. They waited for me, then went to search for me. They were afraid I might have hit out for Bitch Island, but yours truly wasn't leaving the bush on a cold night like this unless I knew where I was going. I had the feeling of being very much on my own out there. I never doubted my ability to make a good camp but I would have liked to have some food. I didn't even have a kettle to melt snow in.

The house where I am staying belongs to an Indian, Boniface. My benefactress is Victoire, young and good-looking for an Indian. Her father was white. I must bring her a present next year.

Fort Resolution; January 26: We were all very sleepy and I didn't get up until 5 a.m. Didn't get away until 8 a.m. I got into the cariole, right under my eiderdown, and never once got out until we arrived at Resolution. My dogs went splendidly and our time was two hours. I was last in.

Conn was busy dashing off a note for the mail which closed at 11 a.m. I did the same. The mail plane is to run three trips a week to Resolution cleaning up all the mail now at McMurray, after that a weekly trip. Riley, the post office inspector, is most enthusiastic about flying in the northern mail. We are entering a new era, for which he should get full credit. We sent off a wire to Winnipeg asking if we could fly where the schedule is convenient. I don't see how they can refuse. Romanet is flying down next week, and Northern Traders is shipping their fur by aeroplane.

We had tea and bread and jam in the house, then I read my mail from home, posted December 23. It came by air.

January 27: I was busy working in the afternoon when the plane was sighted. He circled twice and landed half a mile out, bumped a couple of times, and suddenly came to a stop. The plane appeared to sink down. People streamed out over the lake in a cold, cold wind to see what had happened.

Unfortunately they had come to a bad end. In landing they hit a snow-drift. The undercarriage buckled and let the machine drop. The ends of the propellers hit the ice and were bent right up. The flight is at an end until new parts come in. Punch Dickins, the pilot, said he had seen us out on the lake when he passed over. The aeroplane crew is stopping at Northern Traders and Jim Balsillie is going through to Fort Smith in the morning to wire for another machine to bring in parts. Rags Wilson was there extolling the advantages and pleasures of flying as against mushing.

January 28: It has taken so little time to take stock that we shall probably not be here any longer than we were at Hay River. I only hope we can utilize the aeroplane. It seems to be the only way to travel. I've had enough of dogs.

January 29: The airmen fixed their undercarriage today. Now they are to jack up the plane, which weighs about 4000 pounds, and put the under-carriage on again. They are to try to straighten the propellers. If they can make a good job they will pull out before the other machine gets here. If we get permission from Winnipeg to fly out, which Conn says is unlikely, we may get to Fort Smith on the relief plane. When I think of their flight to Fort Simpson—2½ hours in comfort, compared to our 10½ days on the trail with fatigue, cold, and discomfort—this dog travel strikes me as more absurd than ever.

January 30: Lovely weather, about 15 to 20 degrees below. After lunch Conn and I paid a brief call on Murdoff of Northern Traders. He has a nice house, bright, with lots of windows, decent furniture, electric lights and a furnace. He is partly crippled and pretty deaf but he is a white man, a fact remarked upon by many when comparing their staff to those of the Hudson's Bay Company.

The aviators have been busy on their plane. They put her on her feet and tomorrow they hope to put the propeller on and try her out. Punch Dickins says he will fly out alone without his mechanic or baggage. The news over the radio today says that the fliers have been missing since Sunday.

My nose is healing but is a little sore from the recent frostbites.

C.H. ("Punch") Dickins won the DFC in the First World War; he played a major role in the opening of the Arctic, and the development of Canada's airline industry

January 31: They tell great stories here of Philip Godsell, Romanet's district inspector. His cariole, according to local description, is a regular dog-killer. Godsell makes himself very comfortable, wearing a fur coat, with two eiderdowns in his cariole. His baggage sled weighs about 500 pounds. He left here for Fort Rae with 50 pounds of flour cooked into bannocks, 30 pounds of cooked potatoes, 50 pounds of fresh meat, with butter, jam, and cheese. He also carries a tent and what is known in the north as a B.C. stove!

They taxied the plane close in today. At 8 p.m. they heard over the radio that the news had finally reached the outside and the relief plane will leave Winnipeg tomorrow. Dickins intends to leave for Waterways tomorrow.

Conn and I went to a party at Sergeant Gifford's. Miss Castonguay, an ardent young Conservative from Quebec, was there. We had a very pleasant evening, a good supper, dancing, and a few card games. Hugh and I escorted Miss Castonguay home. She implored us to stay over Monday for another party at Gifford's, then dated us for a walk on Sunday afternoon. The only thing I can see is for us to get out of town on Sunday morning!

It is pretty certain we shall go to Fort Smith by dogteam as the plane has to make a trip for Rags Wilson, Riley, and the fur before it can take us. We will be ready to go before that. Hugh Conn says Winnipeg won't give us permission to fly anyhow.

February 1: The plane got off at noon without any trouble, the pilot and mechanic only on board, no mail or anything else. It circled the settlement a couple of times and left. We heard that they reached Fitzgerald at 1:15 p.m. They expect to be back here on Sunday for Wilson, Riley, the fur and the mail. We may pull out the same day, although it will be a rush to do so.

February 2: I counted all the muskrat today and was 140 short so I had to count them over again. Beastly nuisance!

During breakfast we discussed the white trade which Mr. Mercredi, the manager, says we don't get. Northern Traders give a discount off the Indian prices to the white man, which he is not permitted to do. Ridiculous state of affairs, but fairly indicative of conditions throughout. There is damned poor organization all through the district.

February 3: Busy all day. Conn and I had promised Miss Castonguay we would see her so I had to go and tell her we were too busy. I couldn't get out of a short walk with her. We were invited to a small party in the evening so we dropped in about 10:30 p.m. There was a furious bridge game in session. We had a hand or two, some coffee and sandwiches, and returned home to finish our work.

On the trail; February 4: Didn't get to bed until 2 a.m. For a change I woke Conn up at 5:30 a.m. and we were away around 7:30 a.m., travelled 4 miles on the lake, then took a 15-mile portage. We made a fire halfway across and cooked fish. We hit the big river soon after lunch and reached our fish cache about 4:30 p.m. It was a nice night and we made open camp. Just as we were turning in Jim Balsillie from Northern Traders arrived from the other direction and camped with us. He brought a wire from Commissioner French saying that he preferred us to continue with dogs. Ridiculous.

February 5: Broke camp about 7 a.m. and camped at Alex Beren's place about 6:30 p.m., one hour after dark.

The aeroplane passed over us on its way to Resolution and later on its way back to Fort Smith. We have been on the trail nearly two days going one way. Very exasperating. We feel small.

February 6: Started early and made a long day, 40 miles. The aeroplane crossed us twice today, Resolution and back, while we were between two fires.

Fort Smith; February 10: Aeroplane came over today. I ploughed 3 miles down the river to see them. We got some letters, a few from home. We are well up to date on the news here as Mr. Leggo, the post manager, gets the *Winnipeg Tribune.* Punch Dickins got a great write-up for his Fort Resolution crash. The papers had him winging his way over Great Slave lake in a blizzard while men and dogteams sought warmth and shelter!

Very comfortable with the Leggos, they are both awfully nice and look after us well. Leggo seems to have the trade well in hand here, what there is of it. His store is a model of neatness but there is little profit to be made at Fort Smith.

Fitzgerald; February 27: On hitching up I couldn't find the dog Gaston, who is now my leader. I gave up looking for him and left at 7:00 a.m., and didn't stop for 27 miles. The horse trail is pretty well snowed over. After lunch I did 10 miles on snowshoes ahead of the dogs. When we reached Ryan's camp I was wet with sweat, and felt rather cold after unhitching and feeding the dogs. Charlie Walker gave us a dandy meal and we turned in right after but spent a rather uncomfortable night.

Fort Chipewyan; February 28: Had our longest day of travel of the winter, about 53 miles over rough horse trails. We got the poorest welcome we have had anywhere. Mr. Hooker, the manager, was away. Mrs. Hooker said she thought arrangements had been made for us to stay at McLellans' but Hugh Conn was furious, darned if he would sleep at McLellans', and said he would sleep in the clerks' house. I went to the McLellans' and found the place in darkness. I went to Leo Mercredi's house but Leo didn't even ask me in, although I hinted I would like a cup of tea.

By this time Conn had lighted the stove and we decided to cook some food for ourselves. Then the two clerks came back and Conn moved into one of their rooms. I rolled out my bedroll on the living-room floor. I was certainly all in. I can't understand why neither Mrs. Hooker nor Leo Mercredi asked us in for a cup of tea.

March 1: Conn, the indefatigable slave driver, had us up at 8 a.m. His heart had been fluttering and he didn't know what might happen next. I was furious with him. I got up, terribly stiff and footsore, but I found it hard to settle down to work again.

Gaston, the dog I lost at Fitzgerald, got here ahead of me by air. It cost me $30 for his fare.

March 2: A blizzardy sort of day but it eased up enough to allow the plane to arrive from McMurray with Mr. Hooker and his two daughters—he arrived at 4 p.m. but didn't come to the store until after supper. Nothing seems to worry him. He isn't as alert and on the job as he should be. Conn bawled Mr. Hooker out before the two clerks and he was flabbergasted. He is gentlemanly, quiet-spoken, well educated and one would think up to the mark, yet he doesn't seem to worry at all. I should, with a family to look after. If I had been bawled out immediately, as he was, I would be afraid of losing my job.

After his bawling-out Mr. Hooker sat and talked to Leo Mercredi and me in his office while Conn continued stocktaking. Hooker thoroughly enjoyed his flight. He said how vastly superior it was to dog travel. They made a trip in an hour and a half which takes five days by dog team. I can't see why we must endure this miserable method of travel while other people are flying all over the country.

March 3: Had breakfast at 8:30 a.m. instead of 7:45 a.m., a concession to Sunday, I suppose, then to work for the rest of the day. A whole lot of men came in from Beaver Lodge, where they had put up 3700 tons of ice for the fishing company; they are on their way out with horses. They all boarded at McLellans'.

At 6 p.m. we had supper with the Hookers, roast goose cooked to perfection, several kinds of vegetables, and a delicious steamed pudding. Mr. and Mrs. Hooker, daughters Clara and Laura, the clerks, Conn, and myself sat down to dinner. We chatted for a little afterwards, and then Hugh Conn and I paid a call on Corporal and Mrs. Bryant and spent a pleasant evening talking to them.

March 6: Quite a discussion this morning on how to treat the recovery of Indian debts. This apparently receives a different treatment almost everywhere. There is no uniform rule laid down, although Conn has his own rule for everything. If you have a different view he loses his temper and thinks you are questioning his authority as general inspector.

Dined with the Hookers again tonight, another splendid meal. A dance afterwards. Clara and Laura Hooker are both good dancers.

Western Canada Airways staff: from left, pilot Punch Dickins, agent/bookkeeper Fred Lundy, mechanic Lew Parmenter

Punch Dickins' flight to Fort Resolution inaugurated air freight and airmail service in the North. The previous September, thirty-year-old Dickins, a veteran of the Royal Flying Corps, had made the first flight across the Barren Lands from Winnipeg to Fort Fitzgerald and back, covering almost 4,000 miles in twelve days. Here is Dickins' own description of his adventure at Resolution:

"Experienced one of the worst spells of weather in 18 years and had temperatures down to 62 below zero and 34 below with a 50 mile wind. Had a few troubles, the chief one being frost and ice in the carburetor at temperatures below 30 below zero. The rubber shock absorbers on the undercarriage are not much good at extreme temperatures, freezing solid, and make land-ing just the same as if the tubes were solid in the legs.

"At Resolution I landed in a heavy snowstorm and made a good land-ing but ran over a drift that I could not see and the right leg folded up and then the left. There was no jar of any kind and the passenger thought that it was the normal way for a machine to land. After the legs folded I switched off and pulled the nose up to save the engine but both blades of the prop bent and one blade was cracked about 6 inches from the tip. This blade broke off when we tried to straighten it so we cut the other off and set them at 18 degrees pitch. The legs were fixed by straightening them as much as possible. Then we cut off the cracked parts and inserted water pipes inside and riveted them into place. I flew the ship out this way." *

* From *Pioneering in Canadian Air Transport* (see Bibliography); later quotes from Punch Dickins are from the same source.

March 8: Very cold today. My room at McLellans' is always bitterly cold in the morning, water frozen solid in the jug, and I hate to get up. The glare from the sun hurts the eyes very much now.

The plane arrived at noon, took two passengers, and left almost immediately. He is flying right through to Edmonton with a load of Northern Traders' fur. He left here just when we were going to lunch and will be in McMurray before we have finished eating!

March 9: Miserable day, a regular gale blowing from the north-east. Not quite as cold.

Conn gave Mr. Hooker a nasty time today. It's against the rules for servants, as Conn calls them, to keep dogs, employ relatives, have their own sons on the mess unless they pay for it, and a lot of equally irritating examples. He told Mr. Hooker that the Company even fired one man because he had such a large family, and he quoted the names of men who had been fired without pension after thirty to forty years' service. If I thought the Company was anything like what Conn makes it out to be, the most monstrous institution that ever existed, I would quit right now.

Mr. Hooker tells me Conn has it in for him because of a report he made to the commissioner which wasn't too flattering to Conn, but which Commissioner Brabant said was the best report he had ever seen.

March 10: A beautiful day, quite mild with little wind, a most welcome change. If I lived here this is the kind of a day I would be off with my dogs, but here we are, on Sunday, at work by 9 a.m. Oh well, it won't be for long now.

March 11: Hugh Conn and Mr. Hooker told each other off in good style. Conn did most of the bawling out. Hooker responded by remarking that in the service today you got bawled out whatever you did. I think Conn finally subdued Hooker in the end and I more or less think Conn was right. Things weren't in good shape here, which has meant a lot of extra work for me.

March 12: McLellans' are closing shop so we had our meals at the Hookers', and splendid meals they were. Relations are amiable again. Mr. Hooker told me that never in all his experience had he known a man as thorough as Hugh Conn, but that he doubted the utility of it all. He also apologized to me for having so much extra work to do, the result, he said, of the slovenly ways he had allowed himself to get into. Anyway, Conn's bawling-out seems to have done him some good.

On the trail; March 13: Hitched up the dogs and drove over to the Company house for breakfast at 6:30 a.m., loaded up, and were away by 7:15 a.m. Made a fire at 11 a.m. and had bannock, sardines, sweet biscuits, and jam with tea. We then pushed on and made the big river. About 45 miles today.

March 14: Another beautiful day. I travelled in shirt-sleeves since the sun is so hot. It is very wet underfoot. At Poplar Point we had a meal but pulled out again at 6:15 p.m., and I went ahead of the dogs wearing my snow-shoes. I walked or ran about 8 miles. The moon was three days old and was setting anyway so we had very little light. I was all in but I had to wait for twenty minutes until Hugh Conn arrived with the dogs. I was chilled to the bone. I put on my parka, partly covered myself with my eiderdown robe, and thought I would never get warm. We stopped with an Indian—there wasn't much room—and had coffee, a can of apricots, and some biscuits, and then to bed. Warm at last!

Fort McKay; March 15: I started moving at 5:30 a.m. The Indian woman made some porridge and we had toast and coffee. We were stiff and sore but determined to make it to McKay. We thought we would travel until the going got too soft, then stop until the sun went down. We had an excellent meal and a rest at 11 a.m. so decided to push on the next 19 miles to McKay. It took us 6 hours but I'm glad we made it. Only another 35 miles to Waterways and we'll be all through. We are sure to make the train on March 28 now.

I feel very unsettled. I keep wondering what the future will bring.

THE SONG OF THE ANNUAL ACCOUNTS

We've been juggling formidable figures,
    and statements, and schedules and forms,
With data, with tables, with records, re-
    gardless of sunshine or storms.
We have taken no heed of the hour, our
    meals have been grabbed on the run;
Fam'ly ties have been wholly forgotten,
    we've spared not a moment for fun.
The first rays of daylight have found us
    glued fast to the top of a stool,
While the shadows of evening were falling,
    we'd be busy as kids in a school.
No time have we spared for the "pictures",
    no joy-rides could lure us away;
And the long sunny days of the summer for
    us held no promise of play.
But the labour of weeks is now ended, the
    goal we have striv'n for in sight;
Chaos is turning to order and through
    darkness is breaking a light.
Far sweeter than pealing of church bells,
    or song of the lark as it mounts,
Is the yell that resounds through the office,
    "We've finished the Annual Accounts."

Beaver, December, 1927

(DEPARTMENTAL)   OUTWARD   13170

HUDSON'S BAY COMPANY   Telegram No. 2524
        LONDON   Date   26.3.29

To Messrs.   French
                    Hubaycomte
Addressed   WINNIPEG

        Twofivetwofour   Tuesday

        Please convey to Hugh Conn and Richard Bonnycastle
        the good wishes of the Governor and Committee and
        their congratulations upon returning to Winnipeg
        after accomplishing a journey under winter conditions
        which will rank with the great achievement of their
        predecessors in the Companys service.

                    CHARLES V SALE
                    GOVERNOR

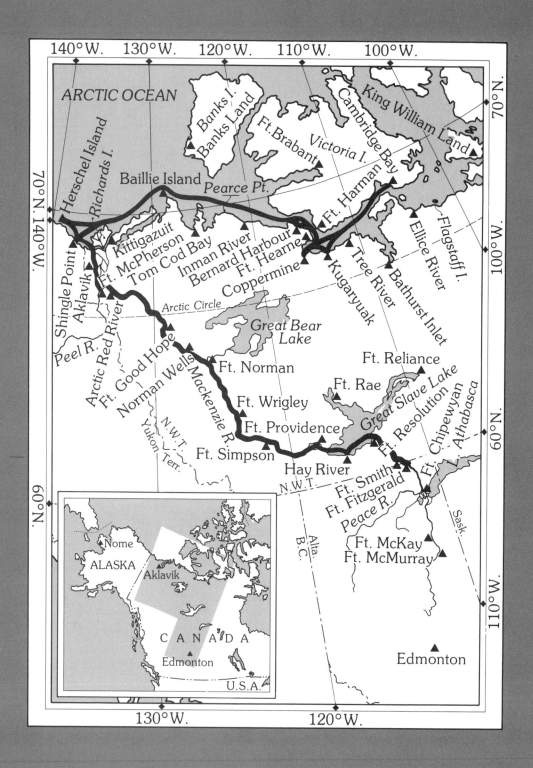

ARCTIC OCEAN

140°W. 130°W. 120°W. 110°W. 100°W.

70°N.

Banks I.
Banks Land
Ft.Brabant
Victoria I.
Cambridge Bay
King William Land

Herschel Island
Richards I.
Baillie Island
Pearce Pt.
Ft. Harman

100°W.

70°N.140°W.
Shingle Point
Aklavik
Kittigazuit
Ft. McPherson
Tom Cod Bay
Inman River
Bernard Harbour
Ft. Hearne
Coppermine
Kugaryuak
Tree River
Bathurst Inlet
Ellice River
Flagstaff I.

Peel R.
Arctic Red River
Arctic Circle
Great Bear Lake
Ft. Good Hope
Norman Wells
Mackenzie R.
Ft. Norman
Ft. Reliance
Ft. Rae
Great Slave Lake
Ft. Resolution
L. Athabasca

60°N.

Yukon Terr.
N.W.T.
Ft. Wrigley
Ft. Providence
Ft. Simpson
Hay River
N.W.T.
Ft. Chipewyan
Sask.

60°N.

Ft. Smith
Ft. Fitzgerald
Peace R.
Alta.
B.C.
Ft. McKay
Ft. McMurray

110°W.

Nome
ALASKA
Aklavik
C A N A D A
Edmonton
U.S.A.

Edmonton

130°W. 120°W.

A Year in the Western Arctic: June 1929–July 1930

3

If Hugh Conn had the slightest inkling of Bonnycastle's antagonism towards him, he gave no sign to his superiors. His report on his trip has nothing but praise for Bonnycastle and the junior clerk, Dick Watt:

> We were held for several days in the ice while travelling by small native schooner from Shingle Point to Herschel Island. The native and his wife and children with whom Mr. Bonnycastle and I travelled were sick. The man was still able to attend to the engine. I took the wheel and hour after hour Mr. Bonnycastle remained at the masthead on the lookout for open leads through the ice, directing me which way to steer. At Herschel Mr. Bonnycastle assisted at digging graves, making coffins, and putting the dead into coffins, and helped to carry them to the burial place and bury them.
>
> I need say nothing more than that Mr. Bonnycastle and Mr. Watt have day and night attended to duty. On very few nights, whether at posts or on the way between posts, have they stopped work before midnight, and were always at work at 8:30 a.m., on several occasions working all night. There has not been the slightest slacking on the part of anyone.

Bonnycastle maintained a diplomatic silence about Mr. Conn in his own report to chief accountant Philip Chester; however he was frankly and uncompromisingly critical of the chaos, incompetence, waste, inefficiency, and obsolescence he had found everywhere in the Company's northern operations. He recommended a total reform and modernization of the Company's business methods, including standardized bookkeeping, uniform trading methods, regular inspections, more capable staff, and the use of aircraft.

The sweeping implications of Bonnycastle's recommendations were politely ignored. Appointed district manager of the Western Arctic in June 1929, he was expected to introduce his reforms singlehanded, by dogteam, travelling from post to post across the frozen tundra during the winter of 1929-1930. It was the most difficult job in the Company: the Western Arctic had lost $183,000 in 1928, putting the HBC itself almost $95,000 in the red. The Western Arctic had been famous for years as the "disaster area" of the fur-trading operation.

The reason was obvious: The Hudson's Bay Company was smug, slow-moving, top-heavy johnny-come-lately to one of the most sophisticated and viciously competitive commercial frontiers in the world. Accustomed to a 200-year tradition of monopoly, the deference of politicians, and a free hand with the natives, the Company found itself up against free-wheeling free traders who had been in the Western Arctic for twenty years when the Company opened its first post at Aklavik in 1912. Its two arch-rivals were T. C. Pedersen, captain of the *Patterson,* and Christian (Charlie) Klengenberg, captain of the *Maid of Orleans.* Klengenberg, who'd come to the north from Denmark as a cabin boy, had built his own family dynasty along the coast, setting up his half-Eskimo sons and daughters and their husbands at a series of outposts reaching as far east as Victoria Island. Both he and Pedersen operated out of west-coast American ports, sailing their trading schooners north to Herschel Island every spring, working east to the Coronation Gulf during the summer, and leaving again before freeze-up via the Bering Sea. They provided a complete department store service for the Indian and Eskimo population, trading kerosene, flour, jam, cotton goods, pots and pans, tobacco, rifles, ammunition, and sewing machines in exchange for furs, hides, whale oil, handicrafts, and ivory carvings. They were mobile and aggressive, able to adapt quickly to the needs of a small, nomadic native population, and willing to accept much less than the 100 to 150% profit margin the HBC considered necessary.

Klengenberg and Pedersen had both come to the Western Arctic on whalers, the great, square-rigged sailing ships that hunted bowhead whales in the Beaufort Sea. The first whaler wintered at Herschel Island in 1889; until the whaling industry collapsed twenty years later, as many as fifteen ships and their crews would spend the long, dark winter months in the ice-bound harbour at Herschel Island. The graves of many sailors who perished on that desolate sandspit can still be found on the gravel beach. Some were frozen to death, trapped on the ice by freak blizzards; some died of sickness or scurvy; some were murdered.

Left, Charlie Klengenberg; right, his son Patsy and wife

C-38499/PUBLIC ARCHIVES CANADA

P7517-362/ANGLICAN ARCHIVES

An Arctic whaler loaded with blubber

P7517-51/ANGLICAN ARCHIVES

Bishop Isaac Stringer and his wife Sadie

The whalers took away a fortune in blubber and bone; they brought booze, debauchery, and venereal disease to the native population. The tiny, remote community acquired a reputation for vice that rivalled Dawson City and the Shanghai waterfront.

News of this Arctic Babylon aroused the compassion of a gentle giant of a man, the Anglican missionary Isaac O. Stringer. In the summer of 1897 Stringer arrived on Herschel Island with his young wife and infant daughter Rowena to establish an Anglican mission and school. Until the RCMP arrived in 1903 to plant the flag and open a customs post, the remarkable Stringers served as sole teachers, doctors, lawyers, counsellors, and peacekeepers to whaler and Eskimo alike. By the time the HBC opened its trading post on the island in 1915, many of the surviving Eskimo were both educated and Anglican. Stringer went on to become Bishop of the Arctic, Bishop of the Yukon, and Archbishop of Rupertsland.

As the Hudson's Bay Company expanded east along the shores of the Coronation Gulf, opening posts at Shingle Point and Baillie Island in 1916,

Bernard Harbour in 1917, Cambridge Bay and King William Land in 1923, the natives they encountered were anything but innocent. Intelligent, independent, and still relatively self-sufficient, they were adept at playing one trader off against another for their own advantage. The Company's most formidable rivals here were Charlie Klengenberg's half-Eskimo children, Patsy, Lena, and Etna, each of whom operated a trading post—Patsy at Wilmot Island, Lena on Victoria Island, Etna and her Eskimo husband Ikey Bolt near Coppermine. Handsome, literate, and thoroughly bicultural, the Klengenbergs could sail like Vikings, hunt like Eskimos, and trade like Eatons. By the time the Hudson's Bay Company arrived, the family dynasty established by the diminutive Dane was already a legend in the north.

At first the Company attempted to imitate Klengenberg's tactics. It stocked its posts with a king's ransom in fancy trade goods and hired former whalers with Eskimo wives as post managers. But the whalers—shrewd, hardnosed, and tough as nails—were contemptuous of paperwork and totally lacking in sympathy with the Company tradition of loyal service and low wages. A warehouse full of food was a bonanza for people who seldom knew where their next meal was coming from, and the whalers distributed it with the spirit of *noblesse oblige* of modern Ali Babas. By 1924 native debt in the Western Arctic surpassed the profit from furs; advances given out were two and three times as large as the payments.

"Records kept at posts by illiterate men are vague and incomplete," reported Inspector Godsell in 1924. "The majority of present post managers appear to be totally unqualified to handle such large outfits as are now being shipped in. There has been a general tendency towards carelessness, extravagance in debt, and reduced gross merchandise profits. The district is conspicuous for the incompetence and undependability of the existing staff. There is a total lack of discipline, every man being permitted to do almost exactly as he desires. Orders are very rarely given and then frequently disregarded. The district manager is on terms of familiarity with all his men, is indulgent to a degree, and lacks the moral courage to face a situation or reprimand an employee."

The district manager, Herbert Hall—an outstanding northern trader and explorer—had no taste for inventories or accounts. "He seems obsessed with the idea that there is going to be a shortage of goods throughout his district," wrote Godsell, who found warehouses full of pyjamas, bathrobes, dancing slippers, tweed coats, silk bloomers, powder and rouge compacts, jewellery, and wrist watches. The dismal little post of Aklavik alone had accumulated more than $500,000 worth of merchandise, with no hope of turning over more than a third of it.

Herbert Hall and the "beachcombers", as Godsell called them, were dismissed. But Hall's intuition had been right: in the winter of 1924 the Company supply ship, the *Lady Kindersley,* was wrecked off Point Barrow and the posts were left without supplies. Cambridge Bay was closed when it ran out of food; other posts ran desperately short. The Eskimos had thrown away their copper knives and become totally dependent on their annual grubstake of ammunition, flour, and kerosene. The RCMP distributed emergency rations of flour, lard, and coal from its caches along the coast to stave off starvation.

Unimpressed by the Company's failure to fulfil its obligations to its Eskimo trappers, the police at Herschel Island were unsympathetic when the Company had Charlie Klengenberg banned from the Arctic coast because he was not a Canadian citizen. When Klengenberg turned up in the *Maid of Orleans* in the summer of 1925, unaware of the new rule, Inspector T. B. Caulkin at Herschel Island was faced with an unpleasant dilemma: Klengenberg argued that without his shipload of supplies his children and their dependents would face the same starvation that the Company's people had faced the previous winter. Caulkin allowed the *Maid* to proceed to Victoria Island on condition that Klengenberg deal only with his own family. To ensure obedience he placed Constable "Slim" Macdonald on board the *Maid*. Klengenberg returned in the autumn. Macdonald did not. He had disappeared at sea off Rymer Point; Klengenberg said he had fallen overboard. There were no witnesses, and an RCMP investigation uncovered no evidence of foul play, but the mystery added a blacker hue to Klengenberg's already shady reputation as the "sea wolf" of the Arctic (he had earlier been tried and acquitted of murder in the death of his chief engineer) and created a legacy of hostility and mistrust between the RCMP and the Company that would endure for years.

"Starvation among the natives must be avoided at no matter what cost," ordered HBC Commissioner Angus Brabant. "Neglect on the part of the Company in this respect has been reported to the government by the police, missionaries, and government agents, causing considerable concern to the London board."

Klengenberg continued to sail to Herschel Island, where his children met him in their own schooners; Hall's successor as district manager, T. P. O'Kelly, lasted little more than a year before his whole staff threatened to resign. His replacement, Gaston Herodier (he whose gastronomic skills later impressed Bonnycastle) proved no more successful at reconciling the Company's appetite for profit with the Eskimo appetite for credit. While the free traders, operating with little overhead, could offer cheap goods and high fur prices, the Company stuck fast to its old policy of cheap fur and dear goods. Fox pelts purchased from the natives for as little as $14 sold in London for as high as $70; profit margins of 180% were not uncommon, and a margin of less than 50% was considered poor.

By 1927 the Company's share of the Western Arctic trade had dwindled drastically; at Baillie Island their post got less than 10% of the fur trapped. The white fox population was decreasing and the Eskimo trappers were incapacitated by epidemics: at Bernard Harbour 60 adult Eskimos died of typhoid and influenza between 1925 and 1927. (The total Eskimo population of the Western

Arctic was about 2,000.) Chronic illness also had a devastating effect on the fur trade.

"Those remaining alive were in such a state of weakness they were unable to go inland for the fall caribou hunt," reported Hugh Conn in 1927. "As a result all are still very short of meat and fat for lighting and heating. It is now too late to get caribou, and fishing through the ice has given such poor returns the natives have to spend most of their time fishing for food for their dogs and themselves. We are doing everything possible to assist them in order to enable them to pay more attention to their traps." He recommended that the price of goods be cut to competitive levels and the price paid for a fox skin raised to $30.

The job of district manager of the Western Arctic had been vacant for a year when Bonnycastle took it on, with Paddy Gibson appointed as his inspector. It was a thankless task. Not only had trading efforts been financially disastrous, but the consequent hunger, sickness, and dependency of the Eskimo population had created a scandal. The Company's feudal paternalism was as obsolete as the dogteam; its selfishness and incompetence had aroused the anger of those responsible for repairing the ravages of free trade. Corporal G. M. Wall described the unhappy situation at Baillie Island in an angry letter to his superior dated July 1929:

> The prosperity of the natives is very much on the downgrade in the past three years. Ten years ago this area was practically virgin country for the trapping of white foxes. The natives had not intensive methods and they could always obtain enough fur to cover their small wants of white man's goods.
>
> With the increase in the price of fur and the competition among the traders to secure that fur the natives were given anything they asked for. During the summer of 1924-25, twenty-six power schooners were brought into the country and in many instances very little paid on them in advance. Large outfits were given on credit, including high-powered rifles, phonographs, cameras, fancy shirts, different brands of canned food, meats, fruits, etc. In 1926 when I took charge of this detachment I was astounded to see the outfits and was informed that $3,000 in credit was nothing, some of the best hunters getting up to $5,000.
>
> The summer of 1926 saw an influx of Alaskan Eskimos and white trappers who had heard of the large fox catches made on the coast. This district was most intensively trapped during the season of 1926-27 and there was not a mile of coastline that was not covered by two or three traplines. The total catch of foxes did not come up to the year before and was divided among a greater number of trappers. In the summer of 1927 when the natives could not pay in full the traders started to cut down a little. The winter of 1927-28 was much worse. The summer of 1928 saw two natives refused any credit whatsoever by the Hudson's Bay Company, not even being given ammunition. Other natives were cut down to more reasonable outfits.
>
> In April of this year the native Annakeena who had turned in 68 white foxes to Mr. McClellan of the HBC was refused credit of any kind, even ammunition to hunt seal. I took the matter up with Mr. McClellan and he informed me that the 68 foxes were put to an old debt and he would not give this native another nickel's worth of goods. I asked him what the native was to do until the next trapping season to which he replied, "It was no concern of mine." I informed him that if any destitute rations were given this native by me a detailed report would be sent to the department concerned and in my opinion the native Annakeena should be supported by the HBC after they had received that number of foxes.
>
> On the arrival of Mr. Gibson, who was making a tour of inspection of the company's posts, I took the matter up and am pleased to say that Mr. Gibson took a more reasonable attitude and gave orders to Mr. McClellan to supply the native Annakeena with staple foods and ammunition.
>
> The majority of the natives are dissatisfied with the treatment they receive at the HBC post here and the prices charged. Last year they were talking among themselves of getting up a petition to ask the government to establish a trading post at Baillie Island. I respectfully draw your attention to the fact that most natives in the district rely now on white man's goods to such an extent that they could not follow their old mode of living, and would suggest some sort of government supervision of the dealings between Eskimos and traders.

Corporal Wall

The HBC had no intention of allowing the government to meddle in the fur trade. Instead, it attempted to re-establish monopoly. In a secret agreement reached in June 1929, the Company loaned $200,000 to Moses Finkelstein, owner of Northern Traders; in return it received 51% of Northern Traders' shares as security, with an option to purchase if the loan was not repaid. Although a public pretence of rivalry was maintained, a close and ultimately expensive partnership was established between the Hudson's Bay Company and its major rival.

Bonnycastle's appointment to the trouble spot of the Western Arctic indicated that the Company was prepared to move hesitantly into the twentieth century. His task of modernization and reform was made almost impossible, however, by the entrenched inertia, conservatism, and colonialism of a monolithic empire which had been doing things the same way since 1670, and by a staff which Bonnycastle dismissed, almost to a man, as weak, lazy, incompetent, braggarts, hypocrites, washouts, ne'er-do-wells, and, in one case, "tottering on the brink of insanity".

His trip down the Mackenzie in June 1929, after barely three months at home in the Winnipeg office, was cold, wet, and miserable, and the driving rain did not improve his temper as he made his way carefully through the minefield of rolling heads left by the flailing of Hugh Conn's hatchet:

> *June 23:* We reached Fort Fitzgerald about 6:30 p.m. and the place is a morass. I went ashore and found the Godsells wouldn't speak to me. They are pretty sore, I expect. George Douglas of Northern Traders asked Godsell if he were going out for a holiday and he replied, "No, for good. They have asked for my resignation."

> *June 24:* We had breakfast at the hotel and got to work on the books afterwards. The mud is certainly terrible. The horses can barely struggle through. The *Athabasca* pulled out about noon with the Godsells on board. Mrs. Godsell actually deigned to speak to me at breakfast!

Bonnycastle was stuck in the mud at Fort Smith, waiting for horses to drag the freight for the *Distributor* over a swampy portage, when he spotted Punch

Dickins buzzing back and forth in his little Fokker monoplane ferrying passengers over the mud to the ship. Dickins was working for Western Canada Airways, a new company owned by Winnipeg grain merchant James Richardson, and he was eager for business. Bonnycastle, who had never yet been up in a plane, couldn't resist the opportunity.

June 30: After lunch Punch Dickins arrived back from Edmonton. Just as he was landing I was handed a wire saying he could take me to Fort Resolution today. I got my toothbrush and boarded the plane. We left Fort Smith at 2:10 p.m. and landed at Resolution at 2:45 p.m. I enjoyed the trip but wasn't too excited about it. I could see all the portages we made in the winter. The river certainly takes a roundabout route. The country back of the river looks most uninteresting, mostly scrub spruce and muskeg with now and then something that looks like a salt plain.

Flying isn't much of a pleasure in a closed-cabin machine. The vibration is pretty tough, the noise is deafening, and the air is none too fresh. On the other hand there is no question about its utility. The plane has revolutionized distance in this country. It is difficult to comprehend.

Dickins flew on downriver and celebrated Dominion Day by becoming the first pilot to land an aircraft at Aklavik:

At Aklavik there were about 300 Eskimos who had never seen a plane, together with about 300 dogs tied up—the din when I shut off the engine and got out was astounding. The Eskimos were very curious and I took some 35 of them up in the machine for $10 each for about 10 minutes. I could have taken more but by the time I had made 7 trips with 42 persons all told I was too tired and called it a day about 11 p.m. This revenue helped the trip considerably. There were some three passengers that were coming out with me but after some hesitation they all backed down. I think they were a bit nervous of the first trip and I have no doubt that after making one or two more trips down there we will still get all kinds of passenger business. I picked up two at Good Hope, including a man with two little boys, one four and the other five, who stood the trip very well indeed.

It was a long grind to make it in four days, however, from Edmonton to Aklavik and back to McMurray. Have put in nearly 45 hours in the last five days and am going north again today as far as Resolution as there is some business waiting for me there and some stuff to go in.

In the Arctic, the summer of 1929 was one of those moments in human history when time seems to be compressed. On the coast, the Eskimos, discovered less than fifty years before in a state of Stone Age simplicity, were taking to the air, while farther south, on the shores of Great Bear Lake, prospector Gilbert LaBine was staking out his claim to the vast deposits of uranium which would build the atom bomb. Caught in the middle, Bonnycastle and the Hudson's Bay Company tried to shore up a commercial empire crumbling under the stress of culture shock.

Company post at
Aklavik

Bonnycastle drove himself harder than Hugh Conn had ever done, taking stock, checking accounts, trying to weed out the illiterate, abrasive, and alcoholic, desperately looking for men who shared his own combination of competence and common sense. His exhaustion, anxiety, and frustration are reflected in terse diary entries. On July 13, in Arctic Red River, he called this "a most miserable trip. Night turned into day. Sleep difficult to get at any time. We arrive at posts at the most ungodly hours and work under rush conditions. It is hell."

Conditions did not improve: the diary for 1929 ends abruptly during a blizzard on Herschel Island, July 25, and his progress along the Coronation Gulf can only be traced from the post journals kept by every manager. F. A. Barnes, manager at Coppermine, reports his arrival on the *Baychimo*.

> August 22nd: *Cloudy with fresh N. W. Winds.* Baychimo *arrived about 6:00 a.m. by our time. Was sure glad to see her too. By rumours it would appear that the Coppermine is going to be a busy spot. R. C. Mission, Gov't. Doctor and two exploration parties locating building sites while Police and two Russians are staking lots for next years location. Aeroplanes are expected shortly by both exploration parties. When the Arctic does boom it all happens in a rush. It is only 15 months ago that I pitched my tent here on behalf of the H. B. C. and considered myself in the light of a modern Hearne. All hands on unloading scows and attending to books.*

> August 23rd: *Cloudy. Wind moderating. Unloading freight and book work. Dominion Explorers erecting storehouse. R. C. Mission laying foundation. Everyone is in desperate hurry for nails, lumber, tools, whatnot, and together with my own affairs in regard to Company business it sure keeps me hopping. Whitefish running fairly well.*

> August 24th: *Clearing up, warmer. Supplied the ship with about 50 whitefish and some smoked salmon of my own curing. Unloading completed by dark and boat ready to leave at daybreak tomorrow. Stayed on board until midnight discussing post matters with District Manager. Brought my new apprentice ashore and said "goodbye" to the old one with many regrets.* Baychimo *will not call here on her return.*

August 29th: *Clearing up and cooler. Aeroplanes expected any minute.*

August 30th: *Clear and cool. Buildings are sprouting like mushrooms at the west end of the settlement and hammers ping merrily.*

August 31st: *Clear and warmer. Interrupted incessantly by natives clamouring for something out of the store. The great event happened around 4:00 a.m., when two aeroplanes came in view to the east. Natives displayed great curiosity, but no apparent alarm. The planes landed on river perfectly, and anchored in front of the house. Proved to belong to N. A. M. E. [Northern Aerial Minerals Exploration] and each plane carried three men. Gave them a hurried meal and entertained them at night with disastrous results to my permit. It is an unusual occasion however. They expect to be here for 12 days.*

September 1st: *I went up in a plane today for 1½ hours, going about 40 miles inland and back. First time I was ever in one, and thoroughly enjoyed it. We had a native with us, and the sensation affected him not the least. Carried on with sorting stock on return.*

Within two years the little boom town of Coppermine would once more be forlorn and deserted as the exploration companies, airlines, and free traders disappeared into bankruptcy. On October 24, 1929, the Great Crash on Wall St. began a decade of world-wide economic depression. Fur prices fell suddenly and drastically, Bonnycastle's ambitious plans were shattered, and the economy of the Arctic reverted once more to survival.

The immediate shock of the Crash went unnoticed in Aklavik: Company staff were more concerned with surviving the winter. Bonnycastle and "head office" could fuss and fume all they liked about requisitions and red ink; the men on the spot had to worry about getting in sufficient meat, fish, and wood to see them through the long, dark months ahead. In a tiny, isolated community like Aklavik, post managers and their wives had to endure weeks of tedium and confinement, and the constant company of a handful of not always congenial

people. Energy and ambition counted for little. Social niceties were more important than bookkeeping, the ability to tolerate solitude more essential than business brains. Bonnycastle's hustle was met with quiet passivity, his admonitions treated with benign neglect; inspections were ordeals to be endured for a week or two, distressing interruptions in the otherwise inexorable seasonal routine.

The calm, complacent tone of Company life in Aklavik is reflected in the post journal for October 1929. As a business record it is worthless, but as a glimpse of a place and a personality—it was probably written by either assistant manager E. J. Stewart, or G. L. Roche—the journal is revealing in its meticulousness, its attention to gossip, and its eagerness to please.

Tuesday, October 1st *35° above zero—9 a.m. Turning colder. Looks like snow. Dull sky overhead.* Liard River *reported to have left Fort Simpson September 26th and is expected daily at Aklavik—making her final trip for this season.*

Bishop Geddes returned from brief trip to Fort McPherson yesterday.

Both Mr. Parsons and Mr. Stewart have been busy opening merchandise—getting both the store and warehouse in shape before Old Man Winter comes to stay.

Settlement very quiet, as all the "huskies" [Eskimos] have left the fort for their trapping grounds and are not expected to return until December, outside of the odd traveller back and forth with a few pelts.

G. L. Roche has been very busy with office routine, as a new counter slip system has been introduced, replacing the usual number of blotters. In fact it would seem that the old 1-10 Day Book has also been abolished and all entries must henceforth be journalized monthly and copies of all journal entries must accompany the usual monthly returns.

Wednesday, October 2nd *40° above zero—9:30 a.m. Cloudy—only slight wind.*

Mr. Parsons assisted by Lewis Kaglik—interpreter—busy sorting lumber and gasoline and putting up storm windows today; Mr. Stewart busy putting store shelves in shape. Milder this afternoon—sun shining through.

As I glance through the office window I see Dr. Urquhart—Medical Health Officer—putting the finishing touches on his newly erected dwelling house.

Thursday, October 3rd *35° above zero—9:30 a.m. Cloudy dull sky with slight rain mist and wind.*

Settlement very quiet—little or no business in the store, although there is ample sundry routine to keep us all busily employed. Mr. Parsons and Mr. Stewart have been busy cleaning stovepipes in store and house—setting up stoves in readiness for the coming winter.

Saturday, October 5th *35° above—9:30 a.m. Dull grey sky—slight mist in spells—evidently trying to snow. Interpreter Lewis Kaglik doing odd chores round premises.* Liard River *with barge arrived here about 8 p.m. this evening carrying a few pieces of freight for the Company post, opposition and others. Left here about 3 a.m. on the first lap of her return journey to Fort Smith—she carried a few passengers for points "outside": Dominion Explorers Corp. employees; Corporal Cummings, R. C. M. P. Fort Good*

Hope—the latter just recovering from a successful operation for appendicitis performed by Dr. Urquhart. A small party of Indians returning to their homes in the vicinity of Good Hope and Arctic Red River comprised the balance of the passenger list.

Sunday, October 6th *Slight frost overnight with thin ice formed on our water barrels outside dwelling house. Quite calm this afternoon with sun shining brightly through. Church parade at 7 p.m.—most everybody attended amongst those few left in the settlement.*

Monday, October 7th *30° above—9:30 a.m. North wind blowing—dull murky sky overhead. Snowing. Old Man Winter paid us a visit overnight—in fact it is probable that he has come to stay. Everything covered by a blanket of snow—first of the season round the fort.*

Mr. Parsons and our interpreter expect to be busy most of the day hauling out our M. B. Little Bear and barge—beaching same before freeze-up. Mr. Stewart kept busy in store and warehouse and G.L. Roche working on monthly statements for September.

Wednesday, October 9th *26° above—9 a.m. Slightly colder with snow flurries. Winter setting in gradually—although the river has not commenced to freeze up yet.*

Mr. Parsons and interpreter shot and killed our two steers this a.m.—our winter's supply of fresh beef. The animals were purchased at Fort Smith and arrived here via last trip of S. S. Distributor.

Ducks and geese have practically all left this vicinity for southern regions. Not much evidence of wildlife round the settlement, with the exception of a few hardy old crows who winter here regularly, and a few sparrows. G. L. Roche finished all monthly returns for September last evening and is now forging ahead nightly with various routine duties of which there is much to be done before the general accounting is actually brought up to date.

Thursday, October 10th *30° about 9 a.m. Milder—sun shining brightly between clouds. Settlement very quiet. Mr. Douglas—Northern Traders Post Manager at McPherson—paid us a brief visit this afternoon and informs us that he is about to have his appendix removed by Dr. Urquhart.*

Friday, October 11th *30° above—9 a.m. East wind blowing—grey unsettled sky. Mr. Parsons and interpreter busy sawing wood today, having the use of the Anglican Mission sawing outfit to cut our winter supply into stove lengths. One of Cpl. Fielding's little girls had a minor operation (surgical) performed successfully this morning by Dr. Urquhart. Having an efficient and capable doctor here so far from actual civilization is proving a wonderful asset to the health of this community and district. A few of the local folk have already been exercising their dogs—giving them short trips in harness round the settlement.*

Friday, October 18th *20° above—9 a.m. Clear sunny morning. A few degrees of frost last night and the river has a thin coat of ice in patches, at this rate the freeze-up should be speedy and enable our hunters to make a caribou hunt. Cpl. Wilson, R. C. M. P. Arctic Red River, and Mr. Beal, apprentice clerk at that post, arrived in the settlement this afternoon with one of the natives, Abraham Stewart, who is now under Dr. Urquhart's* care. It seems that Stewart received a fractured skull as the result of being hit by a capstan while beaching a schooner. They were lucky to make Aklavik over open water as the river is liable to freeze up any day now.

Saturday, October 19th *21° above—9 a.m. Weather about the same—calm and clear. River freezing over at last and should be quite safe for travelling by next week.*

Business almost nil, although there is plenty of routine to keep the staff busy. We learn over the radio that the new winter air mail for northern posts is scheduled to take effect as from November 28th—Aklavik to get three official mails with a maximum of 80 lbs.

Monday, October 21st *15° above—9 a.m. Fine summer morning—calm. Mr. Parsons and Lewis Kaglik left this morning for a caribou hunt and expect to return with sufficient meat for our requirements, in addition to our limited supply of fresh beef.*

Tuesday, October 22nd *20° above—9:30 a.m. Fine clear morning. The river is now frozen over, although a few patches of water are still visible. A few of the children have already been skating near the shore and several of the ladies from the Anglican Mission and Hospital have also ventured on the ice for a spell to break the monotony of long working hours, nursing the sick, etc.*

Joe Greenland, Peter Drymeat, and others have returned from a successful caribou hunt and report having killed fifty. It seems that the herds they saw were in comparatively small numbers.

Wednesday, October 23rd *8° above—Calm and cloudy. G. L. Roche has just completed the task of opening new ledgers—customers and Indians—copying same in detail as from June 1st. Routine progressing nicely. Business quiet.*

Thursday, October 24th *30° above—9 a.m. Cloudy, sun trying to shine through. A few of the natives still round the settlement after their caribou hunt. They also managed to kill a number of mountain sheep, peculiar to these parts, of which the meat is very palatable. It does not taste like mutton, but rather flavours of caribou when cooked. The rams of this species have horns which are curved behind the ears. Unlike our domestic sheep, the hide is covered with short hair instead of wool.*

An open-air "freezer" stands above the dogs' reach

Friday, October 25th 25° above—9 a.m. Calm and cloudy—looks like snow. We learn via "moccasin telegraph" today of the sad death of old Father Lecuyer of the R.C. Mission at Arctic Red River. It seems that he was visiting fish-nets within sight of the settlement when his canoe capsized. A life of self-denial and noble work suddenly launched into the great unknown.

Saturday, October 26th 26° above—calm and cloudy. Father Trocellier left the settlement yesterday en route to Arctic Red River in order to supervise the affairs of the late Father Lecuyer. Cpl. Fielding, local detachment R. C. M. P., paid us a brief visit this morning. Settlement very quiet. Mr. Stewart busy with store and warehouse routine, G. L. Roche still bringing office routine to date. Mr. Parsons and Lewis Kaglik returned from their caribou hunt about 7 p.m. and reported having accounted for 12 animals—which should keep us in meat for a season.

Friday, October 31st 15° above zero—9 a.m. Weather conditions about the same. We all enjoyed a very sociable evening at the Anglican Mission House—conducted by Bishop and Mrs. Geddes last night—recalling the old frivolic custom of Hallowe'en. A number of amusing costumes were very much in evidence—much to the merriment of the evening. Routine same as usual.

After freeze-up natives and white trappers disappeared with their grubstakes to their traplines. The days grew shorter and shorter; in the Western Arctic the sun vanished altogether early in December, though the reflection of its rays often cast a fiery red glow along the horizon at midday. At the trading posts life became a monotonous routine of daily chores until Christmas, when the trappers returned with their families for a week of trading, dancing, eating, and prayer climaxed by a ritual New Year's Day levee at the Company house. In 1929 radio added a new dimension to the Aklavik New Year's Eve, as the post journal records:

Towards evening several fine radio concerts came to us through the air. Numerous messages have already come through CKY Winnipeg to various Company servants throughout the North. The usual New Year's greetings and merriment prevail all over. Although we were only a very small handful "sitting on top of the world" as twelve o'clock midnight approached, ringing out the Old Year and ringing in the New Year, a number of the local folk shot off a few rounds of ammunition. A few hearty cheers intermingled with a few "whoops" echoing from different parts of the settlement. End of another year!

Bonnycastle spent the winter inspecting Company posts along the Mackenzie, travelling by dogteam and, when possible, by aircraft. Mail and freight flights between Fort McMurray and Aklavik were scheduled regularly but weather conditions made air travel extremely unpredictable and hazardous. Flying in the dark by the light of the moon, guided by primitive instruments, landing on frozen, unfamiliar lakes in extreme cold, pilots, mechanics, and passengers took incredible risks, as Punch Dickins noted.

From November 15 to January 15 there is sufficient light for flying only about three hours a day on clear days. Travel away from the main route to Aklavik is not advisable. This is also usually a stormy period and even natives and residents do not travel in December unless it is absolutely necessary. On the Arctic coast away from the river and trees there is very little shelter and the tremendous winds pack the snow into drifts which are both high and hard. It is often difficult to find even a few hundred yards where a machine can be reasonably safely landed.

The deceptive Arctic twilight made obstacles difficult to see, and careful pilots like Dickins took no chances, often dumping their passengers, bag and baggage, out on the smooth ice far from shore: Bonnycastle once walked nine miles from the aircraft to the nearest settlement. Less cautious (or less lucky) pilots sometimes didn't make it; their skeletons were discovered months later in the wreckage of their aircraft, miles from human settlement—victims of laziness, fatigue, alcohol, or the kind of storm Bonnycastle describes in a letter home from Fort Norman in March 1930.

"The last five days we have had the most ungodly blizzard I ever saw. On Tuesday we dared not even cross the river for fear of getting lost—you couldn't see a dozen yards, nor could you face the wind which whipped the snow into your face like sand.

"Wednesday there was a knock on the door about 7 a.m. and a big man, a stranger, came in attired in a woollen windbreaker, moccasins, and breeches. He announced himself as Porsild, a government man (reindeer expert), and passenger on the mail planes which he said had arrived at the landing across the river yesterday, the second day of the blizzard and the worst possible day anyone ever remembered seeing.

"The story is this: they had left Simpson in pretty fair weather and endeavoured to land at Wrigley but found the snow drifted too much, so continued on to Norman. When they ran into our bad weather it was too late to go back, as they did not have enough gas, so they kept on coming. They lost sight of each other and plane no. 1 landed about three miles above the regular landing place directly across the river from here. In coming down it broke a ski, buckled both ends of the propeller, broke the tail ski, and damaged a wing. The other machine landed up near our Fokker. Both pilots had the greatest difficulty holding their machines on the ground, as there was a 70-m.p.h. gale blowing. To weight them down they put mailbags on the skis and also tied them to the wings.

"Porsild was a passenger on plane no. 1. The pilot and mechanic said that if she blew away they'd let her go; they put up a small tent in the bush, lit a blow torch, and spent the night there. Porsild left to walk up to the other plane, where there was a tent pitched with a stove in it. At the first attempt against the wind he froze his thighs so he went back and got a blanket, which he put on like a skirt. He weighs 230 pounds but the wind literally blew him back at times—it took him two hours to walk the three miles.

"When you went travelling you made a great big stew. Young seal was very good. You'd put everything in it, so you could stand a spoon up in it. Then you'd empty all that stuff on a snowbank, spread it around like butter, and let it freeze solid. When it froze you'd beat it with a hammer and put the pieces in empty flour sacks. On the trail you'd take a piece out for dinner and thaw it in the frying-pan."   *L. A. Learmonth*

"In plane no. 2 the pilot, mechanic, and two passengers spent all night in the cabin endeavouring to sleep and keep warm, with little success. The permanent tent had blown down and was no use. They couldn't cross the river which is a mile and a half wide, for fear of losing all sense of direction and wandering around and maybe freezing to death. They waited until morning, and then the storm abated somewhat so they came across and awakened us.

"We got busy at once and put on the kettle and rustled up a couple of dogteams to look for the occupants of plane no. 1. They were found in their tent okay, and the whole gang is now trying to mend the equipment. They have straightened out their propeller and cut a few inches off each end. As soon as the gale goes down enough to allow them to work on their machine they will get the broken ski off and make another. Then they will continue their flight to Aklavik.

"Still the wind blows and the snow flies, although it shows signs of letting up. We watch the weather and will hop off first chance for Coppermine. Dickins is very careful and we don't move until conditions are just right; when we do, we move so fast that a few days' waiting are soon forgotten. I am wondering whether anybody at home is worrying about not getting word from me since last Thursday week. Dickins figures his wife will have started worrying about last Wednesday, unless the wireless messages he sent out blind have been heard by anyone.

"Our machine has weathered the storm okay and only requires a few hours heating up to get under way. Dickins sure is a cracking good pilot and I have every confidence in him, but I shouldn't be surprised if we break a ski at Coppermine, in which case he will be delayed getting back—so there will be no necessity to worry if you do not hear from us for some time. We are well prepared for being stranded between here and there."

Bonnycastle's safe arrival at Coppermine is recorded by Coppermine manager F. A. Barnes in his post journal:

March 23rd: *Clear and light. S. W. Winds. Min. –32°. Messrs. Bonnycastle and Gibson arrived by plane piloted by "Punch" Dickins at 3:00 p.m. Plane landed about six miles W. of Post and left soon after for Ft. Norman. Messrs. B & G started in on mail right away. Much discussing of news. Was certainly glad to see the plane arrive safely after the uncertainty caused by delays.*

March 24th: *Clear and calm. No wind. Min. –28°. Office work and preparations for trip west to Herschel and east to King William Land by Messrs. Bonnycastle and Gibson. A few natives were in with seal.*

March 25th: *Clear and mild. Squally winds. Min. –32°. Max. +22°. Office work. Mr. Bonnycastle left at 6:30 p.m. for seal camp, en route for Bernard and west to Herschel. Several natives in.*

The long, dark Arctic winters were more a psychological hardship for Company men than a test of physical endurance. They were snug and well fed in their tiny posts banked to the roofs with blocks of snow like square igloos. They had meals to cook, books to read, visitors to entertain, and the basic business of survival to occupy the hours.

An Arctic post was constructed like a nest of boxes: first the porch to break the wind, then the large, cold natives' room where the Eskimos came to trade and pass the time, and beyond that the manager's private quarters with its cosy stove. French writer Gilbert de Poncins has left an intimate domestic portrait of Paddy Gibson, with whom he spent a winter at Gjoa Haven on King William Land—as close to the end of the earth as man lived at that time.

This porch was cheerless and dark, its black corners invisible in the feeble light of a single small window.

Next came the natives' room—a long table, benches round the wall, mugs on the table. Here Gibson and I became café waiters each time that a group of Eskimos arrived. Here too the Eskimos camped round the Post collected daily and sat interminably in silence or in laughter. Our immediate provisions were stored in this room—rice, bread, sugar, dried vegetables. At the far side of the room rose a partition built only to within a couple of feet of the ceiling in order that the warmth from the stove in the inner room might come over. Incidentally, that warmth prevented our jams and pickles from freezing and bursting their glass jars.

In the inner room Gibson and I had our living quarters. Here we ate, read, chatted, and mused for whole hours together, each sitting in his own corner while the wind sent the wireless mast swaying in the air and piled up the snow in great drifts. Paddy would go over his accounts and dream of a great day of trading. I would study the Eskimo language, write up my notes and, so long as the season permitted, light would come in through two windows placed opposite one another which, when snow banked the house, lend the effect of great loopholes in a fortress. At the back a second partition, cut by two doorways in each of which a curtain hung, separated this room from the cubicles where we slept, another partition between us.

Paddy had done wonders with his living-room. It was warm and intimate and was the frame within which our life was lived. Here within a hundred miles of the Magnetic Pole there was a kind of bourgeois cosiness that was unbelievable. I used to say to myself that there were no bourgeois places, there were only domesticated souls. One could be an adventurer in New York, and one could also be an old maid in the polar regions.

I had only to raise my eyes to be justified in this reflection. The razor strop hung by the looking-glass, the broom stood behind the door, the pin-cushion rested on the window-sill. Nothing would have been present to remind one of the Arctic if a few white foxes, the "money" that paid for my excursions on the trail, had not been hanging from the ceiling. Scrambled eggs for breakfast? Do sit down, I beg you. The linoleum is stretched taut over the table and awaits your coming. We have a full line of tomato ketchups and fish-sauces.

Really, were it not for the snow bank it would be impossible to tell this house from the average suburban shanty. There were the biscuit-boxes standing in rows on the shelf. Here was the bread in its bread-box, carefully wrapped in a damp cloth to keep it from growing stale too quickly. Chromos hung on the walls, and there was even a vase of artificial flowers—which I would hide from time to time and Gibson would bring out again almost immediately. See the spoons lying in their drawer, and the row of hooks from which hang the skewer, the ladle, the strainer, and the corkscrew. Here is a wicker armchair—salvaged from Amundsen's boat—with its hospitable back and arms; if you saw me sitting in it beside the stove you would certainly say to yourself that I looked like a Paris concierge.

Were I a Hudson's Bay manager I should not change with any shop assistant in the world. What! Get up at seven in the morning, run like mad to the underground, get a dressing-down each time I was criminally late five minutes, lunch in half an hour, and spend my life restless and worrying about my job! Not me! As Post Manager, I should get up when I pleased, take my time over my coffee, hear the natives cough in the outer room, put my head out and say to them, "Hila na-go-y-ok," (nice weather) and shut the door without waiting for their acknowledgement of my greeting.

Each evening was long, calm, and lamplit. I had never imagined such tranquillity. The only sounds that broke upon the silence were those familiar sounds that are so precious in the domestic life of man—the suction of the gas-lamp as it was pumped before being lighted; the crackling of the block of ice as it melted in the water bucket by the stove; the tick-tock of the Big Ben. And there was the singing of the antennae of the wireless mast, a mysterious drone that set me dreaming. Gibson and I would sit face to face, speaking no word, each sunk deep within himself, each at peace with the world, while only the pulsing lamp gave off the impression of life. Now and then one of us would rise and turn the knob of the radio: nothing would come. Nothing would ever come again, and it was well thus. Silence was better than sound.

It was a curious thing that, however long these long evenings might be, we could not tear ourselves away from them. We would sit on indefinitely in that room while the hands of the clock turned, showing that it was one in the morning, then two, then after two. And still we would not go to bed. In the end, Gibson would stir out of his torpor, and it was as if something very heavy had budged. He would half rise out of his chair, put his finger on the perpetual calendar, and the click that would sound in that silence was something almost fateful, made one truly conscious that another day had been released into eternity. We would come to. Gibson would go back and light his bedside lamp while I waited until he called out, "All set!" Then I would put out the big lamp. "Good night!" would float back and forth over the partition between our cubicles, and each would continue to read or ruminate in his sleeping-bag until one lamp went out and then the other, and the only sign of life that remained was the scuffing of a lone dog on the snow-covered roof.

Is there another land in this world where the silence is so total? There is no wind here in the leaves, for there are no leaves. No bird screeches. No sound of running water is heard. No beast is here to take fright and scurry in the darkness. There is not a stone to be loosened under a human foot and roll down a bank, for all these stones are cemented by frost and hidden under snow. Yet it is not that this world is dead: it is merely that the beings who haunt this solitude are soundless and invisible. The fox running through the night over the tundra, the seal marauding in the sea, are as if they were not. And if from time to time you did not see a little white beast caught in a trap, seated and staring at you, you would not know that life existed in this void.

Insensibly, nevertheless, things changed. They changed so gradually that their alteration was imperceptible. Bit by bit this silence that had been so remedial, that had soothed me and laid to rest my frayed nerves, began to seem to me a weight. The horizon was closing in round me. The prison, once so radiantly peaceful, was now unveiling its true face. The visits of the Eskimos grew more rare and the solitude grew longer. But more than this, an almost physical operation of shrinking was going on. I who had come from Outside had first been enclosed by the Arctic. Then my horizon had contracted to the limits of Gjoa Haven; from Gjoa Haven the circle had been reduced to the dimensions of the Post; and now, in the dead of the polar winter, the line I hesitated to cross was drawn in a radius of five feet round the stove. It seemed to me to be true as much of Gibson as of me, that we were forced more and more to retire into ourselves, to live spiritually upon our own resources; and the flame of life within us withdrew farther and farther into a secret hiding-place, our heartbeats grew slower and slower. The day would come when we should have to shake ourselves to keep them from stopping altogether. Sunk deep in this well of silence, we were being stifled by it, we were at the bottom of a pit out of which it was inconceivably difficult to draw ourselves. And yet the re-emergence into the air, into life, had to be attempted.

I went from impatience to restlessness, and from restlessness finally to monomania. I began to rage inwardly, and the very traits in my friend and host which had struck me in the beginning as admirable, ultimately seemed to me detestable. The time came when I could no longer bear the sight of this man who was unfailingly kind to me, whose suggestions were so valuable to me, who, each time that I was off on the trail, would run after my sled at the last minute with still another thoughtful little gift for me. That calm which I had once admired I now called laziness; that philosophic imperturbability became in my eyes insensitiveness. The meticulous organization of his existence was maniacal old-maidenliness and an insult to human dignity.

Naturally, it was the little things that exasperated me: it always is. Vice and virtue have no part in the irritation we feel against those with whom we live in intimate contact. I cannot tell you what a melodramatic object the stovepipe key represented for me. The key regulated the draft in the pipe, and therewith the degree of heat given off by the stove. Heat in a house in the Arctic is obviously of some importance. I always got up before Gibson did, started the stove with the kindling I had chopped the night before, and would let the draft run full blast so that the stove would draw and the room—frozen cold during the night—warm up quickly. This done, if I had been permitted, I should have reduced the draft.

Paddy did not see things as I did. All the time that I was building the fire, shovelling in the coal, setting the table for breakfast, there was silence from the cubicle. But the moment the stove was roaring and the pipe red, I would hear him stir. "Well, well," he would murmur; and having slipped on a pair of pants he would come into the living-room, go straight to the stove, and close the draft with a "We might as well..." that he never finished, so that I never knew whether "we might as well" save the pipe from burning out, or economize the coal, or what was in his mind. The man must have had his eye on the pipe all night, for he was out and at the stove the moment the pipe grew red.

I never said anything, for I knew that if I explained what I was up to, he would smile. I dare say you have seen a stubborn man smile and you know that it is like the smile of a deaf man, of a man who does not want to hear and will not listen. When you see that smile you wish instantly that a special kind of mallet existed for the cracking of such men's skulls.

Then there was the teapot. The teapot stood on a shelf. We drank tea in prodigious quantity and were always reaching for that pot. Now, as it stood habitually behind a tin of lard, I used to change the places of the two objects, putting the teapot in front and the lard behind. And each time, Paddy would put them back in their customary and inefficient order. Whether it was stubbornness or force of habit I couldn't tell; for when I ventured a word he would say merely, "Oh, well...."

It seemed to me I should never, anywhere in the world, meet another such automaton. If you set down the salt-cellar in the wrong place on the table, it threw his whole existence out of gear and sent him into a panic. His life was so regulated that he went through each motion every day at the same moment and in the same order. When he got out of bed, he always began the day by saying to himself, "Well, well." Then, having drawn on his pants, he would go automatically to the stove. After that, he would raise the lid on the kettle to see if the water was ready to boil, and then return to his cubicle. He would come out with a towel, get a basinful of water from the bucket, and wash—always beginning at the same place on his face. That done, he would brush his teeth over the slop bucket. And for an empire, he would not have changed a single one of these motions.

Bonnycastle kept no diary record of his trip west to Herschel Island by dogteam. He took his camera, however, and wrote this account of his first night in an igloo for the Hudson's Bay Company magazine, *The Beaver,* the following spring.

MARCH 1931

The Beaver
An Igloo Night By R. H. G. BONNYCASTLE, *Western Arctic District*

It was after dark on a March night when three dog trains, accompanied by their Eskimo drivers, wives and children, and myself, approached their destination, an Eskimo winter encampment on the frozen waters of Coronation Gulf near the mouth of the Coppermine river. Fairly familiar with winter travel in the bush country, this was my first experience of the barren Arctic Coast in winter. From what I had read and heard, I anticipated that a few indistinct mounds in the snow would indicate our arrival at the snow village, and was amazed, as we rounded the rocky bluff of an island, to see a cluster of bright lights in the darkness, apparently suspended in mid-air. At sight of these, the dogs broke into a gallop, each team heading for one particular light, and at the same time small, dark objects came running towards the sleds. The lights came from seal oil lamps shining through the ice windows of snow houses, and the dark objects were children running out to meet the sleds returning home from the trading post.

My own particular guide halted his team at the entrance to a small tunnel several yards from a knot of lighted snow houses. Pointing to this hole, he indicated that I should enter; which I did, on all fours. Progressing a short distance in this undignified manner brought me to the end of the tunnel, out of which issued three very small holes. I entered the left-hand one, and wriggled through.

I now found myself in a most commodious igloo, about twelve feet in diameter and eight feet high in the centre. It was well illuminated by two seal oil lamps, the light being reflected and intensified by the clean, white walls and roof. A platform, about two feet above the floor, occupied exactly half the area and was covered with deerskins. Blankets and bedding were rolled back on it, against the wall. Other furniture consisted of a board resting on snow blocks acting as a table, two half-moon shaped stone lamps, each on a snow platform and with a sort of scaffolding erected over them made of bits of willow. Pots were suspended from this willow frame and odd garments spread on top to dry. A sort of reservoir, built of snow, against the wall, acted as a receptacle for scraps, and everything seemed clean.

I seated myself on the edge of the sleeping bench, for such was the platform, and removed my outer deerskin garments, which the woman of the house carefully brushed free of snow, folded and stowed away. She then prepared tea over a primus lamp, which we all took, together with hard-tack and jam. Other people—men, women and children—visited us, crowding the snow house and gratefully accepting a cup of tea and a biscuit. They came and went, freely discussing the visitor in their guttural native tongue. On the occasion of a second visitation, the good housewife produced a fine, raw, frozen salmon, which she cut in pieces, one for each person. This everyone ate in their fingers, first tearing off the skin with their teeth. It is a favourite article of diet for these people, and contrary to my expectations, tasted not unpleasant.

By and by, with so many people in the igloo, which, of course, is constructed entirely of snow (not ice, as many think), the temperature began to rise, the weather being comparatively mild in any case. The result was that the snow roof started to drip in places, and I soon felt a trickle of cold water run down the back of my neck. I was much interested in my host's remedy for this discomfiture when I saw him cut a piece of snow about the size of his fist from a block kept handy for the purpose and clap it against the moist spot overhead. The moisture caused the block to stick and further drops, if any, were absorbed by it.

About 11:30 p.m., I wanted to sleep and indicated this by signs. Immediately all guests took their departure, first prostrating themselves on the floor, not from any sense of deference to myself, I discovered, but simply to get on even terms with the door. A nicely fitted snow block was then placed in this opening to keep out the cold, also inquisitive dogs, who had already paid several scavenging visits and were thus confined to the shelter of the entrance porch or tunnel leading from the igloo itself to the outside. Bedding was spread out on the sleeping platform. The seal oil lamps were extinguished, and soon the family and I were settled in our respective sleeping bags, warm and comfortable. Before dropping off to sleep, I pondered the amazing character and resourcefulness of the people who live this life.

These Eskimos had spent the previous few years back from the Arctic Coast, in the Barren Lands, where they hunted deer, living in tents of skin or canvas in the summer and in snow houses in the winter. Each year in March or April, they were accustomed to pay a brief visit to the Hudson's Bay Company trading post at Kugaryuak or Fort Hearne to secure their limited requirements of ammunition, tea, tobacco and other odds and ends, returning immediately afterwards to the interior. This year the deer hunt had failed, and they sought the coast in January in order to seal on the ice, which was their occupation when I visited them. They are not great hunters of foxes and bother themselves very little with trapping or white man's goods, provided they can get plenty of their native foods—deer, fish and seal. They live happily together, having developed the community idea to a high degree.

Chief amongst the many things which amaze a newcomer is the extraordinary efficiency of their snow houses, mud sleds and seal oil lamps. Scarcely anything civilization produces can compete with these three phenomena in their own field. The snow houses cost nothing to build, the only tool necessary is a snow knife, while the only material (snow) is available in large quantities all winter. No portable dwelling could be so comfortable or so well adapted to requirements. The sled, or **komatik,** *which is made of two long planks on edge with cross-pieces lashed on top, is equipped by its ingenious owner with mud runners, extraordinary as this may sound. The sled is turned upside down, and nice pliable mud, like plasticine, previously thawed over a primus lamp, is stuck along the entire length of the runners. This freezes solid, when, with the aid of a plane or rasp, it is made level and smooth. Next, a piece of bearskin is moistened with water and brushed along the surface of the mud, leaving a film which immediately becomes ice. This is repeated until there may be a quarter of an inch of ice covering the mud, giving an ivory-smooth finish with a minimum of friction on snow. The sled is then uprighted and ready for loading up. Enormous loads can be hauled with little effort on account of this lack of friction. The ice wears off and is renewed daily, or sometimes oftener, but the mud sticks on wonderfully provided bare rock and gravel are avoided. If a piece comes off, it is carefully preserved, thawed out and replaced.*

Much could be written about the seal oil lamps. The lamp itself is fashioned of soap-stone. The oil used is secured from the seal, which also provides food and clothing. The wick is moss gathered in swampy places. Everything is home grown, so to speak, and the result provides light and heat for the igloo.

Pondering these things in my mind, I soon dropped off to enjoy my first night's rest under cover of a snow house.

Six weeks after leaving Coppermine Bonnycastle reached Aklavik. He found a poor fur catch, falling prices, and financial ruin. His diary records his frantic efforts to fend off the onset of the Depression; matching daily entries in the Aklavik post journal maintain a discreet silence on Company politics, preferring, more optimistically, to record the coming of spring.

May 6: Tom Lessard, a white trapper, and I arrived at Aklavik about 4 a.m. We had a meal at Mrs. Kost's small hotel and arranged through Jack Parsons, our local manager, to have a room there.

After seeing several people in the settlement and helping Tom Lessard to get his liquor permit released, I wired my arrival home and to the Winnipeg office, then turned in for a sleep. I got up at 5 p.m., had supper, then went to the wireless station where Tom Lessard was giving a party. After staying a short time I paid a call on Inspector and Mrs. Eames and was very warmly received. They are pleasant people and I expect we shall see a lot of them.

May 8: The Fur Trade Commissioner advises me that Captain Charlie Klengenberg now wishes me to buy the *Nigalik* for $35,000 and send his son Patsy east for next year's trade, but they want me to find some reasonable excuse for not putting the deal through. It may be difficult to put the old fellow off without putting his back up, but we must manage it somehow.

The big problem here in Aklavik is debt. Both Indian and white customers are in pretty deep and with the drop in fur prices bringing muskrat down to 60¢ it will be difficult for them to square up. If we can collect our debts we shall make a good killing—sales are high and the mark-up not too bad—but there is a big loss on fur to make up. I made a good stroke by closing Kittigazuit as there is nothing there this year.

Tuesday 6th 25° above—9 a.m. Slight north wind—continues mild. Mr. R. H. G. Bonnycastle and Tom Lessard arrived at Aklavik early this a.m. from the coast and will probably remain here until after first trip of the steamer. Routine progressing nicely.

Thursday 8th 20° to 50° above zero prevailed during the day. Clear blue sky. Pools of water and mud in patches round the settlement. At this rate the snow should melt quickly locally.

Mr. Parsons now busy painting in store. Mr. Stewart bringing costing of merchandise up to date.

Stewart, Tom Lessard, and I called on Inspector and Mrs. Eames, and Tom took his last bottle along. The Eames are very nice. We spent a most enjoyable evening.

May 9: Another beautiful day with the snow going rapidly. In a few more days the riverbank will be dry. Everything goes fine at Kost's. He is a very decent fellow; she talks as much as ever but is motherly and kind-hearted. Tom Lessard is an excellent chap, so we are a happy bunch over there.

I wish they were as happy at the Company house. The same old trouble again. I think Roche is the troublemaker. Claims he is not welcome in the house, that Mrs. Parsons is not going to cook for them after the end of the month, a long rigmarole. He has a mind as large as a peanut and makes mountains out of molehills. I told him so.

Stewart, Roche, and I visited the hospital tonight and called on the young ladies—Miss Bradford, Miss McCabe, and Miss Ball. They are very pleasant and Stewart had brought along a box of chocolates.

May 10: Wire today from district office advising me that Blake at Arctic Red River is paying $4 more for marten than the Company. I wrote Blake by an Indian to tell him to draw in his horns and adhere to our tariff.

I also had an interview with Taylor Pokiak. Taylor has been charged a total $6,828 for a schooner, engine, and light outfit. In addition he has been charged two insurance

Friday 9th 40° above zero—9 a.m. Clear sky with sun warming up nicely. Routine progressing nicely. Snow continues to disappear round the settlement.

Miss Ball, Nurse Bradford, and Nurse McCabe

Saturday 10th 52° above—9 a.m. Fine clear morning. If present conditions continue to prevail locally, the snow and slush should disappear quickly. Numerous flies of the large common "bluebottle" variety have been noticed due to the warm rays of the sun. Everybody busy with sundry routine and spring cleaning.

Mr. Bonnycastle busy attending to various posts in his district. Evenings lengthening out nicely—working daylight now until about 11 p.m.

PA-100575/PUBLIC ARCHIVES CANADA

premiums of $200 each on the boat. He now owes $3,600 according to our books. Taylor claims Philip Godsell told him he could have the works for $5,000, and disclaims the insurance premiums. I cannot believe he is correct, but am obliged to take his word and kiss goodbye to approximately $2,250. In any case Taylor wouldn't pay it, so I might as well give in with a good face and retain his goodwill.

Apparently the stock market is weak and there is to be a General Election in July. Well, the North isn't such a bad place at all.

May 11: At 5:30 p.m. I arrived, half an hour late, for supper at the Anglican mission. Rev. Webster, Nurse Bradford, Mr. & Mrs. McLean, and myself sat down to an excellent meal, after which we went to church and had a sermon from Webster. After church we had quite a singsong and generally spent a pleasant evening which ended with a little supper. And then home to bed—in broad daylight, of course—it is light all night now.

May 12: I had a long talk with Inspector Eames during which I told him all I know about Cpl. Wall. He is going to have a thorough investigation when he gets to Baillie Island and expects McClellan to lay a charge of trading against Wall. The inspector says Wall has affidavits proving that Johnson and McClellan endeavoured to prevent a patrol taking place, which is an indictable offence. So I think the fun is going to be fast and furious this summer.

Sunday 11th *40° to 60° above prevailed during the day. Spring thaw going nicely— patches of grass in places are a welcome change after several months of a mantle of snow and ice. Further signs of spring in the shape of birdlife to be seen round the settlement during the last couple of days—blackbirds flitting round this afternoon and a few robins have also been seen. Church parade as usual at 7 p.m.*

Monday 12th *40° above—9 a.m. Colder overnight—north wind blowing. Clear sunny morning, evidences of spring cleaning and painting in progress round the settlement. Business very quiet, although a few of the natives call at the store from time to time and turn in their rat catch. We still have hopes of a large rat hunt by end of the season, although the fur market prices are in an uncertain condition—especially rats. Office routine as usual.*

I certainly hope Wall gets his. Eames and I discussed things pleasantly and I told him I was sure our men were not all saints, that I was prepared to overlook petty details but any man who interfered with the police would be fired, and so on.

Had a very good meal at Parsons' tonight. He certainly puts on a good front when I am there: I never saw the store look neater, and the books were never in better shape at any post. Stewart and Roche have done their part splendidly. Now if Parsons can collect his debts everything will be lovely.

May 13: Everybody is cleaning up and painting around the settlement. The interior of the store has been done and Jack Parsons is earning $100 on the side for painting the doctor's house. He never mentioned anything about it to me but just goes ahead. The doctor is caulking and painting his boat. People are also preparing for the spring "rat shoot" which will begin from the settlement with the advent of open water. Last year the ice went out on May 27, and this year it will probably go sooner.

May 14: Quite a number of people came in during the night and early morning, and they report a lot of open water upstream, and muskrat emerging. This will be the last visitation on the ice by dogs.

Inspector Eames has definitely decided to ask McClellan to lay a charge of trading against Wall; then he will go right after Wall. On the other hand, the inspector believes

Tuesday 13th 42° above—9 a.m. Clear blue sky. North wind still blowing—ground drying up quickly round the settlement buildings with the aid of a number of drains dug in convenient places. As I write a robin is holding forth lustily heralding spring near the office window.

Wednesday 14th 42° above—9 a.m. Clear fine morning thaw continues steadily. 60° above in the sun at noon. Routine as usual.

Wall will swear a warrant for McClellan's arrest on a charge of instructing a member of the force to desert. So there will be hell to pay, and both Wall and McClellan will probably leave the country.

All the visitors pulled out tonight. Although this side of the river is quite clear of snow and the ground practically dried up, the ice on the river is still solid, merely a strip of water down each side. Once they cross the strip of water they have fine travelling on ice which is still about five feet thick. This is the difference between our southern and northern rivers: southern rivers melt from the bottom and give no sign of their treacherous nature; this northern river seems to melt entirely on the surface, the ice rising as the water level rises.

May 15: A perfectly lovely day, really almost hot. Flies buzzing in the sunshine, birds singing, and what I would like to do is to go out to Pine Ridge and play golf. Got in a moderately good day's work but with quite a number of interruptions.

The police boys are out "ratting" tonight. I am wondering if it is worthwhile to pay $75 for a licence and another $25 for a .22 rifle in order to have a little sport myself. I would need to get at least 200 muskrats to reimburse myself. That may or may not be easy. It was 80° in the sun today—created havoc with the snow and ice around the settlement.

Thursday 15th *45° above—9 a.m. Clear blue sky—slight north wind. Snow practically disappeared in the immediate vicinity of the settlement buildings. General painting and cleaning-up process still in progress. The costing of sales has now been brought up to the end of April in detail. The various monthly percentages of profit on sales might be considered very favourable as well as interesting. A robin, bolder than the others, perched on the fence just outside the office window and gave a brief serenade before flitting away to join the various other songsters. Settlement very quiet.*

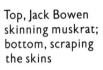

Top, Jack Bowen
skinning muskrat;
bottom, scraping
the skins

May 25: Got up late after a good sleep. The ice down below the Northern Traders' establishment moved a hundred yards or so in the night, so it will not be long before it all goes. Made good progress with my Baillie Island report which is slow work and takes a lot of thinking.

Went to church at 7:00 p.m. and heard an Empire sermon by the Reverend Webster, who isn't the best preacher but means well.

May 26: Awakened at 8:15 a.m. to find the ice moving. The water rose, and the ice with it, and came quite close to where some of the boats were hauled out on the point. No harm was done. The ice all but disappeared in two or three hours but scattered bits ran all day.

Inspector Eames came in to see me about the proposal to create an Eskimo Preserve in the Mackenzie Delta. He wants to quote me in his report to the Deputy Minister, Mr. Finnie, but I told him our commissioner might not like that. He stayed an hour and we chatted about everything. I like him very much.

May 28: Did not get up until early afternoon, and then found Jack Bowen, Frank Riddell, and Nash Leary getting ready to go ratting in the boat *Miss Norman.* I got busy and joined them. They supplied almost everything. All I had to take was my eiderdown, rifle, ammunition, clothes, and some bread.

Jack and I had one canoe, and the others had one. We did our shooting

Sunday 25th 35° to 50° above prevailed during the day. Slight rain early this morning which should help to rot the ice considerably. The river has been rising steadily during the past week. Routine in readiness for stock-taking tomorrow. Church parade as usual 7 p.m. Rev. J. H. Webster rendered rather a good patriotic sermon lauding the great British Empire as she stands so proudly and justly before the world today.

Monday 26th 30° above—9 a.m. Cloudy and raining. The ice has been moving steadily all morning, piled in chunks and just about in its last stages—carrying much driftwood as it passes by our buildings. About noon the river was clear, except for blocks of rotten ice scattered along the shoreline. Slight rainfall prevailed during the day—cloudy and dismal sky overhead. Mr. Bonnycastle, Mr. Parsons, and Mr. Stewart commenced stock-taking this morning.

Wednesday 28th 52° above zero—9 a.m. Slight north wind—clear bright morning. Finished taking stock for this Outfit about 11 p.m. last night. G. L. Roche finished his routine about 5 a.m. this morning, arriving at actual F.T. 4 merchandise figures to date. Mr. Bonnycastle and Mr. Stewart finished the complete rough inventory totals of merchandise about 6 a.m. and then retired to sleep after a good ten hours' steady work since 7 p.m. last evening.

from 8:00 p.m. until 10 a.m. each day, paddling miles looking for muskrat. Then we would return to the boat for lunch, eat, and start the beastly job of skinning; then back to the hunting again, returning afterwards for more skinning. We slept on the riverbank in broad sunlight, and two slept on board. The early mornings were lovely. We got 300 'rats all told—very poor hunting but I thoroughly enjoyed it.

We came across several mink, and a den of foxes where we saw the whole family. All the ducks and birds are mating and raising an awful row with their squawking, calling and flapping.

*Mr. Parsons has been busy putting our motorboat **Little Bear** in proper running shape during the day for the coming busy season. The police and both missions are already busy hauling wood in scow loads and the hum of engines over the river is a pleasant sound once more.*

Bonnycastle with Jack Bowen and Frank Riddell

Friday 30th *60° above—9 a.m. Calm and warmer. Some of the natives brought in word today that two Fort McPherson Indians—young men—were evidently drowned in one of the rivers a few miles from Aklavik. Their canoe and outfit has been found and the police have gone out to look for the bodies. One of the men has only recently been married—a very unfortunate accident.*

Saturday 31st *56° above—9 a.m. Continued fine weather. Several of the natives (Indians) called at the store yesterday afternoon leaving a few hundred rats behind.*

Another drowning accident today—one of the young boys of the R. C. mission, who accompanied the mission brothers with a scow to haul wood during the past few days, fell overboard unnoticed and was carried away by the current and drowned. An orphan Indian boy about fourteen years of age.

June 1: Quite a shock today. A wire arrived from the commissioner informing me that Romanet was out and that John Bartleman is the new district manager.

June 2: Worked hard all day to finish the Baillie Island report, which I finally did at last. I am anxious to get as much mail ready as possible since there is a Western Canada Airways plane due tomorrow.

June 3: Got up late and read over my Baillie Island report, which is ready to go out. I am now starting on the Pearce Point one. Went out in the evening with Pearson, when we got 18 muskrat.

Everyone is out with boats these days and engines of all sorts can be heard day and night. The weather is absolutely perfect, I have never seen anything so lovely. The plane which was due today didn't show up

June 4: Glyn Roberts of Commercial Airways arrived at 4:00 p.m. with a load of second- and third-class mail. This is a trip ahead of the scheduled one, and a race to be down here ahead of Punch Dickins,

Monday 2nd 56° above—9 a.m. Clear sunny morning. An inquest was held at 10 a.m. by Inspector Eames on the recent drowning accident of the two young Indian men, Thos. Wilfred and Alfred Goose, and returned a verdict of accidental drowning. The body of the young Indian boy of the R. C. mission has yet to be recovered.

Glyn Roberts and Bonnycastle

Wednesday 4th 62° above—9 a.m. Fine sunny morning. Office routine quite busy getting ready for expected mail. Pilot Glyn Roberts arrived with one mail plane this afternoon bringing sundry second-class mail only but informs us that Capt. "Wop" May expects to reach Aklavik by Friday with all first-class mail.

who arrived from Fitzgerald at 7:00 p.m.

Roberts quoted Tom Lessard $340 for air passage to McMurray, which is their new rate. Dickins offered the same deal and Tom Lessard is going with him.

Punch Dickins brought in a couple of cases of oranges and eggs. I had some at Pat Quinn's—the eggs tasted good. He also brought the Monday newspaper with him. I am working all night to get certain mail off with the planes in the morning.

It was bush pilot Wop May who located the murderer Mad Trapper Johnson for the RCMP in 1932. But May's adventures went back to World War I; as a novice pilot he was under attack by the Red Baron — with his own guns jammed — when the famous German flier was finally shot down

Thursday 5th *40° below—8 a.m. Cold north wind and cloudy. Changes in the weather last evening—first rainfall this season, for a short spell, with a nasty cold north wind blowing.*

Pilot Dickins with Western Canada Airways plane landed last evening shortly after mail plane—coming right through from Fitzgerald in about 10 hours flying time! We learn that the S. S. Distributor is scheduled to leave Fort Smith on 21st instant.

Sunday 8th *Clear sunny day—getting warmer. Mr. Bonnycastle kept Mr. Roche quite busy all through the night—right to about 3 p.m. this afternoon—finishing off the district manager's correspondence routine. The plane took off about 4 p.m. en route to Fort McMurray.*

Among those of the "white" population who attended Divine Service as usual were Mr. Bonnycastle and Mr. Roche—in spite of the fact that it was necessary to postpone our regular sleeping hours. It might be worth mentioning here that when duty calls some of us are not found wanting.

June 12: Rather a disagreeable, cold day. A number of Indians came in from McPherson and Arctic Red River, including some who had jumped their debts there. We must get hold of them and explain what will happen unless they attempt to square up.

June 13: The people still continue to drift in. Berdette Verville, Cummings, McNealy, Corporal Wilson, Kost, and some others arrived today. Verville paid up $500 after inquiring if we would carry him over to next year in spite of an unpaid balance of $600. I told him we would. By gosh, it's a holy terror, though. Douglas Oneik owes $400. Garrett doesn't like the muskrat prices; I persuaded him to square his local debt at the 60¢ price per pelt and said that I would try to do better on his remaining 2,000 rats when we get to Herschel Island. He still has an outstanding loan of $2,900 on which I am going to charge him 8%. I can see we are going to lose a pile on debts.

The McPherson Indians will probably take their fur back there, I am glad to say. I moved over to Doctor Urquhart's house to sleep.

June 14: Spent a very comfortable night in the doctor's house, a great improvement over Mrs. Kost's. The doctor is the soul of hospitality but a terrible talker.

Thursday 12th *40° above—9 a.m. Chilly north wind somewhat calmer. A few rats keep coming our way from day to day. Routine in progress as much as possible.*

Garrett and his family

Dr. Urquhart

Saturday 14th *Huskies and Indians with their families are still gathering round the settlement. Several schooners can now be seen round the shoreline—rather a picturesque sight—not to mention the large number of dogs strung out on chains round the shore.*

Mr. Parsons and Mr. Stewart very busy in the store today taking in fur on account of outstanding debts.

A dance was held in our interpreter's house between 9 p.m. and 12 midnight. Judging from the brief strains of merriment the natives seem to be quite cheerful in spite of the drop in the fur market.

Sunday 15th *50° to 70° prevailed during the day. Clear blue sky—slight north wind. Warmer during the afternoon. Several white trappers now arrived in the settlement. Const. Wilson of Arctic Red River with Const. Nicolson arrived here from near Fort McPherson, escorting one Louis Poue, a French white trapper who, from various reports and actions, has been considered as being mentally deranged, and evidently had a tough time all alone in the bush. His condition will be taken up in due course by our local doctor and Inspector Eames.*

Church parade as usual at 7 p.m.

Tuesday 17th *55° above—9 a.m. Clear morning. White trappers and natives still gathering around the settlement. Mr. Parsons has been kept busy counting and baling rats in the afternoon in the warehouse. Routine in the store keeps the rest of the staff working long hours.*

Ralph Parsons

June 22: The doctor kept me up most of the night talking about various things. He is a low-down reptile, and showed me a letter to Deputy Minister Finnie from Archdeacon Whittaker complaining about the prevalence of drunkenness amongst the Eskimo, which matter was referred to him to report on or not as he liked. He then asked me if Stewart would be here next winter. I said, "I don't know, why?" He replied, because if he would be, he must report to Ottawa that Stewart had supplied Lewis Kaglick with brew materials, got Lewis to brew for him, and attended brew parties at Lewis's place; if he would not be here for another year there would be no need to reply. The way he put the whole thing was the crudest I ever heard and sickened me. This is just a frame-up between Jack Parsons and the doctor to get Stewart in wrong, although it is probably coming to him. This is acting like a patronizing, loathsome snake in the grass. Surely if there is anything in it this is a matter for the RCMP.

The doctor also remarked, "I wonder why it is the RCMP generally, and all policemen in particular, have it in for the HBC." I said I didn't think they had. He said that Inspector Eames needed watching and had it in particularly for all men who quit dealing with Captain Pedersen of Canalaska for the Company. He as much as warned me to look out for Eames, whom I consider an officer and a gentleman and a friend of mine and who has remarked to me that were he not in the force there is no outfit in the world he would sooner work for than the Company. There was a lot more nasty gossip about people, which I hated, but as I am staying with the doctor, and have enough trouble on my hands in any case, I merely listened and let him bubble on.

Bonnycastle (rear) with Mrs. Eames, Captain Cornwell, Inspector Eames, and Dr. Urquhart

June 30: We had been expecting the steamboat sooner but she didn't arrive until around 6 a.m. on a cold, wet morning—typical of steamboat day here. The large barge has been brought down this far for the first time. The captain found landing difficult with so many small boats lining the riverbank, and smashed into the canoe we had used on the Fort McPherson trip.

The *Distributor* brought a parcel of mail which I was glad to get. Everyone notes the depressing atmosphere. Times are certainly hard, and apparently very much so outside in civilization. It seems both Fort Norman and Fort Simpson have only two bales of fur each. This state of affairs is simply terrible.

July 2: Sleep seems quite a minus quantity this past week. Mrs. Murray and Mrs. Morris, both with young babes, have been given one of the rooms. Our quarters are none too comfortable and it will be a pleasure to be off for Herschel Island. Two babies in here is a bit of a bore, but I feel sorry for the mothers.

July 7: We are a bit cramped with two women in the house, and I am rather annoyed at the way Mrs. Morris expects us to look after her. There are also a couple of lady authoresses. One asked if we could put her up for a day or two at Herschel Island. I said no. To add to my troubles I have contracted a miserable cold, which is a nuisance. Then Wednesday was a day of sweltering

Monday 30th *S. S. Distributor* arrived at Aklavik about 6 a.m. this morning, with a full load of freight for the post and others concerned in the settlement. Amongst those on board were Dr. Truesdell and Mr. Flynn Harris of Fort Simpson; Mr. Finkelstein; Mr. Slater and Mr. Saul, Northern Traders Ltd. officials; another lady writer or journalist—making two now in the settlement as one landed here by Commercial Airways plane a couple of days ago from Fort Norman—Mr. Free, North American Life insurance agent and Tuckett's Tobacco traveller; and several others.

Everybody busy during the day unloading freight and tending to various transportation business.

Mrs. Wm. Murray and child also arrived to join Mr. Murray here, en route to Herschel Island post later.

heat, 84° in the shade, which just about feeds me up with this country.

July 10: Another scorcher of a day, too hot to even cook or eat. The trade to date this year looks like nothing compared with last year. I have slashed it right and left, and think this was the only thing to do. Turned down another trapper today who is broke and wants an outfit. I figure he is not worth two cents.

July 11-14: Two government planes arrived carrying Col. Ford of National Defence, Ottawa, and Mr. Parker of the Indian Department. Mr. Parker brought down a huge parcel of office mail for me from McMurray. It has long been overdue. The planes went on to Herschel Island; I sent a note to Fred Ware to present Mr. Parker with a fox. He is very decent towards the Company and I thought this gesture wouldn't do any harm.

Inspector Eames pulled out today for Herschel Island and we said our goodbyes around the settlement.

Herschel Island; July 15: After fuming about, and several last-minute trips to load the schooner, we finally got away at 3:00 a.m.—with our ladies and babies on board, also Bertram Pokiak and his dogs. It was pleasant for an hour or two, until the engine started heating abominably. We decided to strip the engine down and spent almost the whole day on the job—took off No. 2 cylinder and piston and worked grinding compound into the cylinder and so on.

Gaston Herodier lost his life at Fort Good Hope, at the boundary line of the Arctic Circle, on November 22nd last.

He was a native of France, born in Paris in 1880. In 1903, he left France to join the service of Revillon Freres.

When war broke out he returned to his beloved France. In active service he won several decorations and the rank of lieutenant of artillery in the Vosges, where he was entrusted with a special mission.

Upon his return to Canada, he entered the service of the Hudson's Bay Company, and was sent to open up the most northerly post of the Company, at Pond's Inlet on latitude 74. Then, in 1924 he joined the staff of the Western Arctic district in the capacity of inspector.

He had a very thorough knowledge of the Eskimos. As with most people with whom he came in contact, he was respected and liked by them. They called him *A ta-ta-look*, meaning "Grandfather," and for any one who understands the aborigines, it is a very flattering name.

Herodier never lost his sense of dignity in the North. It might be inspiring to some post managers to mention his determination not to allow the isolation and monotony to get the better of him. He subjected himself to a rigorous daily discipline. This involved the rising at a certain early hour every morning, winter and summer, meals at regular times, and regular exercise, even if it had to be taken without leaving the house. He always kept up certain high standards of living, which are often neglected by persons living permanently far from the beaten track. His house was always kept like a new pin. The setting out of his meals was suggestive of civilization rather than the backwoods.

In 1927, Mr. Herodier was transferred to the Mackenzie river at Fort Good Hope, and now we come to his tragic end.

It was evening and quite dark in that latitude. In the beautiful new dwelling house of Good Hope, three healthy men were settling down to their respective occupations. Upstairs Albert Laferty, the interpreter, was engaged in stretching marten skins just caught the same day. Downstairs, Herodier called Ernest Mills, his clerk, to help him to fix a gasoline

We were ready to resume our journey at 6:00 p.m. when along came Frank Riddell and took us in tow to Herschel Island.

To everyone's surprise the RCMP *St. Roch* arrived today from Vancouver. Everyone on board is fine, and they report heavy ice. They passed Barter Island, 140 miles west of here, last night, and were told by the people there that the *Baychimo* had passed the night before, so she should have been here some time ago. The *St. Roch* works inshore and saw no sign of the *Baychimo*—she must be out amongst the heavy ice.

July 28: The *Baychimo* arrived today. This is going to be a busy summer for me and I will not be able to keep day-by-day diaries since we will be always on the move.

lamp which had been leaking. In the kitchen the bright light of another gasoline lamp was burning cheerfully.

Herodier wanted to put in a good evening's work on his books, and with that in view, he had them taken from the office in the store to the dwelling house. "Pump up the lamp," said Herodier to Mills.

"Well, we had better close the tube first," answered Mills.

"Never mind," returned Herodier, "I will hold the gas with my thumb while we plunge the lamp in water to see where it leaks."

This was a very grave imprudence. Suddenly, Herodier's thumb was released and a strong jet of raw gasoline projected to the ceiling. Being under pressure, the gas was highly inflammable. In an instant, the room was filled with gas, which caught fire as soon as it came in contact with the ignited kitchen lamp. The force of the expansion of burning gas bulged the walls of the house outwardly, jamming all doors and thereby trapping the three men who were inside. It was

shortly after seven o'clock.

Then followed a panic. Mills ran for the fire extinguisher, but in his excitement could not operate it. The flames had now gained so much headway that the best he could do was to try to get out. Every door was tried in vain. Turning back to escape by the basement windows, a trunk landed at Mills' feet from upstairs. The clerk shouted to Herodier to get out, but received no answer. Finally, after several trying failures he managed to crawl out through one of the basement windows, and seeing that his chief was not among the crowd that had assembled, cried out that Herodier was still inside.

Upstairs, Laferty heard a noise like a big wind and then someone yelled. He went to the door of his room and saw Herodier come upstairs and grab his trunk. He asked him what was the matter, but received no reply. The flames were now entering the bedroom. Laferty kicked out the window, but the hole was too small. He struggled desperately, while the flames were burning his face, hands and hair, and finally fell to the ground outside. His burns were taken care of by the mission, who on this occasion, as well as on many others, have shown their devotion to the suffering.

The unfortunate Herodier could have got out the way the two others went, but his sense of responsibility was stronger than his care for safety. His idea was to save the accounts and cash of the post. He ran upstairs, but only succeeded in putting the books in a trunk and throwing it to the foot of the stairs.

Corporal Cummings of the Royal Canadian Mounted Police, who gallantly broke in through the same window, came across Herodier's legs about six feet from the foot of the window. The brave corporal dragged him out and artificial respiration was tried for an hour without success. In a great effort to lift up the body, Corporal Cummings was badly hurt and had to be rushed to Edmonton by airplane later.

Outside, it was cold and calm. One of those wonderful starry boreal nights looking down over the majestic austerity of the Arctic landscape. A small group of men of fantastic appearance under the dancing light of lanterns, carried a burden that made their steps creak on the hard snow. A motley crowd, reverently silent, followed the tragic group who presently entered the historic Church of God. The body was laid down under the solemn arches, awaiting burial.

Gaston Herodier led an unusual life. He was full of vigour and good spirits. Through a momentary imprudence, he paid the supreme price. When he passed away, the Company lost a valuable employee, and I a dear friend.—*Louis A. Romanet.*

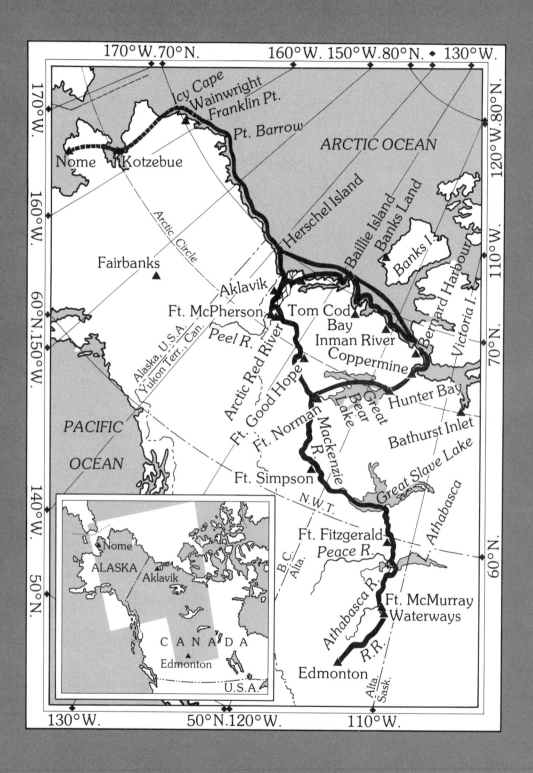

170°W. 70°N.   160°W. 150°W. 80°N.   ♦ 130°W.

170°W.   80°N.

Icy Cape
Wainwright
Franklin Pt.
Pt. Barrow

ARCTIC OCEAN

Nome   Kotzebue

160°W.

Herschel Island

Baillie Island
Banks Land

Banks I.

120°W.

Arctic Circle

Fairbanks ▲

110°W.

Aklavik

Bernard Harbour

Ft. McPherson   Tom Cod ▲
Bay
Peel R.   Inman River ▲
Coppermine ▲

Victoria I.

Alaska, U.S.A.
Yukon Terr., Can.

Arctic Red River

70°N.

150°W.

Ft. Good Hope ▲

Hunter Bay ▲

Great
Bear
Lake

PACIFIC

Ft. Norman ▲

Bathurst Inlet

140°W.

Mackenzie R.

Great Slave Lake

OCEAN

Athabasca

Ft. Simpson ▲

N.W.T.

60°N.

Ft. Fitzgerald
Peace R.

B.C.
Alta.

Athabasca R.

Ft. McMurray ▲
Waterways

50°N.

ALASKA
▲ Nome

Aklavik ▲

C A N A D A

Edmonton ▲

U.S.A.

R.R.

Edmonton ▲

Alta.
Sask.

130°W.   50°N. 120°W.   110°W.

A Tough Summer on the Arctic Coast, and the Wreck of the *Baychimo*: 1931

4

Bonnycastle's first year in the Arctic was an outstanding success. By writing off useless merchandise, closing posts, enticing the best white trappers away from Captain Pedersen, and persuading the Klengenbergs to join forces with the Hudson's Bay Company, he reduced the loss for the Western Arctic to little more than $6,000. He also proved himself to be an astute, and lucky, trader:

"When the *Baychimo* arrived at Herschel Island, Bonny had to bid against Captain Pedersen for a lot of 1500 white foxes," says L. A. Learmonth, post manager at Cambridge Bay. "Bonny bid $39.50 a skin. Pedersen bid $40. Pedersen got the lot, $60,000 worth of fur. When Bonny got back to the ship, word came on the wireless that the price of white fox had dropped to $22.50. By the time Pedersen got back to Seattle the price was down to $12. He sold the whole lot to the Company for $12 a skin."

Bonnycastle's achievements won him special mention in Commissioner C. H. French's annual report for Outfit 259:

May we particularly draw your attention to the Western Arctic District report. To us it gives real satisfaction and speaks well for its manager. Being new he has yet to learn many things, one of which is that his post managers are not all as good as he pictures them. After he finds that some of them have "let him down" in some particular, he will then commence to get their real measure.

Before returning north in the spring of 1931, Bonnycastle was feeling confident enough to become engaged to Mary Northwood, eldest of the four daughters of Winnipeg architect G. M. Northwood. The wedding date was set for October 17. Bonnycastle hoped to get the jump on the opposition by flying down the Mackenzie early in March and meeting the trappers coming in for Easter with their winter catches. After inspecting the Arctic posts on the *Baychimo* during the summer, he planned to return on the ship to Vancouver in September, arriving back in Winnipeg a week or two before his wedding. The plan seemed to be a model of good timing.

Fort Resolution; March 10: Western Canada Airways called for me at the MacDonald Hotel, Edmonton, at 8:30 a.m., before I was quite ready to leave. I rushed my packing, addressed the mail I had stayed up all night to finish, bundled up my city clothes to express back home, and got downstairs before the other passenger did.

I wore Eskimo snowboots with one pair of duffel socks, the police trousers I had acquired, heavy underwear and shirt, golf sweater, suede leather jacket, and woollen toque. Even then I was none too warm at the airport, where Punch Dickins had the machine all ready to go when we arrived. We got away about 10 a.m. and flew to McMurray in about 2¾ hours. It was cold in the plane. We were glad to get out at McMurray for lunch. Dickins and his mechanic, Len Parmenter, took on some express and refuelled. Our bags had been weighed at Edmonton. Mine were 60 pounds over the allowable weight; they only charged me for 50, but that was enough at $3.10 per pound, making $155 plus my fare of $460—$615 all told.

We left McMurray in cold but beautiful weather. I wore deerskin pants, an improvement, but my feet were still cold, especially my heels. I sat with Punch Dickins in the cockpit. The view was splendid and I could watch all the instruments. We circled Chipewyan and landed at Fitzgerald in about 2½ hours. We stayed a short time and took off for Resolution, making it in little over an hour. I went right up to the store and warmed up. We had a supper of caribou meat and potatoes, and after I had a shave I fell asleep in my chair.

Fort Simpson; March 11: We only made Simpson today, as weather reports from Norman are poor. It was a very cold day but I dressed warmly with deerskin socks and soles, skin pants, and parka. The fur reports along the river are most disappointing although the partial opening of beaver hunting will help a great deal. Sixty permits, each to take 15 beaver pelts, have been issued at Fort Providence. This means about $13,500 in revenue to the Indians which will be reflected in our business.

Jock Milne met us at Simpson and took me up to his house. His wife gave us a splendid meal of moosemeat. Milne certainly keeps the post nicely, and has a good eye for business, keeping his debts down. They have electric light here but it is expensive—cost this outfit has been $800.

Arctic Red River; March 12: Very cold morning. We got away by 9 a.m. I sat with Dickins in the cockpit; it is cramped but I could see everything that goes on, and a good view of the country. Flying is just like driving a car except that you hardly ever have to do anything like turning the wheel or putting on brakes. You just fly for miles without doing a thing. The engine never missed a beat in spite of the intense cold.

We landed at Fort Norman in 2 hours and 40 minutes for the 300 miles, and were glad to warm up in a tent which had been used that morning by

Wop May. He must have passed us en route as he went south. Patsy Klengenberg and Otto Torrington were passengers with him. Then we took off for Fort Good Hope. This was the coldest spot on our trip—51° below. We landed across the river, threw out the parcels, and took off again without waiting for people to come over. I never felt such a bitter wind as when I put my head out. It's marvellous how the engine functions and lubricates in this cold.

We made Arctic Red River in 2 hours for the 200 miles and decided to stay here for the night. We were very glad to get a good meal, and went early to bed.

March 13: Too foggy to proceed so we remained here all day. There is very little fur here. It is better at Aklavik, I am told.

Aklavik; March 14: Flew to Aklavik via McPherson. Everyone was on hand. Lewis Kaglik most opportunely arrived last night from Baillie Island but the news from there is the worst possible: the fur hunt is a failure and the debts are the highest imaginable. I don't know what is going to happen there. There is just a chance that the Banksland hunters have done well and the fur hunt may pick up this month, but we can't come out in any way except badly in the soup. The only thing to do is face the music and clean up properly. It's terribly discouraging.

Started to work on the Baillie Island requisitions and other odds and ends to send back on the plane. The requisitions came to $31,000 but with Bill Murray's assistance I cut them down to $20,000. I wrote numerous letters and when I came to enclose the requisitions I decided they were still high, so Murray and I did an all-night job and cut them down to $10,000. That's an awful cut but I can't justify a larger order.

March 16: Breakfast at 8:30 a.m., prepared by Bill Murray—porridge, coffee, bread and jam. There can be no complaint about economy here. Plain, satisfying foods are eaten with no fancy canned fruit, which is just as it should be.

Garlund came in and wanted more credit. I told him he had the limit so he said he would pay cash! Lecombe brought in 26 mink, 3 lynx, 15 foxes, and some ermine. He agitated for a 25% discount on goods but I allowed this only on sugar and flour. He did bring in some fur and will continue if he gets what he thinks is a fair deal. Corporal Fielding came and asked Murray to give him a draft for $75 and charge it to his account, Bill told him he would have to deposit that amount first and he went away mad. We must educate these people to realize we are not a charitable institution.

March 17: If all goes well, this day six—seven, darn it—months from now will be a very interesting one for Mary and me.

The Alsatian which Bill Murray brought in last summer has a litter of pups, three weeks old, which are kept in the kitchen. They set up a most ungodly row early in the morning and act as a splendid alarm clock, but it gets tiresome after a bit.

Donald Greenland has set himself up as spokesman for the Indians and says they will not turn in their muskrat for under 50¢. I gave him quite a spiel on what controlled prices and said if the Indians didn't want to trade with us we could quite easily close the post. After long and learned discussion he departed. He returned to say *he* had explained everything to the Indians and they would trade with the Company. We laughed behind his back, knowing that Donald is a deadbeat trying to get into our favour for more debt.

We put in a good day stock-taking and in the evening the McLeans, Miss Ball, Mrs. Fielding, Hersey, and Hancock dropped in to listen to the local broadcast from UZK. We played ping-pong and cribbage and had a snack— a rather pleasant evening. Everything is going happily, if only Baillie Island were not such a nightmare.

March 18: The days are lengthening—only ten hours of darkness in the twenty-four.

After supper we took a break and went on a snowshoe tramp for three miles up Pokiak Creek. The snow was terribly deep. Afterwards we dropped into Fieldings' and had some ice cream. As usual I went to sleep sitting there. I get very tired towards night and cannot keep awake.

March 19: Started up the fire in the store to warm things up a bit as it is very cold writing in there.

A few muskrat are coming in and Bill Murray is paying $1 for three. He sure gets his fur right and I think handles things very well. He is a little hasty on some points and not too easy to handle but I would sooner have him that way and producing results than very amenable to discipline and not able to make money. There is a little fur coming in every day and we are getting it cheaply. They report mink and lynx are plentiful this year.

Lewis Kaglik is getting a bit obstreperous. He is anxious to buy methyl hydrate to drink and got after Jock Kilgour, one of the clerks, to sell it to him, offering cash. Bill Murray will not allow Lewis anything so he is threatening to go back to Baillie Island forthwith. He hasn't said anything about it to me, but I will give Lewis a piece of my mind if he does.

March 20: Very cold but clear and bright. We worked upstairs in the unheated warehouse. By tomorrow the inventory should be complete.

Rev. Murray dropped in this afternoon and wanted to know if we could issue orders to natives in payment of labour etc., and have them redeemed at cost plus 25% or thereabouts, to the extent of $500 or $600. As the mission needs all the assistance it can get, Bill Murray and I decided to allow a

20 % discount on orders which are redeemed in goods other than flour, sugar, gas, and oil. This is a knotty problem which we should have a definite ruling on.

Called on the girls at the hospital and found them most cheerful. The social round here is quite a chore. I still have to call on the parson, the McLeans, priest, and sisters. They are all most pleasant people, but after working all day a rest at home is usually more pleasant than paying calls.

Everything is going splendidly and the days just seem to slip by. We are going to do well at Aklavik this year, which is most encouraging.

March 21: The Herschel Island patrol arrived with Inspector and Mrs. Eames. I dropped around to visit them after supper and found them most cheery. They are a very fine couple indeed and I shall be glad to see as much of them as I can before I leave.

Two of our post dogs died today. Apparently they had been suffering from worms all winter. Bill Murray gave them some medicine he had from the doctor and followed it an hour later with a strong dose of Epsom salts. It was too much for them. But they were skin and bone anyway.

March 22: Reports continually reach us from the Indians of 50¢ muskrat at McPherson. Old Attoe told Bill Murray he was proposing to go there to trade on account of the better price and what did he think about that. Bill didn't think much of it, especially as the old man had kept 50 muskrat from last year in spite of having unpaid debts. The old fellow agreed to stay with Aklavik when he was assured prices here would be the same as McPherson. I sent District Manager Bartleman a wire suggesting he instruct McPherson to bring their prices to three pelts for one dollar until the

The fan-shaped hitch — one of many styles of harness

spring sale, when we could raise our tariff if the market is strong.

I spent most of the day writing to Windy about the clothes I want him to get for me. It is very pleasant contemplating these matters.

March 23: Had a reply from Bartleman agreeing with my suggestion for the control of fur prices. I decided to pull out for McPherson in the morning with Stan Mackie, who is returning to Arctic Red River.

We finished costing the inventory. It came to something over $44,000, considerably less than we had anticipated. However, it works out about right considering the sales.

March 24: Looked out at 6 a.m. There was a strong south wind blowing so I decided to return to bed. When we got up at 8 a.m. we saw the police were hitching up at the barracks. If the weather is good enough for them it is good enough for us, so Mackie, his two Indians, and myself pulled out approximately one hour behind the police.

I drove the Herschel Island team of six dogs and found them pretty slow. Travelling once more with dogs affected me with varying emotions. First I though it was lovely to be out again—the river, woods, and lakes were beautiful. But after rather poor going, urging the dogs forward all day long, I was tired before we made camp in Charlie Snowshoe's empty cabin at Oneiak's place, 45 miles from Aklavik. The Indians who are with us are Jimmy Thompson and Stephen, a one-legged man, but both are okay. The cabin wasn't comfortable. Mackie and I shared a pole bunk; I placed my deerskin on it and got into my robe.

March 25: It was a nice day and we had a decent run to the mouth of the Peel River where we had dinner at Stephen's house. After that we separated: Stan Mackie followed the Mackenzie to Arctic Red River, the two Indians remained, and I went up the Peel River to the Husky River by myself. I found the trail easily enough and arrived at Blake's about 7 p.m.

Blake made me very welcome and showed me his dogs and some of his furs. After supper he distilled some alcohol from a brew of raisins he had going and insisted on me drinking some of it with him. I never saw such a dirty hole as Blake's house. It is terrible, dead rabbits, ptarmigan, and muskrat lying around and dirty clothes all over the place. He has six boys, the eldest eighteen, so they should all make useful trappers in time.

March 26: We went over the cancellations in Blake's requisitions, reinstating some and adding others. He is quite amenable to reason and realizes the necessity of getting his balance in order. If muskrat are plentiful, as we anticipate, he should have $12,000 worth of fur to give us this year. So if we give him, say, $7,000 worth of goods, his balance will be $5,000 less next year.

March 27: It took me nearly 3 hours to make Fort McPherson this morning.

Roman Catholic priest
with his students

I arranged with our man, Jack Parsons, and Bill Douglas of Northern Traders, to make muskrat three for a dollar. I also saw old John Firth who is getting pretty feeble. I returned to Blake's, stayed an hour, and pulled out for
the mouth of the Peel River which I reached about 10 p.m.—40 miles for
the day and I felt pretty tired. I camped with Jim Fintor and he made me
comfortable.

March 28: A howling gale from the north. I was undecided whether to pull
out but made a break for it about 11 a.m. I had an awful job finding the trail
in the blizzard. An Indian caught up with me about a mile out and broke
trail for two miles. Labouring along on snowshoes, I finally made Oneiak's
place about 5 p.m. I soon lighted the fire but had difficulty getting dry
wood. I got to bed at 8 p.m.—my first night alone in the wilderness. Fairly
comfortable.

March 29: Still blowing. I was up at daybreak, lit the fire, and cooked tea,
meat, and bannock. Pulled out at 8 a.m. and had a cold ride to Harrison's—
15 miles in 4 hours. Froze my face a bit. Plugged on again. The snow was
very deep on the portages, and hard for the dogs to negotiate, but I had
Chein in the lead and he followed the invisible trail fairly well. I eventually
reached the camp of some German woodcutters and had some food with
them before going on to Knud Lang's. Lang did me awfully well—caribou
steaks, macaroni and cheese, canned fruit, and coffee. It was great. We
played chess well into the night. Travelled 30 miles today.

Aklavik; March 30: Miserable day—snowing with a head wind. I had a worse job than ever finding the trail, but halfway to Aklavik I met teams coming the other way so had a trail to the settlement, which I reached in six hours. My face is pretty badly frozen. I am glad to be back. I couldn't have had worse weather for my first trip alone. I don't dislike travelling alone, there is a certain pride of accomplishment in getting along unassisted.

April 1: Mrs. Murray took advantage of the date to fool Bill Murray and Jock Kilgour by altering the alarm clock. She got them up two hours ahead of time!

A bright, mild day—it would have been much pleasanter if I had had this kind of weather for travelling instead of those filthy storms. They say they are among the worst this winter. The scabs are forming on my chin and cheeks and I shall be able to peel off dead skin soon. In the meantime I look a bit patchy.

I went down to see the R. C. sisters today but they are in retreat.

April 2: Checked up on post expenses today and found them very high indeed. It is not all Murray's fault because most of the expenses were incurred by Jack Parsons. There are some expensive articles of household furniture which I never should have allowed to come in. We can't help what has gone before, but the budget for next year's expenses is less than half this year's. Bill is of the opinion he can operate on the budget okay, and I believe he will.

It was an awful shock to me to find Billy Phillips in debt to the extent he is. He owes us $11,000 and I thought it only $4,000. I am afraid we shall not get more than $5,000 of fur this year from him, which is disastrous. I don't know how I shall explain it.

The Eskimos have started to come in for Easter and are camped in our native house.

Constable "Frenchy" Chartrand arrived back from Baillie Island with the police patrol. His news is not a bit encouraging—the fur catch amounts to little or nothing, and debts are colossal. It is going to be a tough proposition. A clean slate from now on is absolutely our only salvation. We must take our present losses and close down tight on debt in the future. The outlook is most discouraging but, by God, I am going to clean up.

April 3: Today is Good Friday. I wonder where I shall spend it one year hence; perhaps Mary and I shall be able to play golf, or have a picnic.

The native people had a dance tonight which we looked in on for a short time. They had square dances. I participated in one—found it pretty strenuous. They do enjoy congregating at Christmas and Easter. They are a jolly crowd, especially the Eskimos, and fine people to trade with.

April 4: More people arriving for Easter. There are dozens of dogteams

around now and our native house is packed to the doors. There are quite a few white trappers in too.

Bill Murray is splendid at saying no, much better than I could possibly be. Old Oliver came in today to get $5 for collections tomorrow. He is way in the hole and has only two cross foxes at home. He brought nothing in. Of course he has had hard luck, losing Donald last fall, one of the finest lads in the Delta. Bill Murray had a long talk with Oliver, explaining how he must get along on practically nothing. The poor old man has always traded every pelt with us, and we should never have let him get in so deep last summer.

There was an Eskimo dance with drums tonight which was quite good to watch. The place was packed with people sitting on the floor all around the walls. They sing and beat the drum one after the other, men and women, several together or singly, getting up and interpreting the words of the song in motion. There is much laughter at the end of each dance.

April 5: Today being Easter Sunday, I declared a holiday. In the afternoon I went along to call on the R. C. sisters. They really are wonderful people, and the Sister Superior is a peach. They brought in the two little Eskimo girls we brought from Coppermine last summer, about six and eleven years. The eldest, who could not speak a word of English six months ago, can now read well, write splendidly, and even add and subtract quite rapidly. It is remarkable. All the children in the school seem most happy and are apparently well cared for; I am to go on Tuesday to see them.

I went to the hospital for supper with Miss Bradford, Miss McCabe, and Miss Ball, then attended church at 7 p.m. for Holy Communion. After church I spent an hour with the Eames and had some ice cream at the Fieldings' before winding up the evening with a game of bridge with Bill and Mrs. Murray and Fred Ware.

Mrs. Murray is splendid. When anyone is going on a trip she sends them off with bannock, doughnuts, cakes, etc. She even made a cake tonight, after 10 p.m., for Fred Ware to take on the trail tomorrow, and she has already made doughnuts for my forthcoming trip. She wouldn't let me go to the hospital this afternoon until she had ironed my clean shirt at the last moment. She and Bill fight like cat and dog. Bill is a brute but she stands up for herself fairly well.

April 6: A very cold day—Inspector Eames said the official thermometer touched 44° below last night. Fred Ware pulled out for Herschel Island with Constables Chartrand and McDowell. Chartrand asked the inspector if he could take his concubine Kenelli along with him. He was flatly refused, of course, so he turned around and hired Charlie Stewart to take her. I never heard of such gall. I imagine he is liable to be cashiered for it.

They are quite busy in the store. The Eskimos intend pulling out tomor-

Frenchy Chartrand

"The dance began with the man swaying slowly and beating the drum from time to time as he swayed on motionless feet. Then he turned slowly round and round, gazing at the onlookers and apparently trying to win their participation. After a moment one of the women (his wife) began a high-pitched lingering chant, and the man's pace quickened. Each time that he hit the drum with his heavy stick, it pivoted round his left wrist, and as both drum and stick were very heavy, and the drum was often raised above the dancer's head, the dance was in part an exhibition of endurance and the dancer was required to go on until complete exhaustion. Then, in a ceremonial gesture, he would pass the drum to some one else.

"As usual—and especially here, where many of the natives had adopted some of the white man's ways—it was the old men who knew the tribal rites best. Ailennak must have been sixty years old, yet when he took up the drum an extraordinary agility began to flow through all his body. To this he added immense spirit and a remarkable sense of pantomime, so that he, in dancing, became the amorous bear he was seeking to simulate in a mixture of the burlesque, the lascivious, and the solemn. He handled the drum as if it were a fan behind which his impudicity was hidden, and the constant and unceasing repetition of the drum-beat sent his audience into a sort of trance. After an hour of dancing and drumming, the men and women round him had been worked up to a pitch of hysteria. The more lubricious and exhilarated the old man grew, the more the entranced women fell into an ecstatic rigidity. Standing with closed eyes, rigid to a point that seemed to simulate rigor mortis, they chanted an endless refrain on two notes while Ailennak bounded, crouched, sprang up again, and then squatted with glazed eyes as if never would he be able to come out of his delirium. The drum seemed to grow larger and larger until it filled the igloo, and as it rose in the air and fell again each time to earth, an intolerable impression of its weight was suggested by the rise and plunge of the drum. Now and then the old man seemed about to stop for lack of strength. Then the whole audience would come suddenly out of its trance and shout to urge him on. He went on till he could do no more, and all of a sudden he stopped dead, the drum hanging from his inert wrist. The air seemed to clear at once; the distorted faces and rigid bodies became normal; but the effect was still to send the audience back to their tents to continue their erotic exercises."

Gilbert de Poncins

row after their dance tonight. I had supper with the Eames and then took them to the Eskimo dance. It was quite good only there were too many white men there.

Bill Murray and I drew up a proposed authorized advance list. It allows the biggest white man $300 credit and the Indians practically nothing. Eskimos get a little more: Allan, Tom Elanik, and Garrett, $1,000; a few others $500; most $250 to $300. This is a revolutionary policy for the white men.

April 10: On Tuesday I went to see the children at the mission school. First they sang me a song of welcome and then read aloud, spelled, did calculations on the blackboard, wrote letters to me in their copybooks, and made up accounts as with the Hudson's Bay Company. They are very smart, Indian children of nine being able to read quite well. Afterwards the Sister Superior gave us afternoon tea. The sisters are wonderful and if there were not so much religion mixed up in it their work would probably be all to the good.

Tuesday was cold but the Eskimos all pulled out. I took some moving pictures of several of the teams. The Easter trade has not been very large but about $1,000 of debts have been collected—all to the good. Apparently both McPherson and Arctic Red River have made muskrat 50¢ so we shall have to follow suit. We are also reducing prices on many lines here, which should help the trade.

On the trail to Baillie Island; April 11: Lewis Kaglik and I got away about 9:15 a.m. We had a small toboggan and our load, though high, was not heavy. We had a fine grubstake—150 bannocks, 50 buns, cooked beans, caribou, bacon, jam, butter, tea, milk, and coffee. Our seven dogs started off fine, though the state of the trail was not good and our load prevented us both riding together. We took turns running and riding. At noon we stopped and ate some cooked meat with a couple of buns, and some coffee from our thermos. Then on again up creeks, across lakes and portages in the brilliant sunshine. I wore both goggles and eyeshade.

I thought the trail was the only life when we started out but it didn't seem so after 3 p.m. When we got to Noel's place about 5 p.m. my feet were beginning to feel like lead and my legs were stiff. Noel has a splendid house, warm, clean, and bright. Some girls had tea ready for us and we ate hot meat, beans, bread and jam. It all tasted fine. The girls also took our wet shoes and duffels, shook them out, and hung them up to dry. Splendid service. We enjoyed selections on the Victrola and one of the girls played the accordion. Just as we finished eating Noel and his wife arrived from the fish lakes where they had been jigging. They had quite a few jackfish, including a huge one, so I took two snapshots.

I sit on the floor in Noel's house, writing to the strains of the gramophone, while all the Eskimos are playing cards. They are a happy, contented crowd. The children are playing around or watching me write. A short time ago Norman came in by dogteam after looking at his traps. He got 8 muskrat. He was followed by Owen, a great, strapping, cheerful swashbuckler with 23 muskrat. The girls ran out to see what they had on their sleds, and made tea for them. They ate fish, muskrat, bread and butter— apparently any quantity—and are on the second two-pound tin of jam since we arrived. They are sitting in a circle now playing a sort of Eskimo rummy, chafing each other and laughing. Two young girls are sewing. This is the best Eskimo house I have seen, real flooring, oilcloth walls, a couple of beds and mattresses and several bunks, all kinds of fur clothing, calico parkas, bright blankets. Duffels and moccasins are drying on lines over the stove. Old John Kobegan lives here with the crowd. He is just a bum and is too old to trap anyway, but they keep him in comfort; it says a lot for them.

April 12: Had a frightfully hot night. There were ten of us sleeping in one small room and I woke in the night bathed in perspiration. Didn't have much sleep either—we didn't get to bed until midnight and they started getting up around 6 a.m. We all had breakfast together, seated in a circle on the floor around an oilcloth spread with all the dishes, a couple of big bowls of porridge, a pan of baked fish, bread and butter, two two-pound tins of creamery butter going at one time, jam, tea and coffee. I provided bannock, bacon, and a pan of beans.

We got away about 8:30 a.m., the whole crowd seeing us off. Owen came five miles with us, driving me in the cariole. Lewis Kaglik has been doing his best to get me to hire someone to drive me. I wouldn't give in— perhaps foolishly, because we had a pretty hard day running and I am stiff and sore tonight, almost as stiff and sore as I have ever been.

We made Dick Eckhardt's place after noon. I sure was tired. He gave us some stew, tea, bread and butter, and fruit. We spent two hours there and discussed world topics, and then set out for Amos's place 15 miles distant. About 5 p.m. we saw the last small stand of timber—nothing but willows north of there. Tomorrow we will see the last of them also. I was awfully leg-weary, running and riding short spells, before we reached Amos's place about 6 p.m.

There are three families here. We ate immediately in one of the houses, seated on the floor in a circle, with grace spoken before and after eating. There was ptarmigan broth with macaroni and barley, boiled caribou and ptarmigan, bread, butter, and tea. I cleaned up some broth and ptarmigan which was excellent. We then went to Amos's house, where I changed footwear and had a shave. I feel much better now although drowsy and stiff as a poker. The Amos château would not get a prize for cleanliness but

it is warm and light. There were four frozen foxes and one muskrat hanging up to thaw. One fox had the back of its head missing, having been eaten in the trap by another fox. We saw a fox on the river today and numerous tracks of lynx, foxes, rabbits, and ptarmigan.

April 13: We got away from Amos's place at a reasonable hour and kept on travelling downriver. It widened out as we neared the sea, great expanses of white snow with fairly steep riverbanks. The going was heavy, with deep snow. I walked the last 20 miles to Porsild's on my snowshoes. When I got going I felt as if I could go on for ever—absolutely tireless. Before reaching Porsild's we had tea from our thermos bottle, plus a tin of frozen strawberries which tasted excellent. Although we were hungry, our palates were too jaded for anything else.

I beat Lewis to the reindeer camp by half an hour. Bob Porsild came out to meet me, fearing something was wrong when he saw a man coming alone on foot. He and Mrs. Porsild gave me a warm welcome, took me to a room all ready for me, lit a stove, and brought some warm water. I certainly was all in, and one sock was red with blood where my snowshoe tie had taken the skin off my toes. It was 11 p.m. by now but we had a good meal and soon afterwards I hit the hay with the greatest delight. It had been a perfect afternoon for me. The high banks of the river, with undulating snowdrifts stretching 5 to 10 miles between bends, made a lovely scene in the spring sunlight.

April 14: The Porsilds have a fine house built right up on a ledge of the riverbank which gives them a splendid view up and downstream for miles. We walked around the place and I took some pictures from the hilltop. Porsild is all ready for the arrival of his 3000 reindeer from Alaska next year. Mrs. Porsild, a year out of Denmark and evidently expecting a child, is cheerful and bright and keeps things neat and tidy. Bob lets her do all her own work while he smokes a cigar. I can't understand that; she does deserve a little help with the dishes. We visited Bob's fish-net out under the ice and got a couple of fish. In the evening we had a game of three-handed bridge.

April 15: I started out for Tuktoyaktuk with seven dogs and an empty toboggan. Rode all the way and arrived at 11 p.m., pretty hungry. There was an awful crowd in Chief Williams' house but they made room for me. Lewis got busy and cooked us some bacon and beans. The people here have very little food, and apparently fish are scarce in the Husky Lakes. All they had, as far as I could see, was a little flour and an old white whale head which nearly made me sick to look at. Thirty of us slept in one room, all over the floor, beds, and everything, men, women, and children. This life isn't all it's cracked up to be!

April 16: Made our longest day—60 miles to Atkinson Point. We arrived late and all in, having run half the distance. I cursed myself for leaving my snowshoes at the Porsilds'.

We stopped three times for tea during the trip. Tea is certainly a wonderful pickup on the trail—you can be dead tired, stop for a ten-minute rest and some hot tea, and then get up and run 10 miles.

Ole Anderson gave us a good feed of pea soup. I don't think I was ever so tired, so I decided to spend tomorrow with Ole.

April 17: Had a very much appreciated rest today talking to Ole Anderson. He told us all about his expedition to the high Arctic islands with Stefansson and their journey over the polar ice. We discussed every topic under the sun, and both enjoyed it. I promised to send him a copy of Stef's *Hunters of the Great North.*

April 18: A long, 50-mile trip to Dalhousie. It was late when we reached Ole Anderson's trapping cabin. We got a good fire going and ate a big meal. Lewis is certainly a first-rate fellow to travel with, even if he is not much of a worker around the post. He is cheerful, energetic, and good to his dogs. I was very tired before getting into my eiderdown but cooked some rice for the morning.

Baillie Island; April 19: Crossed Liverpool Bay from Cape Dalhousie and got to Baillie Island half an hour before midnight. This has been the hardest day yet, very little riding and plenty of rough ice to scramble over with deep snow all around it. We were eight or nine hours out of sight of land and spent the last 25 miles breaking trail ahead of the dogs. We travelled by compass and, except for one deviation, hit the south-west sandspit without any trouble. There is very little darkness now but everyone was in bed when we arrived. Bill Johnson was up first and Margaret and Pat Wyant soon followed. They made me some hot soup, which tasted very good, and I got to bed two hours after midnight. I am thoroughly glad this part of the trip is over.

April 20: Slept until about 10 a.m. and felt much better, though a bit tough still when I got up. Pat had his sourdough flapjacks on the stove and they tasted good with maple syrup and coffee.

We spent the day discussing business, looking over statements, and getting up to date on everything. The debt situation is the worst possible. There is $44,000 outstanding in native accounts alone, and $25,000 in white customers' debts. Much of the former, probably $30,000, will remain unpaid this year, while a good $10,000 of the latter is absolutely worthless. Beside these there are the Horton River accounts of $21,000 against us. It is simply terrible and I don't know how I can explain it. The responsibility is mine because I did not set specific limits on the debts which could be given

Company store and residence at Baillie Island

out. Then I was victimized by McClellan who, deciding to quit his job, outfitted Berdette Verville with a jolly boat and motor when I had said he could only get a small outfit. Pat Wyant then came on the job and the sky was the limit. Of course we were expecting $30 for white foxes and a good fur year, but even so we were unreasonably generous. I cannot estimate the final results at better than a $45,000 loss.

Margaret and Pat Wyant

Pat was very subdued and willing to co-operate in reducing debts, expenses, and so on. I am pleased about this; I was rather afraid he might be insistent on having his own way, which would make things awkward for me. I see that if I make my instructions quite definite they will be followed. Bill Johnson will see things are kept up to date in the accounts line, so Pat will always know where he stands and not get out of his depth. I believe he will make out okay after this year. But I am very doubtful if I can weather the storm. I imagine I will have to send in my resignation along with my report—it will be such a bad one, and will reflect so much on me. I really do not deserve another chance. My only hope is that I believe I have turned the corner and taken the right steps to remedy things in the future. Moreover, the sad experience I have gained should fit me to carry on in the future as well as, if not better than, a new man. My only saving grace will be the soundness of the instructions I leave for Baillie Island between now and the summer.

I am sleeping in the attic, a poor place but somewhere to get some rest. By Jove, I want to make a success of this business, though it will take an awful lot of good fortune to compensate for the failure I've made already.

April 21: The weather is mild, up to 40° above zero, and the snow is getting soft around the buildings. There are not many natives around. They have no fur and are in debt so are not making any purchases.

April 24: Busy on inventory. There is a terrific stock, and McClellan has ordered in some extraordinary articles and quantities. I thank my stars I cut down his requisitions the way I did. Next summer we shall have to do some heavy transferring to other posts—but it takes years to accomplish things in this country.

The Eskimos are getting a lot of seal at the floe edge these days. We are going to take a run out on Sunday and take a crack at them. Sometimes I feel pretty blue. The heavy loss here is most depressing and the way the house is kept is not very elevating to the spirits. Sometimes I feel as if I were a slave up here and wonder why I came. But if I last another year I think I shall see great benefits from the policy I am putting across now. I hope I do, because I do not want to leave the country a failure.

Heavy rain last night and the snow sinking fast. Foggy and drizzling. We are feeding very well—getting a lot of seal liver, which is certainly as good as beef liver. We are also going to eat seal meat.

April 25: The inventory is quite a long one, 55 pages, and there are enormous quantities of unopened goods. Much surprise was evinced when several bales and cases were discovered to contain the same goods ordered for this year. Fortunately in most instances I had cancelled them again.

Very mild all day. Pat worked on his ice house and Margaret went with him, so Johnson and I had a little peace and quiet. This is a terrible house, filthy dirty. Margaret is just a native who is always anxious to be cutting up seal or something like that and leaving dirty dishes all over the place. She wears a dirty rag of a calico dress and never by any chance combs her hank of hair. It makes me sick. Too bad such a good fellow as Pat should marry a wreck like her.

April 26: Finished the inventory, which came to $38,000—much less than we had expected.

At 4 p.m. Pat, Bill, and I went out seal-hunting to the edge of the floe. We went with Pat's dogs in a dandy little sled he made. We travelled about 7 miles, all riding in the sled. It ran very easily through rough and smooth ice. The rough ice was the loveliest green or blue imaginable. Finally we came to the open bay, about a mile wide with ice drifting along in it. The Eskimos, Tonoamik, Annakeena, and Lewis, were out there and had several seals. They stand on the ice at intervals close to the water, wait for a seal to appear, and shoot it when it comes up to breathe. One came up near us. Pat and Bill both shot at it and missed. Next time Bill got it through the head. We shouted for Lewis; all the natives came over and Lewis took a small canvas boat and retrieved the seal. We stayed another couple of hours but only saw two misses so we came home at 10 p.m.

April 27: I fired Lewis Kaglik today, letting him down fairly easily. He is to leave on April 30 but get wages and rations for May. Lewis took it all right.

I am revising our price list here, reducing prices. The losses last year are terrible—I shiver every time I see them—and I feel obliged to offer my resignation as a result of the catastrophe. It is very unfortunate, with everything practically set for our wedding.

April 28: Several of the natives came over from Cape Bathurst and Pat

Eskimo home at Baillie Island

explained how much debt they are to get until the next trapping season. They were satisfied. I prepared a list of goods to be shipped to Aklavik, being unsaleable here.

McClellan let me down terribly before quitting his job. I was far too soft with him. The more I go into the debt question here, the more depressed I feel.

April 29: We are $7000 short on merchandise, which is unsatisfactory. Johnson and I spent the morning unsuccessfully looking for it. I feel sure it is shortages from the *Baychimo* which will show up—nobody could steal that much.

Listed the advances to natives next season with Pat; we are sure holding them down. The white customers' debts are a caution but we are cutting them down too.

May 2: It remains light all through the night now although lamps are needed indoors for a couple of hours.

Alex, Lester, and John Reuben were in with very little fur to put towards their debts. Pat took what they had and gave them a good talking-to regarding future small advances. They took it very philosophically. They contend they can pay up when they get a good year's hunting. I believe they can if prices also rise a little. Lewis Kaglik, whom I fired, is now hauling wood since his coal ration has been cut off.

Inspected the underground ice house which Pat is having built in the permafrost. It is a good one, a hole or shaft 10 feet deep widened into a chamber at the bottom. There is a small house on top through which entry is made.

Pat's wife, Margaret, is very busy sewing for the trip—she is to go with us as far as Horton River. She spends most of the day scraping sealskins, chewing soles, and sewing boots. She sits on the floor all day and never cooks or washes a dish. She is strongly native in her attitudes and way of going about things.

Only two more days until we pull out. We sit up very late at night here, and get up late, which is bad—but it is difficult to do otherwise with daylight almost all day long.

May 4: Very busy all day writing out my instructions to Pat Wyant: five foolscap pages covering every point I can think of. I am getting everything down in black and white so there can be no comeback whatsoever. Also I made Pat sign the list of authorized debts as a sign he would not exceed them.

The weather has been very mild and fine for travelling. Pat is getting ready for our trip. I have cleared up all my notes for my report and packed all my papers, heartily glad to be finished here. Before going to bed I checked the weather and found the wind blowing strongly from the east—right into our faces.

On the trail to Letty Harbour; May 5: Got up at 10:30 a.m. and found the weather unchanged—still blowing from the east. We had breakfast, packed our belongings, and managed to pull out at 1:30 p.m. Pat and I each drove a team of four dogs. Pat had the grub and duffels while I had my own gear plus Margaret, who rode on my sled because my four dogs were faster than the others.

We only got as far as Whale Bluff, 20 to 25 miles but far enough. The wind, though not very cold, was dead ahead and unpleasant. I had to run a bit and watch the sled in rough ice. Never being able to let go of the handle-bars was most tiring. Having Margaret on my sled is also a nuisance.

At Whale Bluff Pat Wyant keeps a tent in an old cabin. We camped there—most uncomfortably. The place was cramped and dirty and the child, Sigrid, which Pat takes on his sled, was an infernal nuisance. We fed on bacon and beans, fruit, hardtack, and coffee. The few doughnuts I had saved from the Aklavik–Baillie Island trip were a godsend on our arrival. Tommy Chichi and Teddy Oshokok came along after us but camped a few miles farther on; they gave us four ptarmigan which we are going to have for breakfast. I was thoroughly glad to turn in, although the floor was hard and very cold. Life in the Arctic did not seem very good.

May 6: After our ptarmigan breakfast we got away about 11 a.m. It doesn't matter much what time we start now as there is light almost all day long. It was a brute of a day, a strong wind nearly straight ahead and a nasty drift. The snow melted when it struck our faces. It formed into a thin film of ice which you weren't aware of until your hand went there, as it often did, to scrape the ice away. It froze particularly on my chin. As we had a great deal of rough ice to negotiate I couldn't face away from the wind, which meant a frozen nose, chin, and cheek. I don't think I have ever had a more misera-ble day's travel. We reached Horton River in about 7 hours.

Fred Carpenter, his wife and baby were occupying a house belonging to Pat Wyant. Roddy and family were also staying there. Edward's family came in and out and with Sigrid, who is a perfect brat, they made the place a bedlam. Fred Carpenter is a good lad and trapped 93 foxes this winter. Rolled in on the floor again and glad to do so. The reports of the very mea-gre hunts are discouraging.

May 7: Pat Wyant and I left Horton River about 10:30 a.m. with eight dogs on the one sled in an east wind, which was pretty uncomfortable, especially after my face was frost-bitten yesterday. We soon lost sight of land and didn't pick it up again until 6 p.m., after 7½ hours of most miserable travel-ling over sea ice with small drifts of loose snow on it. We made a couple of stops for coffee. It was nice to sit down with our backs to the wind and take a few minutes rest. I wore dark goggles and was warm enough with a single *artigi* and deerskin pants.

After sighting land to the south we decided we were too far south and hauled north, although it was hard to keep the team leader's head directly into the wind. Two or three hours later we spotted land and came up to a small sandspit. We searched the horizon with glasses and decided we were still south of our day's destination, which is Tom Cod Bay. We again headed north. The sun was down and objects and distances were most deceiving: we mistook sticks for schooner masts and mounds for houses and everything was all wrong. We crossed deep bays, rough ice, points of land, and still no sign of Tom Cod Bay. At 1 a.m. there was still nothing doing. We stopped at a big snowbank, lit the primus stove, and had coffee. We are running two days into one now.

Pulled out again feeling much better. At 4 a.m. we were crossing a huge bay when I spotted a tiny streak on the land. We headed for it, reaching it in about half an hour. It turned out to be a schooner mast; there were two schooners there, but no houses. Pat decided that what we had seen some time ago were articles on the roofs of snowed-under cabins, so we made our way back and sure enough found two cabins buried in the snow. It was now 5 a.m. Dogs and men were dead beat and very glad to find a place to flop. I dug my way into one shack and found it had leaked in the thaw and was all covered in ice—floor, stove, bunks, table, and everything. I dug a six-foot hole to get on even terms with the door to the other house and found it in fine shape inside, clean and tidy with a good stove and nice floor, kettles, etc. I lit a fire, melted snow, and made tea while Pat unhitched and fed the dogs. The sun was up by this time. We have been up for 22 hours, travelling 18 of these. The tea, hardtack, and fruit tasted divine and we rolled into our bags absolutely exhausted. I rolled off my deerskin mat onto the floor but was so tired I didn't even notice.

Letty Harbour; May 8: We had 10 hours' sleep but mine wasn't as sound as it might have been—I had nightmares about the Letty Harbour debts and worried all night. We got up at 5:30 p.m. to find the wind still blowing in our faces but very little drift. We had bacon and fried hardbread and coffee, and a good wash in warm water. Then we cleaned up the cabin, packed our goods, loaded the sled, and pulled out, the dogs doing fine in spite of their long day yesterday.

We headed inland across country travelling from hill to hill; from each high knoll we would look ahead to the next and then make for it. The going was splendid, mostly large lakes with hard snow, and as luck would have it we came out right at Letty Harbour, exactly where we were heading for, after about five hours' travelling. We arrived around midnight and found Stewart in bed but soon got him up and cooking something to eat. We talked for a few hours, as we had slept a good deal the night before, then lay down to rest.

I feel pretty rotten, system upset with trail grub and irregular hours and yesterday's terrible travel. Eyes are sore with a touch of snowblindness, face burned up with exposure, and chin broken out with frequent frostbite. In addition big debts, especially Billy Thrasher's, just about broke my spirit. I scarcely know whether I am standing on my feet or my head, and feel very depressed.

May 9: I spent the day doing very little. My eyes troubled me a little. They are inclined to be granulated and discharge at night; that gave me a headache, and the reaction after the strain of travelling against the wind for four successive days made me a bit groggy.

I read over the personal mail I have with me, which cheered me up, helping me to realize there is a big world outside my little one. Thinking constantly only about business gets one in a rut so it is difficult to see beyond one's own immediate worries. I do not expect to write to Mary until I get to Bernard Harbour as I shall be up to my ears until then, and I would sooner get through my hard work and travel.

May 10: A nice day. Wyant left to return to Baillie Island this morning, while Stewart and I started on the inventory right away and got all the stock down on paper by suppertime. After supper we dropped over to the R.C. mission and chatted with the brother for a bit—Fathers Trocellier and Griffin were away hunting caribou at the bottom of the bay with the natives. I would rather not see them as they are always looking after their own interests. Their latest idea is to move down into Darnley Bay and for us to move with them. Last year they pointed out what a wonderful place Letty Harbour is and how ideal for a trading post. I would never think of moving an inch unless it was to abandon this part of the country altogether.

May 11: Porridge, bacon, toast, and coffee for breakfast. Stewart feeds us very well, caribou meat, dried potatoes, and an odd pie, quite a contrast to Baillie Island! The wind is still blowing hard from the east. This is the seventh day of it. I never saw anything like it.

Pearce Point; May 13: I hired Colin to take me to Pearce Point. Just before we pulled out the brother from the mission brought me two big ham sandwiches and two packets of figs for our trip, which was very thoughtful of him.

We had a pretty good trip, though as usual we had a head wind which burned our faces or froze them, we weren't sure which. Shortly after midnight we saw a couple of seals sleeping on the ice beside their holes. Colin loaned me his rifle to stalk one, telling me to shoot from the shelter of some rough ice he indicated. When I got close to the rough ice the seal still looked half a mile away so I went closer and closer, stopping when the seal raised its head to look around, walking on when the head went down again. I found it impossible to gauge the distance although I was well within range—that tiny black spot dancing in a wilderness of blinding white might have been a mile away to my eyes. Then the seal saw me and dived down the hole. So I returned to the sled disappointed.

The early morning was lovely. We arrived about 4 a.m. to find Swagger Henriksen, Harry Siles, and Fred Jacobson and his son Ted just getting up to welcome us. They gave us bacon and eggs and all the news. The principal item of discussion was the new $15 tariff for white foxes—it had been $20 up to our arrival at Pearce Point. Karl Peterson is the only one with a fair hunt, 70 white foxes, but he is terribly in debt—$3,600 this year plus $5,000 from before—so I can't see how we can ever collect. Swagger gave me his bed and I had a fair rest, though it was too sunny and hot to sleep very much.

May 14: This place is certainly changed from last year, when our buildings were the only ones and there was no one else for miles. The big catches of last year brought trappers galore, white and native, and the police also moved from Baillie Island. It is now quite a settlement and absolutely ruined by the crowd, who have made very meagre catches. Swagger and Harry are both going out this year and we are closing the outpost. Everyone is leaving except the police, and Karl Peterson and his partner.

I told Peterson I would pay him $1,000 for his 60 white foxes and then he could get $400 credit plus $200 for his partner. He nearly hit the roof but I could do no better so we finally made out a list of the $600 worth of supplies he needs. His balance will now be $7,500 and I hope someday this may be cleared off. It is an awful blow to find he owes so much. The commissioner will be wild and I don't blame him.

May 16: Spent all day finishing the inventory and checking prices. It hasn't been easy to work in such a small house with such amazing old characters as Henriksen and Jacobson yarning away. I sit and roar with laughter at them all day.

On the trail to Bernard Harbour; May 17: Five months to October 17!

We left Pearce Point with two teams of seven and five dogs in a heavy snowstorm which melted as it fell on us. The dogs were eager to go and leapt into their collars when they were being hitched up. We saw seals, squirrels, ptarmigan, three geese, two caribou and wolf tracks, so spring is here.

We travelled on the sea ice, and near the Roscoe River we saw another

Fred Jacobson

caribou track leaving the ice for the land, evidently at some speed. This was extraordinary as all deer are supposed to be pretty well inland. Farther on young Teddy Jacobson saw something trotting up and down the beach and thought it might have been a dog they had left on their way to Pearce Point, and Fred said it must be a cross fox, but I knew it was a big grey wolf. I grabbed Fred's rifle and took a standing shot at him. I was about four inches above his back and he made off. Later we saw where the caribou had left the land with the wolf after him.

We slept in a tent, 6 x 8 feet, and cooked our caribou over a primus stove. The floor was covered with ice from the thaw so we put down sealskins first, then deerskins, and the three of us slept under one eiderdown.

May 18: Sunny and hot, but fairly fresh snow made slow going. Saw dozens of seals sleeping on the ice. It would have been great fun stalking them.

At Tinney Point, Teddy and I slept outside on a bare patch of ground. The sun was on the upgrade as we went to sleep and it sure warmed up. Behind us were the snow-covered hills with ground showing here and there; before us was mile upon mile of ice as far as the eye could see, all snow-covered, some places level as a billiard table and others rough with ice broken by fall gales, here and there a ridge 20 to 30 feet high formed by pressure.

May 19: We passed Croker River which was throwing water. We unknowingly crossed some very thin ice covered with a thin layer of snow, where the river ran pretty fast below. It was a crossing of a couple of miles, but we arrived safely.

We reached Inman River around 7 p.m., glad to finish that leg of our journey. We found Fred Jacobson's house in order but his wife sick; he thinks she may die. She wouldn't be much loss anyway as she is the laziest, most quarrelsome brute I ever saw. We had a good ptarmigan stew for supper but Inman River is the worst place on the coast for country food. Jacobson's family is a terrible one, six awful kids. Louis and Teddy are good trappers but all are frightfully extravagant and waste more than they eat. Their combined catch last year was 150 white foxes. Jacobson is way in the hole.

May 22: Henry Jensen said he would take me as far as Art Watson's place, 75 miles away. I had been worried how to get there, and was figuring on borrowing some dogs from Fred Jacobson and going alone.

We travelled until 5 a.m., making 40 miles, then camped, ate, slept for five hours, got up and travelled again. It was a terrible day with poor visibility and heavy pulling. We were hungry when we reached the outcamp.

The Lord only knows how we discovered it—nothing except an occasional black rock or basking seal could be discerned. We could not get into the camp—it would have meant an hour's digging, and we had no shovel—so we made a stove from a coal oil tin and with a little blubber and wood managed to heat some canned meat. Then we went on to Art Watson's place, another 3 hours. Mrs. Watson rustled us up a good meal and Art produced his last bottle of rum. He has 140 to 150 white foxes and is requisitioning $3500 of goods.

Bernard Harbour; May 23: Slim Purcell brought me the 35 miles to Bernard Harbour. We had an enjoyable 8-hour run across country. I felt really at home with the worst worries behind, a decent house to live in, nice chaps, a good bed, and a scant 100 miles from Coppermine. Ray Ross and Billy Joss are both fine. Scotty Gall has come here to run our schooner, the *Aklavik*. There are only one or two Eskimos around so all is quiet.

May 24: I read the mail Paddy Gibson left here for me. It is not encouraging; conditions at eastern posts are poor. The trade here at Bernard Harbour has been a failure as elsewhere—only 200 white foxes—but there is no great amount of debt, which is hopeful. Ray Ross keeps a really clean, bright house, something I haven't seen since Aklavik. We are inclined to be late in going to bed and late to rise. I want to fight this as I am convinced it is not good.

May 25: Breakfast at 11 a.m.—porridge, coffee, toast, and marmalade. I am busy collecting my notes and getting up to date before starting the post work here. I have really no need to rush now, as I can reach Coppermine easily, though I have plenty of work to do writing reports on all the posts I have visited.

Billy Joss and I had a little golf practice out on the bay back of the house but the snow was pretty soft.

Scotty Gall

May 26: Another glorious day. We had breakfast much earlier today and are getting back to a regular routine gradually. I spent the day going over stock item by item with Ray Ross. There is a terrible stock situation here, and it will take years to get it down to a reasonable basis. There is much of a saleable nature but more prosperous times must come before it will move.

I went over the *Aklavik* with Scotty Gall. She is certainly a fine schooner and has a dandy engine. It is a pity her carrying capacity is so limited and she is leaking so badly. I am going to hire Gall as an engineer, at probably $125 per month for the summer and then a nominal $25 for the winter.

May 28: Weather perfect with a soft, spring-like feeling and birds singing cheerfully. It would be glorious outside now. All we have here are bare patches of ground showing up, water appearing on the ice, and slowly diminishing dirty snowbanks. The radio news was all wars and rumours of wars.

May 29: The *Aklavik* is leaking faster now and a great deal of pumping is necessary. The leak seems to be around her stern post and deadwood. During the day it appeared her bow was higher, and this was correct—the bow had floated up clear of the ice but the stern was still solid! This made us apprehensive of the keel being sprung. Gall tried to locate the leaks in order to plug them, but water seemed to make all along the deadwood. We pumped her every little while.

Evidently she was leaking very badly last summer, and this caused the stern to freeze solidly into the ice. When the bow rose it must have opened the seams aft. She should never have been left in the water last fall. She is now almost filled with water. We decided to leave her that way until morning as she cannot sink, being still supported by ice.

May 31: Very weary and stiff today after a strenuous day caulking yesterday. There is no change in the *Aklavik's* position. She is full of water to the level of the water outside but is still in her ice cradle, and it is almost impossible to do anything. We decided to give her a couple of days to thaw free, then commence baling again and build a watertight bulkhead across the stern to keep the water back there. Ross and I continued to work on the post business and are making good progress.

June 3: We repaired to the schooner early and everyone manned the pumps and baling buckets. But try as we might, we couldn't get the water down low enough. It is most discouraging.

We had to quit work about 10 p.m., as it was getting dark and we couldn't see what we were doing, particularly under water. We had only managed to get the water down about a foot below the top of the engine. We weighed the bow down by putting three boats across it and filling them with water for extra weight—this may prevent the bow from rising, which causes seam leaks and drains the water back to the stern. If the bulkhead doesn't work I don't know what we can do. We haven't got the tackle to haul her out of the ice. We may have to buoy her up with drums and things and wait until the *Baychimo* arrives, and have her hauled out then.

June 4: Down to the schooner around 9 and in three to four hours we had finished our bulkhead to our satisfaction. We were delighted to find we could take the water down quite easily, and with the help of the natives baled her nearly dry with two pumps and two drums. It was heavy work but we didn't mind when we could see the water level dropping. In about

four hours we got most of the water out but found that she was still leaking quite badly underneath our bulkhead. This was a disappointment, but we decided to build a second bulkhead on the next rib but one. While this was being done we had to keep pumping.

At midnight, after hours of hard, back-breaking labour, the new bulkhead was complete. Water still came in, but not much, and we caulked a few leaks around the deadwood. We left her at that—all utterly fagged out after sixteen hours of it. The boat is in the worst possible mess. The engine-room is coated with oil and everything is wrack and ruin where we pulled up the floor, the interior of the cabin, and the deck. However, she is afloat, and that is the main thing. All else can be repaired, though she cannot operate this year as a proper ship's carpenter must repair the hull. We are feeling much happier tonight, and I have visions of getting away for Coppermine in the near future after all.

June 6: Up in good time this morning but terribly weary. I do not sleep well at nights. I am thinking about business while in bed, and dreaming about it in all sorts of distorted ways. Apparently I shall make Coppermine okay. Scotty Gall is going to take me about 15 miles down the coast to a native camp, where I shall be relayed to Cape Krusenstern. There I hope to get a native to take me down to Coppermine. It will seem strange travelling by dogteam with all the snow gone off the land, creeks in full flood and water all over the ice!

On the trail to Coppermine; June 8: Packed my things and gave the word to pull out. This travelling through six inches of water is new to me, but the dogs seem to enjoy it and paddled through all the water they came to. Before long we came in sight of open water a mile or two off shore but we are sticking to the shoreline.

Our small sled ran easily and we rode all the time. In four hours we were at Kavintuk's tent where he and his new wife are living with an old widow and some children. We went inside and found it spic and span. We were given a feed of boiled fresh trout with no trimmings, not even salt, and tea without milk or sugar, and we produced our ham sandwiches and biscuits and shared them. About 9 p.m. Kavintuk hitched up his seven dogs to a big sled and I said goodbye to Scotty Gall as we pulled out for Krusenstern.

There was a young girl back in the tent and I am pretty sure she died as we left to pull out. I watched her closely. The way her eyes turned up under the lids and the general appearance of her face gave me the impression that she cashed in then and there. I didn't draw attention to it as it would only cause complications and do no good. The woman made a remark which may have meant "She is dying," and I let it go at that. Poor kid, they can do so little for them when they are ill and the people accept death philosophically.

Eskimo tent at Cambridge Bay

Kavintuk's team was pretty slow and we stopped quite a number of times while he stalked seal or I shot at ducks with my .22. Each time it was "no kill". Kavintuk even shot at ducks on the wing with his rifle. He must have used the better part of a box of cartridges, in spite of their cost and great value to him.

We rounded Cape Lambert and passed over some very dangerous ice, I'm afraid—there were blue patches of water showing. I believe we should have gone on the land. But the portage over to Krusenstern was lovely— we left ice and water and went about a mile over turf and gravelly patches. I had experienced nothing like it since last autumn, and it was delightful to feel my feet sinking into spongy growth. There was the odd pond too, with ice in it, sometimes ducks, other birds singing and the sun coming up.

June 9: The dogs pulled our sled up and over a hump and we found ourselves at the buildings. Bill Seymour, the post manager, gave us breakfast and I had a good sleep, and then I went over to Avakana's tent to see if he would take me to Coppermine. William Kuptana, Bill's chief man, came along as interpreter. But Avakana's dogs had sore feet, and neither Smokestack or Okituk felt inclined to go. William said they were afraid of the water, and said he would go himself and take his small twelve-year-old son for company and assistance on the way back. He has made a lot of dogboots since the ice cuts their paws so late in spring.

By 4 p.m. we were ready to pull out. Bill Seymour gave us a dandy feed of roast goose and packed a good lunch for us to take along. Bill has a nice house with the window in the roof, and Lena, the neatest-looking Eskimo girl I ever saw, slim and neatly dressed. William Kuptana's wife does most of the cooking and housework.

William hitched his seven dogs to a 16-foot sled onto which we loaded a 17-foot skiff. We piled all our gear into the skiff and got in ourselves, riding in comfort while the dogs paddled merrily over ice and through water up to a foot deep. We crossed cracks in the ice here and there, choosing places where the crack wasn't over 6 to 8 feet wide. At times we shoved the sled across the crack, using it as a bridge, then hauled the dogs through the water. The ice was covered with water but nothing high enough to go over my boot-tops when I ran. At 6 p.m. we stopped and put on the dogs' seal-skin boots, 28 of them—it took us 45 minutes. It was darned cold now so I put on my deerskin pants and tied the belt around my parka. Seems strange on June 9!

William shot at seal several times with his Mannlicher rifle but got none; he blew the head off one but it sank. I shot one with my .22 but it either dived or sank. At Dead Man Island we made coffee and ate the cold goose Bill Seymour had given us. It was getting on towards midnight when we left there—of course the sun never came anywhere near setting, but it was freezing and that made it hard on the dogs' feet. Two weren't pulling at all so William cut them out and we left them to follow at their own speed. William's son went to sleep in the stern of the skiff, I sat amidships, and William sat in the bow.

Coppermine; June 10: Soon after midnight I wore a hole in the heel of my left water boot and got a miserable wet foot. We were heading for the big island about 20 to 25 miles from Coppermine. When it showed up as a line on the horizon I wondered if we could reach it in two hours, but it took twice that time. We stopped, cooked, and dried our footgear in the sun.

Rounding the island we came in sight of the Coppermine settlement, the buildings like dots at regular intervals. The way ahead was dead smooth with no water on it. We climbed halfway up a cliff to see where the Coppermine River was throwing water. It was positively hot, no wind and the sun well up at 6 a.m. Away down below the sled and dogs looked like miniatures in black, the perfectly smooth white ice stretching for miles with the hills in the background. The scene was glorious. We looked through glasses and noted the river running near the buildings but there was only a lane of water between the ice and the land farther down from the settlement. We didn't stay long on the hill—we felt too sleepy in the warmth after 22 hours on the go, including 14 hours travelling. The sun was so warm and the going so perfect I slept halfway to the settlement.

As we approached, it looked as if we might land near the wireless building by using our boat for the last hundred yards. But as we got closer we found the ice getting pretty rotten, all candled, and all of a sudden a fast current of water was running just in front of us. The ice showed every sign of collapsing. William grabbed the lead dog and we doubled on our tracks as fast as we could turn the sled and beat it!

We approached the settlement again about half a mile below. There the ice was okay to the water's edge. The water extended about a hundred yards from shore and was only about 24 inches deep at most. So we floated our boat and tied the dogs on behind. But the boat grounded, and it was too heavy for us to pull so we hitched the dogs to it and tied the sled on behind. The water got deeper and the dogs had to swim. It was the funniest sight I think I have ever seen—five dogs in harness swimming to beat the band, towing a skiff with us in it, the big sled floating placidly along behind.

We were soon ashore, dogs, boat, and sled. The dogs could not pull the sled along the beach with my gear on it so I left it all there and just took the dogs to the settlement. It was amusing driving dogs hanging on to a long rope behind them. They nearly pulled my arms out by the roots until I thought to walk ahead of them and thus maintain a reasonable walk to the settlement.

Coppermine at last, and am I glad to get here! It is a wonderful place, grass and turf, willows and water and hills with a glorious spring-like feeling, a regular jump from winter into summer. The post buildings are lovely, all freshly painted white, green, and red. Barnes gave us something to eat, we chatted, and I sent telegrams to the fur trade commissioner, Mary, and home. Then I turned in on Barnes' bed and had four dandy hours of sleep, after having only five or six in 52—during which time I travelled 90 to 100 miles.

I got up at 5 p.m. and chatted during the evening, getting abreast of the news. Reverend Webster, the Anglican missionary, dropped in. I think I am going to enjoy my stay. I have stacks of work to do.

June 11: Barnes moved the dining-room table into the office so I have plenty of room. Just by turning my head I can look out across the river and the bay to the islands in Coronation Gulf. I can't get over the feeling of leaping into summer. It's great. I put on some lighter clothing—feels nice.

Champion hunter and family, Coppermine

Father Fallaise of the R.C. mission dropped in, and I paid a visit to their mission. I have a very comfortable bed upstairs and they keep good hours here so everything is splendid for work.

June 12: Did a washing today, which took some time but was necessary. I am also going to wash my sweaters, trousers, and snowshirt as they are all in a terrible mess from working on the *Aklavik*. For a while today we had a really hot wind, just like "outside" during the summer. I visited the fish-net with Barnes and Savage, the assistant manager. There were seven fine salmon trout, one quite large. They never eat fish here, but I am going to when the others pull out upriver and leave me here alone.

June 13: Finished a telegraphic report to Winnipeg, which is unpleasant. I coded it and got it away, then got off another regarding my proposal to establish at Read Island. The two of them took up most of the day.

A loose dog came around and started chewing up one of Barnes' pups. I drove it off but a few minutes later it was worrying another. I again drove it off. The next time it returned I put a .22 bullet through it. It didn't return a fourth time! I was annoyed because I thought it had killed the pup, but the pup seems to have recovered okay. I believe it was Dr. Martin's dog, so there will probably be a row.

I mapped out a program of hard work which will take me until July 1, the earliest date I can get away. Barnes and I have had some great discussions regarding the trade in this part of the country, but I can't see any way to make it pay with fur prices as they are. We can cut down expenses but our revenue is so limited.

The weather is calm as can be, grass getting green and everything so peaceful.

June 14: The ice still hangs on in the river but is expected to break up any day and go under the sea ice in the bay. I worked on my *Aklavik* report, but I find it difficult to recall the details. My notes are not as complete as they might be.

It is a corker how nice and mild it is now. Barnes and I sat on the back step after supper and revelled in the balmy air. I am told there is a dead dog under the doctor's house—the one I shot yesterday evidently cashed it in. It's a good job the doctor is "outside".

The old medicine man brought me a present of a fine salmon this afternoon. Apparently he is an old scoundrel. It's a funny thing that I always revel in a good feed of Coppermine salmon but they never eat it here, they prefer canned meat. I'm going to cook a piece of fish for myself tomorrow.

June 15: Gerry, the Cambridge Bay interpreter, arrived today with some mail. Paddy Gibson writes that King William Land has 3000 white foxes but unfortunately they cost an average of $20.50 as our advice about lower fur prices failed to arrive there until April 30. Still, this means we have had good sales.

Jack Kimpton added a note that the commissioner is chafing for my brief report on the trade. I'm afraid it will not please him. I'm terribly worried sometimes whether I shall survive for another year. I must.

I cooked my piece of salmon today and found it delicious. I even had some cold—the best eating. Quite a bit of ice moved out of the river here so it is clear all the way across.

June 17: Four months from today is THE DAY.

Another wire from Winnipeg announced a district managers' conference on November 10 and asked for suggestions for the agenda. Why they should ask me up here I can't imagine. It is a good sign to be asked, though, and I am quite bucked up about it. The conference definitely puts a finish to our honeymoon by that date. As it does give us three weeks I think we shall be okay. That will probably be about the right length of time.

June 18: A fine day with the ice moving nearly all day. Barnes and Savage left for fishing upriver tonight, leaving me all alone. It is nice to be alone.

June 19: Received a wire last night saying that Western Canada Airways would be in next Thursday, a week earlier than I had expected, so now I am in an awful rush to finish my work. I got up before 8 a.m., had the dogs watered by 9:30, and then got down to work. Had lunch at 1 p.m.—cold boiled Coppermine salmon-trout, cocoa, bread and jam; supper at 6:30 p.m.—fried eggs, macaroni and cheese, toast and tea.

Had a wire from Mary saying she got my letters and had sent one in here for me. Glory be! She sent twenty-four to Aklavik, which is lovely. Wire from Jack Kimpton saying the fur commissioner is peeved regarding my increase in estimated loss. he is thinking of paying E.W.W off this summer. I hope he doesn't pay me off! My brother Hum added a note that stocks are shot to hell and general conditions are pretty punk. I'll say they are! I'm worried now as to whether I'll have enough cash to be married, but I guess everything will come out okay.

Worked hard all day and now must hit the hay. It's just midnight.

June 21: Midsummer day. The sea ice is a good mile from here now, and there is a hot wind blowing again today. I got up at noon and cooked a rather poor breakfast on the primus stove. Next time I'm going to use the kitchen stove. Then I washed up, swept the house out, and watered the dogs. I like this batching. I can think without interruptions and get a lot more done.

June 23: Nothing but work, work, in preparation for the plane this week. They are coming all too soon for me. I shall not be ready for them, which will reflect on me as I should have everything ready, tons of material. However I can only do my best and if it is not satisfactory, well, it is just too bad. Reflecting on what I have to face in Winnipeg is not a bit encouraging. It is a sad story I have to tell.

June 25: Western Canada Airways were due today but no sign of the plane. Every time I hear an outboard motor I look out. Working long hours.

June 26: At 6 p.m. a plane was overhead before I knew it, and Bill Spence piloted his blue and yellow monoplane to a lovely landing in front of the post. Pete Norberg and Patsy Klengenberg were on board. I thought Patsy looked splendid and in good spirits. He gave me a bottle of Scotch and offered to take down the warehouse at Rymer Point. Pete Norberg says conditions are terrible outside.

They left shortly after for Rymer Point. I gave Spence mail for Mary; he said he would drop in again to pick up the office mail on his way back, but he flew far to the west of here on his return!

June 27: I have been terribly depressed going over my reports, they are so bad. I wrote a personal letter to Mr. Ralph Parsons, the fur trade commissioner, admitting my responsibility for the failure of the past year but expressing confidence in my ability and my desire to stick with the job. I have learned my lesson.

June 28: Busy from 9 a.m. to midnight. I must have everything ready for the next plane going out and also be ready to leave for Fort Norman pretty soon.

July 1: Two N.A.M.E. planes arrived with Gordon Duncan and Mr. Channing, president of Hudson Bay Mining and Smelting Company, on board.

Mr. Channing and
J. C. Rogers with
Bonnycastle

PA-10128S/PUBLIC ARCHIVES CANADA

Mr. Duncan and Garfield Smith with Bonnycastle at NAME (Northern Aerial Minerals Exploration) camp at Dismal Lake.

PA-101273/PUBLIC ARCHIVES CANADA

They brought mail, including one letter from Mary. They went on to Richardson River to observe transport possibilities there, but will take me to their Dismal Lake prospecting camp tomorrow, so I am working straight through until then.

Dismal Lake; July 2: We pulled out for the N.A.M.E. camp at 6 p.m. today, six of us crushed into the cabin of one Fairchild along with quite a load of supplies. It was a wonder we managed to take off.

The camp is quite picturesque, a number of round silk tents on a plateau halfway up a hill. The surrounding country looks lovely, rolling and green. We had a dandy sleep under canvas.

Fort Norman; July 4: Took off after lunch for Great Bear Lake. We landed at Hunter Bay about an hour later. We heard about the recent uraninite find [Eldorado] from the geologist there. Went on to Norman, a lovely flight over the lake which was a deep blue and had floating ice in it. The 300 miles were covered in about 2½ hours. We arrived in a squall of wind and rain which shook us up a little.

Here I am in the timber country again, quite a queer sensation after being so long on the coast. Spence and another pilot are here with two planes and may go down to Aklavik if they can get return passengers. They are wiring Aklavik to find out. I could fly down for $125.

Mr. Channing is flying right through to Winnipeg and took my mail; he should reach there in two or three days. He promised to phone Mary and say he saw me. I think he is an awfully decent man.

Down the Mackenzie to Aklavik; July 5: There were no passengers going out from Aklavik by air so it was a canoe for yours truly. I got hold of Pat

Bonnycastle and Mr.
Duncan at the bornite
trench at Dismal Lake

PA-101281/PUBLIC ARCHIVES CANADA

Coombs, and borrowed a 22-foot canoe and a 10 hp Johnson Seahorse motor from the Northern Traders. Pat is going downriver with me and will return on the *Distributor*.

We pulled out at 6:20 p.m. for our 500-mile jaunt. The river was like glass and we slipped along at about 10 miles per hour. Forty miles downriver we stopped at the oil wells and boiled a kettle, then pushed on again. It is a lovely day, real summer, everything green and nice and warm.

July 6: We ran all night, taking turns sleeping and steering. It did not get dark. About 4 a.m. we shot through the centre of the Sans Sault Rapids in some very rough water. After cooking breakfast we pushed on through the Ramparts and into Fort Good Hope about 10 a.m.—175 miles in 16 hours, about 13 hours of running time.

We pulled out of Fort Good Hope at 2 p.m., in a rainstorm. I steered while Pat had a sleep. At 3 p.m. we stopped and ate on the riverbank in the hot sun, then once again down the big river, the engine running beautifully, the big canoe slipping through rough and smooth water alike. At 11 p.m. we again stopped to eat—it was lovely resting on the beach while we boiled our kettle. Then we pulled off again and ran straight through the night.

July 7: About 9 a.m. we sighted a white speck way ahead in the mirage, which speedily resolved itself into the *Distributor*. She stopped in midstream, and we came alongside and had our canoe hoisted in the boat falls. I stayed on board for a couple of hours and saw the various passengers; there was not much news. I decided to continue the journey, but Pat Coombs remained on board, so I had the 75 miles to Arctic Red River to do alone. All the passengers lined the deck to see me off.

I had a marvellous ride. I sat right in the bow, with a long rope to steer by, and fairly roared down the river. I got very sleepy and kept dropping off, but I came into Arctic Red at a good lick and had all the populace speculating as to who the new arrival was until I stepped ashore. I did the 75 miles in 6 hours flat.

After inspecting the posts at Arctic Red River and Aklavik, Dick Bonnycastle arrived at Herschel Island on July 20, 1931. He settled into the usual weary routine of taking stock and inspecting books while waiting to be picked up by the *Baychimo*, stuck in the ice north of Alaska. He was also preparing for a personal inspection by the fur trade commissioner, Ralph Parsons. The fur trade had not prospered at Herschel Island and the weather was, as usual, wet and miserable with snow squalls and howling winds.

For a few days in August, however, the eyes of the world were focused on

The Lindberghs in Aklavik with Ralph Parsons (right) and unidentified man (left)

this tiny corner of the Arctic wilderness as the famous aviator Charles Lindbergh and his wife Anne flew across the Barren Lands and landed to refuel at Aklavik before flying west across the Bering Sea to China. Bonnycastle recorded their progress.

August 8: We had a game of ball in the evening and in the middle of it Hersey ran out of the wireless station shouting, "The Lindberghs are coming!" and would be here in ten minutes. It was a nasty night, with fog and rain to the west, but they came in low and fast. I was sure they would land and I would have the pleasure of putting them up in the commissioner's bed. No such luck. They kept on going and gave us a wave as they passed over. The plane looked a beauty, open cockpit and beautifully streamlined.

I ran in to see Hersey, who was working Mrs. Lindbergh. He said, "What shall I tell her?" I wrote a note: "Thanks for the hand wave." She got it and replied, "Thanks, sorry we couldn't stop." Hersey continued to work her for two hours until she made contact with Point Barrow. Modern science is marvellous.

The Herschel Island post was as spic and span as it could possibly be when Commissioner Ralph Parsons arrived by native schooner on August 12, 1931. He immediately closeted himself with Bonnycastle, Fred Ware of the Herschel post, and Bill Murray of Aklavik, to thrash out the troubles of the Western Arctic. Bonnycastle's diary is silent until three days later.

August 15: Very busy. Wonderfully satisfactory conversations. Criticism unstinted but only where it is due. Very happy over the way things are going. I was bold enough to ask my fate. It is to be postponed for a week, which means I shall be okay.

August 17: Bill Murray is proving useless and making no effort. We sent a wire to Winnipeg asking if Bonshor could be made available to come to Aklavik by the last plane in September. I am satisfied this is the only course. Murray has let me down badly. Mr. Parsons is splendid, he has good ideas and is encouraging and energetic. We shall go ahead under his coaching. We had a meeting with the Eskimos today and Mr. Parsons and I both had a few words of exhortation to say to them.

August 18: We held a bargain day at Herschel today. Mr. Parsons and I routed through the Shingle Point stock and cleaned it out, threw out old junk and gave away others. The bargain counters were crowded all day with people making purchases for 50 cents and $1 and getting a present with each. It was a red letter day on the island and no mistake.

August 19: A pretty stiff session today. We all went through the mill for fair. Every word Mr. Parsons said is true. It cuts pretty deep but it can't do anything but good. Blowing a howling sou'wester from early morning until late at night. It has been like this for 48 hours now.

August 20: A howling blizzard blowing with snow all over the place and drifts a foot deep here and there. It is hard to see. The water is high and the dogs are marooned. We put somebody's bitch dog in the warehouse to have pups—there is one already. Moved a lot of dogs onto dry land, beat off one dog that had killed another, shovelled snow out of the store and warehouse. No one is moving around much. I never saw worse weather. Eskimos sticking to their schooners bobbing up and down in the harbour.

August 21: The blizzard continued unabated, with drifts as much as six feet deep. At noon Captain Cornwell reported the *Baychimo* at Point Barrow and expecting to reach Herschel Island in 75 hours, ice permitting. This is great news.

Mr. Parsons gave me mine today! He told me he had decided a change of management was necessary up here but he is going to give me another chance, though I don't deserve it, as I am young enough to mend my ways. I am terribly relieved to get off this way and shall certainly not let him down. As a result I was able to wire Mary that we could go ahead with our plans, which is wonderful.

August 25: No *Baychimo* all day; she got within 27 miles of here but was stopped by fog and ice. The news tonight is that she is expected to move as soon as the fog lifts a little and that the ice is going fast. We shall surely have her here before morning.

This is my birthday. I got a wire from Pater which I was darned glad to get. It sounded most cheerful.

August 26: We were awakened at 4 a.m. by shouts and yells and I stuck my head out the window to see the lights of the *Baychimo* bearing down on us. We all got up at once, except Mr. Parsons, and I went down to the beach. First Mate Coe came ashore to see that the beach was clear for mooring. Shortly afterwards they brought her alongside and tied up and I went aboard to welcome the captain and officers, and Jack Kimpton.

They commenced discharging right away. Mr. Parsons and I went on board and discussed things with the captain. We decided the ship could only go as far as Coppermine and made our plans accordingly. Had a very busy day attending to a thousand and one matters. One thing I noticed was a great deal of bootlegging going on; I told Mr. Parsons and he suggested I approach the captain and warn him it must stop at once or I would take it up. I did so.

After leaving Herschel Island August 28 to deliver the year's supplies to Baillie Island, Bernard Harbour, and Coppermine, the *Baychimo* ran into heavy ice and lost three days' precious travel time. Captain Cornwell wanted to return to Herschel Island, unload the supplies for the eastern posts, and return to Vancouver before the ship was caught in the winter ice. Commissioner Parsons persuaded him to give it one more try—"egged him on without taking any responsibility", as Bonnycastle saw it—and on the night of August 30 the *Baychimo* reached open water and steamed full speed for Baillie Island. The ship arrived at Coppermine September 6 and Ralph Parsons flew out to Winnipeg, leaving instructions that Bill Murray, Fred Ware, and Pat Wyant were to be relieved of their posts. Bonnycastle returned to Herschel Island on the *Baychimo* September 12 and the ship prepared to leave on its homeward journey around Alaska the following morning.

On board the "Baychimo": September 13: When I turned in last night I hoped to wake up many miles towards Point Barrow and our ultimate goal, Vancouver. I awoke fairly early to hear the wind howling around my cabin, but jumping up to look out the porthole I discovered to my great disappointment that we were still fast to the beach with a strong nor'wester blowing. There was nothing for it but to go back to bed and imagine that the ship will never get out and we will have to winter at Herschel Island, thoughts which certainly ruined the prospect of any more sleep. After an hour of backing and shouting and swearing and cutting cables with the propeller, the engine-room telegraph rang for full speed and at long last we were under way for the final leg of our voyage through Arctic waters. Point Barrow reports a calm there. Hopes run high.

September 14: Woke up at 4:30 a.m. to find us still on the move but working ice. I got up and spent half an hour on the bridge watching our progress. The staff, myself included, did a good hour's work before breakfast. The office was as warm as toast, but the rest of the ship was pretty chilly and the decks were covered with frost. Everyone was working full tilt all day although my interest in our progress is so great that I spent a good deal of time on the bridge seeing where we were going.

At 12:50 p.m. the captain anchored the ship to allow the brisk wind to open the ice a little before proceeding. The ice pans were heavy and miles long so there was little we could do but wait. It was galling to be sitting still so I went aloft to the crow's nest to survey the situation. When the captain tackled it again we got ahead much better. About 6:30 p.m. we rounded Cross Island, usually considered a bad place; we were much relieved and did not mind when we anchored an hour later with darkness coming on. Good reports from Point Barrow—no ice in sight.

September 15: Woke up to find us punching quite a bit of heavy ice and sculling around a great deal, but about 7 a.m. we got into clear going and the engines were rung up for full speed ahead. The captain told the chief engineer to give her all he had, as we had 24 hours' work to do in half that time. We should thump along. We hope to be up to Point Barrow by midnight.

No such luck. Here it is 9:40 p.m. and we have been anchored since 5:30, 85 miles east of Point Barrow. It is most exasperating. After lunch we had to work heavy loose ice, dodging around and over it, and finally the ice

forced us into three fathoms of water. After sculling around there, very slowly, the captain decided it was too risky and down went the hook for the night. A man with a little guts could have had us on the other side of Point Barrow today. I can see no reason why he couldn't have kept going— we are only drawing 14 feet aft and he is always talking about how he worked the ship in 2½ fathoms when he was coming in fully loaded.

It is a very dark, cold night—temperature 24° with snow flurries. Pans of ice are drifting past the ship and the officer on watch is pacing the bridge over my head. It is cold for the sailors in the chains these days. Mate Coe told me they have only been given six issues of rum this voyage, whereas the captain was given ten gallons. It's a damned outrage there isn't a drop for the men working late in the cold—especially when the stuff was put aboard for the purpose, only to be bootlegged by the old man.

Tomorrow we should reach Point Barrow and with any luck be well down the coast by night-time. I hope we are, I'm awfully anxious to wire Mary. I'm sure they want to go ahead with our marriage arrangements as soon as possible, so do I, but we can't buck the elements. But we are practically certain to get out now.

September 16: I joined the captain at the masthead and had a thoroughly enjoyable morning up there, although it was bitterly cold with a westerly breeze and occasional snow squalls. We had to work quite a bit of ice and I took some movie pictures from the crow's nest. Just before lunch I thought I had sighted the buildings of Point Barrow, in honour of which I executed a war-dance in the crow's nest, but I found what I had seen were not houses but merely hummocks on the land. The ice became heavier and finally, after working her into three fathoms, the captain was obliged to anchor. There was nothing else for it. We simply couldn't work the ice ahead and the few leads led north or nowhere. We are still 22 miles from Point Barrow. It is exasperating but in another way it is a relief—being so close to Barrow there will be sufficient good accommodation and provisions in case of accident.

I worry about my wedding. I know Mrs. Northwood will want to get the

Bonnycastle and Mary
Northwood at the time
of their engagement

invitations out but I am tied. I can't advise her to go ahead—we are not out
of the woods yet—but I don't want to postpone things because we run into
the Fur Trade conference. I am very much betwixt and between. I'll wire
how things stand tomorrow.

The ship is moored fore and aft to a small pan of grounded ice to safe-
guard us against being pushed up on the beach. This is no place for a ship
but there is nowhere else we can go—except back to Herschel Island.

The work is going along nicely and the staff put in a whole day. We must
make hay while the sun shines, before we get into rough seas in the Bering
Sea and the Pacific.

September 17: We are anchored in the same place as last night, not having
moved all day. No change except that a lot of new ice has formed in the
floes and around the ship. The rigging and topsides are coated in ice. The
captain and I viewed the pack from the masthead and decided we could do
nothing but wait. We all felt pretty blue this morning. While trying to put
on a brave face, I think everyone, including myself, considers the prospect
of spending the winter at Point Barrow not so pleasant.

One month from today is the date set for my wedding. I intended wiring
Mary today but held off in the hope I shall have good news tomorrow. This
uncertainty is terribly awkward. I pray tomorrow may bring better luck.

September 18: We got under way at 3:30 a.m., and at 4 I got up and joined the
captain at the masthead. The ice-fields of yesterday had completely evaporated. But we hit one little jackpot, a hefty, solid chunk of ice we couldn't
shake off for 40 minutes. We worked to port and starboard; it turned with
us. We went astern and it came too. We charged other ice and it wouldn't
budge. It was most exasperating.

The next incident came immediately afterwards. To get back on course we had to swing for an opening between two ice pans—and on account of the relative weakness of our stern we must be careful not to back into even a small piece of ice. We came astern for a few revolutions of the propeller, then rang for full speed ahead. Instead of "full ahead" the engineer put her "full astern". To our consternation we moved back pretty fast, but struck nothing. Again the mate stopped the engines and telegraphed "full ahead", and again they gave her "full astern". We rushed backwards past ice pans of all sizes on both sides, but wonderfully no damage was done. This time the mate spoke to the engine-room down the tube and called for "full ahead". Again we got "full astern"—we fairly flew out of the ice, the ship describing a wide arc and encountering the only free passage there was. It was a miracle we did not wreck the ship, strip our propeller, and carry away the rudder. There was no explanation from the engine-room when the mate frantically rushed down. They just blundered. The old *Baychimo* bears a charmed life.

We reached Point Barrow and rounded it, hauling up to the village about 10 miles to the south-west and anchoring inside a pan of heavy, grounded ice. Outside, the floe was moving steadily to the north-east. Down the coast, as far as the eye could see, there was nothing but solid ice right against the beach.

Point Barrow is justly the last place on the continent in my opinion. The ice comes right to the beach, winter and summer, it is exposed to gales and low temperatures year round, there is not a bit of shelter or scenery, just cold and damp and gravel. There is a government school with one teacher, a hospital with nurse and doctor, a wireless station, one main trading post—and natives. We were no sooner at anchor than we were boarded by a crowd of Alaskan Eskimos in whaleboats who came to see the ship and their fellow countrymen who had been working on her on her eastern voyage. They brought 800 pounds of frozen reindeer meat, ordered ahead by wireless.

I wired Mary tonight telling her that we are here and waiting for winds to clear the coast. As things are so indefinite they may think it desirable to change the date for the wedding. Any other date will suit me, but I must attend the Fur Trade conference November 10-12. It's too bad things are so topsy-turvy. I know everybody involved will be terribly put out.

September 19: We are still in the same place. The outside ice is packed in tight against the coast and there is positively no open water in sight other than the strip where we are anchored. The temperature was 13° this morning, which must be the coldest weather this ship has ever encountered. This is not at all pleasant.

Heavy snowfall last night makes the water around the ship very thick with slush. It has the look of syrup, and is trying hard to freeze. As a matter of fact there is a lot of young ice between us and the beach already. Saw thousands upon thousands of ducks tonight, flying south. The captain and third engineer were on deck with guns, and I had a couple of shots at a seal but missed. We cannot help speculating on what we shall do if frozen in.

I suppose everything will come out for the best, but I am so used to looking forward to things that it seems I can do so indefinitely without ever reaching my goal. If we get frozen in here, that will be the last straw. What a year!

September 20: Not so cold today, about 20° and overcast. Nothing but solid ice out to sea as far as the eye can see, not a drop of water except the lead we are in.

A wire from Mary tonight saying they have fixed the wedding date for October 31. It will mean a short honeymoon but we shall make the most of it. My spirits have risen. Now for the old ship to hurry and get out.

September 21: A phenomenon has occurred! A light north-east breeze came up this morning and freshened towards noon. At 1 p.m. there was no movement in the vast body of ice; by 4 there was a good, wide lead running parallel to the shore. The wind is blowing quite hard and we expect that by morning we shall have a clear run out. A start is to be made at daybreak. The very wind we have been asking for has come!

This afternoon we heard a great hullabalooing. Looking out the porthole I saw a whole line of whaleboats, one behind the other, passing the ship. The natives had a bowhead whale in tow, an enormous monster they had killed. Kimpton and Coe and I went to watch them cut up the carcass. They had towed it alongside the grounded ice and were cutting it up and hauling it onto the ice in pieces. It must have been 35 feet long. They were pulling one fin off with block and tackle, twenty or thirty men pulling while the others chopped and probed and dug to get the fin joint free. Blood spurted up from the cuttings—it was an awful mess, and the smell something to be avoided at all costs. The wind is liable to carry off the ice they have the beast on so they can't quit work until it has all been cut up and the meat taken ashore. It is a godsend for the people, food for men and dogs aplenty.

September 22: What a day! What a day! We hove anchor around 3:45 a.m. and tried to proceed inside the grounded ice which prevented us reaching the great sea of water. We pushed ahead in the teeth of the gale, with only 2½ fathoms of water under us, but finally the water shoaled up on us and we got no farther. The ship was turned about and we headed back to be imprisoned again, but on the way a piece of ice grounded under our stern and kept us for 2 hours before we got free, the wind rushing past laden with snow and sleet, the sea heavy with thick slush. I dozed in bed, restless and uneasy. From time to time I jumped up and looked out my porthole, only to return to my bunk and my nightmares.

I got up at 6:30 a.m and found we were nearly back to our old anchorage off the village. The captain finally decided to put the ship into the ice— heavy stuff cemented together with young ice and grounded here and there with great solid pans. The ship, light and high in the bow, was difficult to handle. We made little progress—the wind swung the ship, and with our weak stern we couldn't back up to much advantage. But we penetrated a few yards of the scant 200 separating us from clear sailing to Vancouver and home.

Then began one of the darndest performances I've ever seen, as we tried to break through the barrier of loose ice-pans cemented together with new slush ice and jammed tight by onshore currents and winds. Every little chunk we put behind us got in our way, because if we backed into these they might cut our propeller blades clear off. In this little predicament that required patience and commonsense the captain swore at his officers and men in a most unjust fashion, became panicky and pessimistic, and was altogether most objectionable and impossible. We would gladly have thrown him overboard as an obstacle to our salvation.

By noon we had made 25 yards at best, and that only because Scotty Gall and O.D. Morris went out on the ice and pushed small pans away from our stern.

By suppertime we had made over 100 yards. The captain, having lost his head completely, would try anything anybody suggested. He had men on the ice with ropes towing pans out of the way, he was porting and starboarding and doing everything but making a good run at it. I have never spent such a galling, depressing, maddening day in all my life. I went in to supper thoroughly depressed—darkness in 2 hours, fully half the barrier yet to be cleared, and the captain still fooling around with wire, ropes, gunpowder, etc., when a little bunting ahead would always give some results.

Then the chief engineer came forward to the bow where we were standing. We pointed out to him how bunting made progress, so he encouraged the captain to do this, and every time he went ahead we would shout out, "Ten feet," or "Six feet,": always gaining, just to keep him at it.

Finally he did manage to get a couple of fairly good runs, and made some headway, and in less time than it takes to tell we had made 50 yards and split the remaining ice ahead, making a crack which ran to open water. We took our men off the ice, backed up a bit, got fair way on the ship and, behold, we were through!!

Such a wonderful feeling of relief to everyone! We gave three blasts with our whistle, let off three detonators, swung the ship on her course, and rang for full speed ahead. I *think* we are safe for a clear run. We have thought that so often, and been disappointed, that we hesitate to think anything. I shook hands with the captain and congratulated him, whereas I had been reviling him inwardly all day. Other people shook hands with him and with each other and everyone is happy.

As I have been writing we have been running full speed in the snow and darkness. All of a sudden I heard the engine-room telegraph ring and felt the ship quiver fore and aft. We had charged into ice. It brought the ship up short but we backed out and have now resumed our course, although at reduced speed.

September 23: Approaching Cape Belcher after breakfast, we found that hard-packed floe ice was in tight against the beach. All we could do was return some 15 miles to a fairly safe anchorage off Franklin Point and await another favourable wind to open leads to the southward again. This last set-back is quite a jar to our hopes and I am depressed over it. It will be most extraordinarily awkward if I don't get back to Winnipeg by October 15.

We encountered miles and miles of young ice today—dead smooth, slushy stuff, very clogging—and it was all the ship could do to steam through it. If it thickens much more we may not be able to get to open water. Tonight the wind is southerly but it is only a breeze. What we want is a roaring sou'easter. I pray we get it soon. We have nine days' coal for steaming left, and lying around like this we use about half a day's steaming. Everyone is discussing ways and means of wintering, jokingly on the surface, but there is a distinct current of uneasiness.

September 24: I got up just as they were heaving the anchor and found that a fine southerly wind last night had dispersed the ice which was surrounding us, so we proceeded up an inshore lead—only to find the big ice still packed in tight on the beach about 6 miles this side of Cape Belcher. A big offshore lead looked very tempting—it would probably take us right out beyond all difficulties—but we couldn't get into it. The intervening ice is only a quarter or half a mile wide but it is solid and completely beyond our ice-breaking capabilities. We are as impotent to reach it as if it were 1000 miles away.

We finally dropped anchor for the night at 5 p.m. We are in a cul-de-sac which will probably not open again this year. Our coal is getting short—only eight days' steaming left. The position is getting very serious. To make matters worse there is a strong west wind—this will bring in more ice than ever.

A wire arrived from the commissioner asking our position. I wired him tonight. I also wired Mary. It will upset her and her whole family. I am beginning to feel rather desperate, but there is nothing I can do except pray that we may get safely and quickly through.

September 25: No movement today whatsoever. The big open lead seen yes-

PA-100651/PUBLIC ARCHIVES CANADA

"Our Captain, short, rotund, with a reddish face, clean-shaven and with little fluffs of scanty hair, a man from Kent, born to the sea, a bull-doggish type, aloof, not to be crossed if one can avoid it, a small man who has to stretch his arms to hold the binoculars over the canvas windscreen of the bridge, with fat hands almost childlike emerging from the gilt cuffs of his jacket; a man with an unimpressive flat tenor voice, sometimes petulant, peevish, sometimes unexpectedly good-humoured, but most often, to the fo'c'sle, hard and indifferent."

D.W. Gillingham

terday closed up this morning, not a drop of water to be seen. The young ice seems to be making fast also. It seems to me we haven't a ghost of a chance. The captain and I discussed ways and means of building houses ashore, heating them, and so on. There is a lot of lumber in the ship, what with hatches and the lining of the holds and so on, and there is also a good bit of canvas which would help make warm shacks. Yesterday and today we have seen dogteams passing up and down the beach, evidently natives hauling wood, and there appear to be some houses two or three miles up the beach. We both figure we have two weeks' grace before it will be necessary to abandon hope of release. The captain says we have 120 tons of coal; lying idle we burn three tons a day, so that would be roughly 50 tons used for a two-week wait. It would still leave plenty to steam out if the ice opened during that interval. I am quite optimistic, although I have my weak spells of doubt.

I must be putting on weight. We do eat a lot and take no exercise, and the food is really good. We have breakfast at eight, dinner at twelve, tea at three, supper at five, cocoa and sandwiches at nine. And the office work progresses satisfactorily. It is a glorious opportunity to get things cleaned up.

Everybody watches the barometer and the smoke from the funnel incessantly. The slightest sign of a favourable wind is hailed with delight. Yesterday three of us climbed over the bow and went on the ice. It is terrific stuff—you can almost get lost among hummocks 12 to 15 feet high. The ship looks puny in comparison.

September 26: I shouldn't get discouraged on the first day of our fourteen days' grace, but I must confess this waiting and uncertainty produces the worst feeling in the world.

Everyone was out walking on the ice this afternoon. It is not very safe and bends under our weight. Three walked up to the native village and reported the presence of three wrecks there. The ice is supposed to be packed right down to Wainwright, Alaska, just as it is here. Measures have gone into effect for saving coal: one boiler has been banked, and steam drawn off the winches; lights are to go out at 11 p.m. It is not a very cheerful prospect. The captain thinks we are here for the winter and is kicking himself for going east of Herschel Island. It is just a month today since the ship arrived there, but to all on board it seems like the longest month in our lives. I hope and pray we make a move soon.

September 27: The situation has not improved one particle, in fact it is worse. The grounded ice has moved 20 or 30 yards towards us. But everyone keeps very cheerful. While there are a few skeptics, everyone says, "Oh well, of course we are bound to get out eventually." None of us is so darned sure about it at all.

I must confess I haven't the slightest idea what we can do if we do get stuck, whether build houses ashore with what we can tear out of the ship, move down to Wainwright, walk back to Point Barrow, fly outside, or what. The ice inside the lagoon where we are anchored would make a splendid landing place for an aeroplane, I believe. But I don't know how soon they would be able to leave Nome or Fairbanks on skis. Got in a splendid day's work.

September 28: No change in ice conditions. Temperature 28°, nice and mild. This waiting is terribly trying. I get impatient at times; at other times I am fairly calm. We just don't know what to make of things right now. The ice is packed in so tightly that it seems we must have a very strong and lengthy wind to clear passage, and that may not come. We can only trust in the Lord. I *do* so want to be married on October 31.

A wire tonight from the commissioner asking, in the *unlikely* event of the ship having to winter, (1) If she can winter safely in her present position, (2) If we have sufficient provisions and clothing, (3) When it is probable a plane could land here, and (4) Any other useful information. As for (1), the ship cannot winter safely here as there is no suitable harbour. (2) We have enough clothing on board, duffel parkas and pants and mitts, and we believe there is enough food if supplemented by reindeer meat which is supposed to be available in large quantities. (3) We believe the salt-water ice in the lagoon will support a plane in a couple of weeks, but I am doubtful how it will be for landing on account of the friction; even a sled will not slide on it.

Mr. Parsons evidently considers sending in a plane at first opportunity, which means I would get home by November 15. In spite of all this we believe our east wind can't be far away. We cannot think we are going to be stuck here after all.

September 29: Shortly before noon we observed a party of four people approaching the ship. They turned out to be Jim Allen, the trader from Wainwright; his half-breed daughter, a graduate nurse from 'Frisco doing medical work up here; and two native Alaskans. Jim Allen is an old-timer up here, a big, burly fellow, and is supposed to know all about everything. Born in 'Frisco, he came north with the whalers thirty-six years ago. He has wintered all along the coast in whaling ships as far east as Baillie Island. He reports the ice very heavy all down the coast to Bering Straits. He thinks our chances of getting out are pretty slim, but says the ship is in as good a place as any around here and should come out all right next summer.

Allen really came to solicit our business if the ship has to winter. He is prepared to supply everything we are short of, including 12,000 pounds of reindeer meat at 10¢ per pound. They would also be able to provide quarters for about half our crew down there.

I elicited the information that there are two aeroplane companies operating out of Nome which would be willing to fly in any time. The steamer *Victoria* is due to leave Nome on October 25 for Seattle, so it seems to me we could easily fly our crowd down there by that date and get outside after all. Allen doesn't want the ship to get out, though, as we would be a gold mine for him if we had to winter. He even advised the captain that he should start getting provisions ashore now, but the captain said we needn't give up until November 15.

I sent a long wire to Winnipeg saying that a plane could land here about October 15 and mentioning the names of the companies in Nome, also the sailing date of the *Victoria*.

I have a sore leg. The mate was trying out some detonators and let one off while I was moving away. I felt a couple of pellets hit me, one in the leg and the other in the posterior. The first made a slight mark but it has stiffened up the muscle a bit. I let nurse Kate Allen look at it in case there is something which would set up a poison. She said she could find nothing, so I suppose I shall survive.

September 30: A lovely day, clear and sharp. This calm, clear weather is going to make a lot of ice. There is quite a bit of open water offshore; it leads nowhere, but all it needs is a good gale of wind.

Jim Allen and his party left this morning for Wainwright and we all walked ashore on the ice to see them off. Afterwards I walked along the beach for about a mile and found the skeleton of a wreck that had been a whaling ship. This would provide a little fuel for the winter, but not much. My leg, where I got blasted, troubled me a bit.

I wired Mary tonight telling her I could not reach Winnipeg before October 21 at the earliest. I am afraid this wire will cause some consternation. I can't say anything else. It is wretched.

The wireless news from England was quite interesting today. I was astonished to find the pound sterling down to $3.91. It referred to Arthur Henderson as leader of the Opposition in the House of Commons, Austen Chamberlain as First Lord of the Admiralty, and yet Ramsay MacDonald as Prime Minister. It also referred to the unprecedented nature of the National Economy Bill. Apparently the financial strength of England can't be as much greater than other countries as we thought. It is all very disturbing.

Everyone on board is quite resigned to wintering in, or almost everybody. We concede that the ship has a chance to get out but not a great one. All are cheerful. We keep the office going full blast, and this is a great comfort; our accounts are further advanced than ever before at this date.

October 1: Preparations against wintering in are going forward and the mate is at present engaged in making a *komatik* for hauling stuff ashore. We find there is quite a lot of lumber of various kinds on board ship.

A native came up from Wainwright with a load of brant and eider ducks from Jim Allen. There were 530 pounds in all. The captain paid 23¢ per pound.

News reports from England are most disquieting. The political situation is obscure but seems to be pretty critical: increased taxation, a coalition government or something, ministers conferring with the King, and so on. Then there have been big riots in Glasgow, banks closed in India—the world must be in a hell of a state! It is awful being cooped up here and ignorant of what is going on. Probably we are lucky enough but I should like to be near the people I love.

October 2: A fairly bright day with occasional snow flurries. The pool of water near our stern is now practically frozen over. It looks very wintry.

The following wire has just come in:

Would like to make bid for business to take your passengers off ship please send confirmation

Pacific International Airways

I am going to advise the aeroplane company to refer this to the Winnipeg office. This is most encouraging news.

I do hope we get a little action soon. It seems such miserably hard luck after looking forward to getting back for so long, and with so much reason, to be balked like this when Mary has got all her things, the wedding date has been set and postponed once already—oh, it is simply rotten.

October 3: A bright, cold morning, brilliant sunshine, sparkling snow. This would be an ideal day for flying—I hope we get more of them. It does *not* look as if the *Baychimo* will move from her present anchorage again this year. The captain gets more pessimistic each day. The question is: What will happen to the ship? I doubt very much if she will come through it. There will not be a pound of coal for manoeuvring next summer. This is going to be a costly matter for the Company.

There was a big football game this afternoon alongside the ship. I took some movies. The ice is now a foot thick and makes a good field.

October 4: Blowing a gale all night and most of the day. Bitterly cold. The mate issued winter clothing to the crew today—duffel parkas, wind pants, skin boots, and mitts. They certainly needed it, being what they call "parish rigged" with very little clothing, and their quarters beastly cold. The engineer made a "bogey", a stove made from a small drum, for the fireman's fo'castle. It must have been hell before.

There is quite a discussion going on about equipment for the proposed house ashore. The captain wants to buy a range and heater from Jim Allen;

I want him to move the galley range ashore and make extra heaters out of oil drums. But he may have to buy the range as the galley stove burns 200 pounds of coal a day, which is extravagant.

Got in a good day at the office.

October 5: The captain has decided to cable the London office advising them that October 10 is the last date we can entertain hopes of getting out. After that we shall have only 70 tons of coal, daily diminishing. If we go down the coast we risk being held up somewhere out of coal entirely, which would mean abandoning ship, a total loss, escaping ourselves with nothing more than the clothes on our backs.

The captain got a wire from London inquiring the insurance value of cargo, furs, etc. At 10 p.m. I got a most interesting wire from the Winnipeg office:

As we wish to make absolutely certain that annual accounts and certain passengers listed hereafter connect with boat from Nome, and as we presume you can make arrangements more expeditiously, we authorize you to make arrangements direct with transportation company for one trip of plane. Ascertain price of one or more trips to bring out any of the crew that master wishes sent out and latest date planes could leave Baychimo *to connect. Keep us fully advised of your arrangements.*

It was a great relief to get this as it means we are going to get out of this jackpot whether the ship gets out or not. The captain wants to send out ten men and I want all my men out. Two planes will take the crew and another my men.

October 6: The coldest morning so far—2° below zero at 7:30 a.m. It is a lovely sunny day but making lots of ice.

Discussions are going on as to how the house should be built. They are going to have quite a job building with only hatches, odd bits of lumber, and tarpaulins. At my suggestion they are thinking of making it 15 feet by 45—the hatches all being 15 feet long—with three rooms inside: a room for the sailors, galley in the centre, and a room for the officers at the other end. I believe they can make a good job of it although it may be a bit dark inside. The floor will have to be put in after from scraps of lumber and it will be hard to keep clean. Captain Cornwell is a terrible man, bull-headed, overbearing, and knows it all. He is going to be hard to get along with this winter. I want to help him all I can with his building, and have my own men help, but he will not listen to advice and insists on going his own way.

The district staff went ashore to pile driftwood. It is not all good, some having rotted, but quite a bit is okay. I tested the lagoon ice and found it to be six to eight inches thick, quite good for a plane to land on. It was a glorious morning to be out and perfectly lovely walking back to the ship across the smooth ice all covered with a mantle of sparkling snow.

Got a wire from Alaskan Airways quoting $1,500 per trip, four to six passengers, their proposal depending on good landing conditions on *wheels*, which amazes me—I never thought they would fly on anything but skis at this time of year. I am not going to make up my mind yet. I must wait for the captain to abandon hope first, as he says he will on October 10. I do hope Mr. Parsons is agreeable to flying out the rest of the men. They cannot very well stay here. Some of them who do will draw their pay. Though I can't figure out whether we really are obliged to pay them wages until they get out or can cease payment now.

October 7: I advised the men going out on furlough that there will be no wages paid after October 31. This got them going—they had expected they would be sitting around here drawing wages all winter if the Company did not give them transportation out. So now they think they will charter a plane between them to get them to Nome, if the Company will pay their fares south from Nome. I am wiring the commissioner tonight, and I imagine he will agree to it.

A wire from Alaskan Airways saying they reserve the right to withdraw their bid if no planes are available on October 12. It is a bit worrying and gives rise to the fear they may possibly back out altogether. I will not feel safe until I get to Nome.

I have wired Mary saying definitely I cannot make it for October 31. It is awful but I am powerless. My only fear now is that there may be a slip-up and the planes may not come. How I pray everything will come out right!

October 8: The captain and mate went ashore with our men after breakfast to get the uprights for the house set in place. The captain seemed to think our chances of getting out were as bright as they ever have been. The truth is that things are no different from what they are most days. The men on board were busy getting coal etc. up on deck.

Great excitement tonight! I was in the wireless room after tea—I had just got a wire from Mary saying everything was all right, the wedding could be on November 21 or 28, whichever I liked—when Sparks asked if I had noticed the ship shaking. I had not. Just then Jack Kimpton stuck his head in and said the young ice was cracking up. Sure enough, a large crack was opening right from the ship's side towards shore. Some sailors were playing ball out on the ice and hurried on board immediately. The wind had shifted to north-west and was now moving the pack in, the ice slowly heaving and breaking alongside. They went ahead on the main engines to relieve the strain on the rudder but we moved quite a few yards towards shore; it was a good thing the ice was no thicker around us. I got a few things ready for going ashore in a hurry, and told Kimpton to do likewise.

The captain figures the situation is very poor. He thinks the ship will never stand the winter if a little wind such as we had tonight can bring

such pressures. As I write the pressure has evidently eased and there is no movement, but another 100 yards will put us aground. We can do nothing about it, being packed tightly in new ice. Not very cheerful. They are keeping steam on all night in case of emergency, so we have lights. The captain says he will look the situation over tomorrow morning, and if there is no improvement he will give up at once and start building ashore.

October 9: I slept with my clothes on but the precaution was not necessary, and this morning the wind had calmed down a bit. All the smooth ice is broken up, rafted and shoved around, and we are pretty close to the beach. The captain says we shall be aground in another 100 feet but he can't move the ship at all as she is jammed in, fore and aft and athwartships. He started all hands hauling lumber ashore. The sled they built proved useless—it

would not slide on the wet salt ice—so everything had to be carried. They also found that the uprights they put up for the house yesterday are too close to the beach, and the ice pushed up to within feet of them, so now they have to be moved.

Got the following wire at 10 p.m. from Nome:

Can send 3 heated cabin planes carrying 11 passengers and 350 pounds baggage round trip 12 hours flying time. Runways should be 1600 feet clear paralleling wind for capacity loading. Rate for three planes $140 per hour. Advise start early account changeable weather. Can give fast service but must have decision soon also length runway available and date ready.

—Northern Air Transportation

This sounded wonderful at first glance, but on reading it again I thought it might mean $140 per hour for each plane, which would be more than Alaskan Airways. I dispatched a wire asking for confirmation that they would charge $1,680 for taking out 11 men and 350 pounds baggage. I will then decide which company to give the contract to and wire them at once.

All hope of our getting the ship out has been abandoned. The captain and I walked over to see the progress being made on the building. They are getting on quite well with the walls. The hatches are hard to get ashore, being so very heavy, but the house is shaping up better than I expected. I think it will be okay. Jim Allen came up from Wainwright tonight. He is going to lie over for a day or two and let them use the dogs to haul stuff ashore.

October 10: Good news! Northern Air Transport advised that my first interpretation was correct so I accepted their terms for two trips and ordered a quantity of supplies the captain wants.

In the daily press broadcast from England was an item about the *Baychimo*: "Trapped in the ice, within the Arctic Circle by 1000 miles, the London steamer *Baychimo* may have to spend the winter there. Arrangements have been made to take off the passengers and some of the crew by aeroplane." They have pretty quick information regarding the aeroplane transportation, since I only completed the arrangements this morning! I wonder if there will be anything in the Canadian papers?

Work on the house is proceeding but the captain is terribly interfering, intolerant and intolerable. Nowhere, except as master of the ship, could he get away with his vitriolic abuse and overbearing manner. He knows nothing about the house going up but instructs, criticizes, and butts in until no one knows where they are. First Mate Coe is bound he will go out. He complains bitterly about the cold he suffers in his feet, and says if the captain keeps him here he will be sorry for it. So we had a showdown with the captain and Coe is going out instead of the third mate. The captain sent a wire saying Coe was suffering from cold feet—it did sound funny.

We have everything packed and ready to go. There is much weighing of baggage since everyone's limit is 30 pounds. And our district office books and records are pretty heavy. I am hoping we shall not have to leave Fred Ware behind. There is not much hope of him getting out on the second trip, which will have a full load of crew members.

October 11: Rotten luck! Point Barrow wireless has broken down and Sparks can't raise him at all. I expected to hear from the aeroplane company advising when they would be here. Nothing came until 2:30 p.m., when I got a message saying they would not carry free freight up but would do so at 20¢ a pound—there was nothing to do but agree, as their rates are so cheap, so I wired acceptance but cut our order quite a bit. I expect to hear in the morning when they will arrive.

Everyone worked hard on the shore camp today. They have all four walls up from the hatches, three tiny windows let in, a door cut, and canvas over the biggest part of it, double canvas on both sides. It is quite a large place and will be a success. But it is hard work getting the materials ashore, and Jim Allen's dogs had to quit for sore feet after hauling a few loads so now they must haul the rest by hand, half a dozen men to a sled. The pulling is better today with the cold weather but still it drags.

Captain Cornwell is the limit. He was terribly abusive to Mate Coe, who says little. He knows he is going out and cares about little else, but he is bitter about the captain and you can't blame him. Cornwell thinks only of himself and no one else.

There is a chance we may have the planes here tomorrow. The sooner the better. I want to get to Nome and away from here where our rooms are ice cold and everything is topsy-turvy.

October 12: I went over to our landing strip after breakfast to clear the snow off the runway markers. The captain came along, quite a struggle for him in all the clothes he wears! I took an axe to cut a hole in the ice and a small can to carry water. The idea was to pour some water on each of the sacks marking the runway so that they would freeze down and not blow away. The captain dipped the water and poured it on each sack, fairly beside himself with rage because I had brought a can instead of a bucket. First he got his hands cold and dropped the can over his feet, then he got his mitts wet and dropped it again. I had a good laugh at his expense. He is a scream the way he flies off the handle.

There are about two inches of snow over the ice which is about a foot thick. It should make ideal conditions for landing on wheels.

Disappointment! Instead of the planes turning up this afternoon I got a wire inquiring our exact location for customs purposes, and also the depth of snow. I gave them the latitude and longitude, and the depth of snow as 1½ inches. Tonight is fine and clear. I hope tomorrow will see them arrive.

October 13: No luck again today. At 3:30 p.m. I got a wire from Northern Air Transport saying, "Rush answer our wire 10th regarding freight rate. Planes waiting." This was extraordinary because my answer went five minutes after I got their inquiry two days ago—the message had evidently gone astray. It is a pity. We are losing a lovely day for flying. I intend to find out who is to blame.

A wire from Ralph Parsons saying he wants his two bags sent out, so that means we shall not be able to take Ware on the first trip. The weather isn't so fine tonight, it is snowing, but it may be okay tomorrow again. I hope so.

They are getting on well with the house. Built on the porch today, also part of the captain's lean-to and wireless station. There is not quite so much bickering now, as everybody has been jumping the captain and helping him shut up a little. I remonstrated with him gently this morning to good effect.

I made a start on my annual report today, though it isn't easy to settle down to anything when I expect to hear the roar of the planes. I am restless to get out.

October 14: Sparks advised us about 10:30 a.m. that the planes were ready to take off from Nome on receipt of a favourable weather report from Barrow. We were quite excited and started looking for them after lunch. However we got a wire reading as follows: "Planes in Kotzebue tonight. Have passengers on field at 12:30 on 15th. Planes will return to Kotzebue at once. Advise Barrow of weather early." We are happy about everything. We shall get all our gear out on the ice in good time, with everyone standing by, so there will be no delays.

They have built a 15x15-foot addition to the house for the captain. I can see it is going to be pretty darned cold—it is built against the porch and can't be made weathertight. They do some foolish things and it is no use saying anything to them.

The weather has been a little heavy today and inclined to snow, but there are some northern lights tonight. It looks more hopeful for tomorrow.

October 15: It dawned quite a decent day and flying prospects looked fine so I gave Sparks a good report to send to Nome. But Nome reported snowing and blowing and the third plane tied up there, and we couldn't find out what was happening at Kotzebue. I spent the morning getting ready in case the planes should get through but not really expecting them. However, the captain ordered dinner at 11:30 a.m. to give us a chance to get on the ice with our bags by 12:30 p.m. We were sorting things on deck when Kimpton called up and said he saw a speck in the air away to the south-

(1)Second Mate Shorty Somers, (2)Captain Cornwell, (3)Purser Patmore, (4)Bonnycastle

west. I ran up on the bridge, and sure enough, it was a plane! It was marvellous to see it.

We were rushing around getting our baggage ready when somebody shouted he could see a second plane. Soon they were circling the ship while we were getting everything down on the ice. The machines landed at the place we had marked out for them. I got there as soon as they had landed and found two nice Stinson-Detroiter monoplanes. The pilots said they were anxious to get right back to Kotzebue while the weather held.

All the others from the ship arrived and helped unload. They carried several hundred pounds of supplies, as well as a supply of gasoline in tins which was immediately put in the tanks. One plane could only take five and the other three so it became apparent we would have to cut one passenger in favour of our district office books and records. I drew lots to see who would come besides myself, Kimpton, and Patmore; Ross, Henriksen, Gall, and Brabant were the lucky ones. It didn't take long to say goodbye. After stowing the baggage we climbed aboard, cranked up, and were off.

I had a very comfortable, upholstered seat in the big machine, beside the pilot, with splendid vision all around. Our wheels ran over the ice and we took off a few minutes after the others. The runway was perfect.

It was marvellous to be in the air again, a lovely, independent feeling. The ship below us looked so puny and small. We slid straight down the coast at about 90 miles per hour. We saw a small lead off the ship, then all tight to Wainwright. There were a few offshore leads off Wainwright but from there down to Icy Cape nothing much, and the ice was tight in at Blossom Shoals. I don't think the *Baychimo* had much of a chance to get out.

We followed the coast at about 2500 feet, the frozen ocean on one side and the snow-covered land on the other, everything white. From Lay Point we struck straight south, gradually getting further inland. I followed our course on the map all the way down. Not long after leaving the coast we struck a range of mountains. It was pretty darned risky—more than 100 miles without a landing place, peaks towering up 4000 feet with deep valleys and precipices below us, clouds and fog low down on the mountains obscuring visibility. But a narrow opening between the mountains showed up as we went along. The Wasp engine never failed. God knows what would have happened if it had!

We watched the other plane all the time. It was usually 1000 feet above us and way off to one side. Once we lost sight of it, and it gave me a nasty feeling for a minute until we wheeled and picked it up on our other flank, sailing along above us. We reached Kotzebue just before darkness with only 20 minutes of gasoline left, 3½ hours after leaving the *Baychimo*. We had covered 320 miles. I was thankful to reach the ground, as was the pilot and everybody else.

We were soon in a very comfortable restaurant-roadhouse place run by an Eskimo woman, eating a wonderful meal of fried ptarmigan, mashed potatoes, corn, fruit, cake, and coffee. I never imagined we would find ourselves so comfortable—a big house, clean as a whistle and warm and bright, excellent cooking, and two nice-looking girls, halfbreed daughters of the house, to wait on table. There is a player piano and a gramophone and fine clean beds. Quite a change from the *Baychimo*.

This is just an Eskimo village but there are about thirty white people here, missions, hospital, school, wireless, and a couple of roadhouses and well-stocked stores. I bought a few odds and ends to send back to the ship tomorrow as the planes figure on relaying everyone down here before moving us on to Nome. We are praying for fine weather.

October 16: A blizzardy day with no flying possible. We are very comfortable here, though, and there is no need to worry. I am managing to do a little work but there is a lot of noise going on all the time. I got a wire from Mr. Parsons asking how much extra it would cost to bring out the furs, so I wired him giving all the information. The boys went to a picture show put on for their benefit but I stayed home to do a little work on my reports.

October 17: Today was supposed to be Mary's and my wedding day. Instead I am miles away.

Snowing heavily; the boys spent the day playing the player piano and gramophone. There is much laughter and jollity; I think it is good for the two girls, who lead such a secluded life here—especially Esther who is a very hard worker. Tomorrow if the weather is fine one plane will start relaying us to Nome while the other two make two trips north to the *Baychimo*.

R. H. Bonnycastle (right), who was on the icebound Baychimo, Hudson's Bay company steamer, ended an eight-months' trip through the Arctic on arrival in Winnipeg this morning. He reached Nome, Alaska, by airplane, with J. Kimpton, who returned with him, and twenty-two others, and escaped confinement in the Arctic until next July. He is seen when greeted by his brother, C. H. Bonnycastle, at the Canadian Pacific station.

Long Dreaded Menace of Arctic Is Discounted by Returning Winnipeggers

The Arctic, locale of reams of adventure fiction, was stripped of a deal of its glamor today by R. H. Bonnycastle and J. Kimpton, just returned to Winnipeg after a long and arduous journey through its icefields.

They barely escaped a winter's imprisonment in ice and snow, and that was an insignificant incident to them. They were only concerned with the long time of their journey out of the north into a warmer and more inhabited land, and were very thankful it had ended this morning.

Once again in Winnipeg, they discredited the common belief that the Arctic is a place of privation, hardships and hazards, but they know the strange beauty of endless miles of ice and snow, where water glistens in the vast whiteness occasionally, where there is neither habitation nor vegetation.

The Arctic has changed. The wonders of this age have removed the perils. An airplane can always take one out, which was their experience; radio makes communication with the rest of the world always possible.

Tall and fair, young Mr. Bonnycastle, who is manager for the west Arctic region for the Hudson's Bay company, left Winnipeg eight months ago. He went directly north, by plane, paddle steamer, and dog team until he reached Herschel island.

Mr. Kimpton, stocky and dark haired, went to Vancouver four months ago, embarked on the Hudson's Bay company steamer Baychimo, sailed the north Pacific to the northernmost point of Alaska, where the ship turned and steamed through the ice lanes of the Arctic ocean to Herschel island.

Mr. Bonnycastle joined the Baychimo on its return voyage. It was late reaching Herschel island, being delayed by ice. Off Point Barrow, Alaska, a solid icefield entrapped the steamer, and northeast winds, which would have awaited until Sept. 23, when planes were requested by radio messages to Nome.

Two Northern Airplane Transport planes carried out twenty-four men in a series of flights, leaving behind the captain of the Baychimo and the crew of seventeen men.

Mr. Bonnycastle and Mr. Kimpton travelled down the coast from Nome to Seattle, and came on to Winnipeg by train.

The captain and the men remaining with the ship have an usual Arctic winter ahead of them, Mr. Bonnycastle said. They were prepared for it, a building having been constructed of tarpaulin and lumber carried on the ship. Airplanes carried in ample provisions. When the snow had covered their dwelling they will have no real hardships to bear, he said.

WINNIPEG MAN TELLS OF ARCTIC SHIP'S PLIGHT

R. H. C. Bonnycastle and Party From Baychimo Reach Vancouver

[By Canadian Press]

VANCOUVER, Nov. 3.—The hazards of the Arctic are minimized with the advent of modern inventions, according to the story related by R. H. C. Bonnycastle, Winnipeg, manager of the West Arctic district for the Hudson's Bay Co.

Mr. Bonnycastle, together with J. O. Kimpton, also of Winnipeg, and 17 members of the S.S. Baychimo, which they left icebound, southwest of Point Barrow, Alaska, in command of Capt. S. A. Cornwall and 16 of a crew, who will stand by until ice breaks in the spring, arrived in Vancouver last night from Seattle, where they disembarked from the S.S. Victoria, Monday.

Mr. Bonnycastle and Mr. Kimpton will arrive in Winnipeg Thursday morning.

Nothing Spectacular

Fresh from months of life in the northland, Mr. Bonnycastle refused to acknowledge there was anything spectacular or particularly adventurous about their experience.

He told how the Baychimo had left on her annual visit to the company's Arctic trading posts, and owing to the lateness of arrival at Hershel Island, plus unfavorable winds and early freeze-up, the vessel became icebound.

Mr. Bonnycastle paid tribute to the efficient way two planes made three return trips from Nome to the Baychimo, a distance of 600 miles, and safely landed 19 of their party, all but three of whom made connection with the S.S. Victoria, last boat south this season.

The second to last plane arrived just three hours before the ship sailed. The last plane missed the connection, but the three passengers will be brought out by a U.S. cutter.

Live In Shack

Capt. Cornwall and members of the crew who are left with the Baychimo have built a substantial shack from material from the vessel, and with additional provisions taken to them from Nome by plane, will weather the winter without difficulty.

Late getting into the Arctic, the vessel steamed far east into the northern ocean. Then, turning west, the Baychimo tried to beat the forming ice pack into the Bering sea, but too late.

A few hours after it was certain the vessel was frozen in for the winter, radio revealed her plight.

TWO MEN RESCUED FROM ARCTIC NOW ARE ON WAY HOME

Bonnycastle and Kimpton Were Taken From Ice-Bound Baychimo

(Canadian Press Despatch.)

Vancouver, B.C., Nov. 3.—The hazards of the Arctic are minimized with the advent of modern inventions, according to the story related by R. H. C. Bonnycastle, of Winnipeg, manager of the west Arctic district for the Hudson's Bay company.

Mr. Bonnycastle, together with J. O. Kimpton, also of Winnipeg, and 17 members of the steamship Baychimo, which they left icebound, southwest of Point Barrow, Alaska, in command of Captain S. A. Cornwall, and 16 of a crew, who will stand by until ice breaks in the spring, arrived in Vancouver Monday from Seattle, where they disembarked from the steamship Victoria this morning.

Mr. Bonnycastle and Mr. Kimpton left for Winnipeg Monday night.

Fresh from months of healthy outdoor life and obviously elated over the prospects of arriving home in a few days, Mr. Bonnycastle refused to acknowledge that there was anything spectacular or particularly adventurous about their experiences. In a quiet and reserved manner he related how the ship Baychimo had left on her annual visit to the company's Arctic trading posts, and owing to lateness of arrival at Herschel island, plus unfavorable winds and early freeze-up, the vessel became ice-bound.

Mr. Bonnycastle paid tribute to the Northern Airplane transport of Nome, Alaska, for the efficient way in which two of their planes made three return trips each from Nome to the Baychimo, a distance of 600 miles, and safely landed 19 of their party, all but three of whom made connection with the steamship Victoria, last boat south this season. The second to last plane arrived just three hours before the ship sailed. The last plane, with three of the crew, missed connection with the Victoria, but they will be brought out on the United States cutter Northland.

Captain Cornwall and members of the crew who are left with the Baychimo, Mr. Bonnycastle said, built a substantial shack from material from the vessel, and with the additional provisions brought to them from Nome by the planes, will weather the winter without difficulty.

Men Aboard Ice-Locked Ship Face Long Winter in Arctic

Nome, Alaska, Oct. 21.—(AP)—Seventeen men, the captain and the crew of the ice-locked ship Baychimo, face a long and hazardous winter far north of the arctic circle while the Baychimo's passengers, "rescued" by airplanes, are far away to the south.

In a hastily built winter house on the beach the men will spend the eight or nine months until the sun again melts the ice in the far north. No village lies within 30 miles.

The plight of the little band, commanded by Capt. S. A. Cornwall of London was described today by passengers brought out by airplane. The passengers will sail for the south soon on the last ship of the season to leave here.

"We are surely glad to arrive at Nome," H. G. Bonnycastle of Winnipeg said, on stepping from a plane a week after having left the Baychimo." These fliers did great work, over hazardous flying country and in arctic conditions."

He referred to pilots Vic Ross and Hans Mirow of the Northern Air Transport company, who began the rescue work soon after all hope was given up of freeing the Baychimo. It was caught in the ice shortly after leaving Point Barrow; several weeks ago.

Bonnycastle said the Baychimo, a Hudson Bay company trading ship, rests about a quarter mile from shore. She has a chance to winter through, members of the crew believe, if the shore ice does not move or she is not crushed by incoming floes.

In addition to Bonnycastle, six other Canadian passengers arrived here yesterday. Their flight south from the Baychimo was broken for several days at Kotzebue by severe weather.

Eight more men, several of them members of the crew, were at Kotzebue today and seven more hope to be flown from the ship.

SAVED BY AIRPLANE IN NORTH

R. H. Bonnycastle and J. Kempton Brought Out From Ice-Bound Baychimo

EXPECTED SOON

Stranded in the midst of a wilderness of Arctic ice and snow for the past three weeks, passengers on board the Hudson's Bay boat, Baychimo, are expecting to reach civilization again within the next few days. Three airplanes are passing back and forth between the ice-bound boat and Koetchi, a point inland, 250 miles distant, and midway between the boat and Nome, Alaska.

Among the nine passengers on board were two Winnipeggers, R. H. Bonnycastle and J. Kempton. Interest is especially keen in the return of Mr. Bonnycastle for he is a bridegroom-to-be for whom the wedding has now been postponed several times because all the efforts that the most gallant bridegroom might put forth is of no avail to the grim determination of the north to hold in its grip the boat on which he now safely landed by Alaskan post.

FARTHEST NORTH FLIGHT SUCCESSF

Edmonton, Sept. 19.—Flying Coppermine, on Coronation gul Walker bay, on the northwest ner of Victoria island, and retu between breakfast and supper W. A. Spence, well-known no pilot, successfully complete farthest-north commercial fl the history of aviation, according to word received

The brilliant flight took over 150 miles further no the epic flight of Pilot W bert with Major L. T. Bu 1930. It covered 600 mi bleakest Arctic wastes.

It was made with Insp nycastle, of the Hudsons pany, who wished to visit Bay outpost and bring in out any preliminary accepting the job as m of routine work, Spen Fairchilds machine w hopped off at dawn.

Crossing Coronation lay across Dolphin an Wollaston peninsular island, over Prince Al Minto inlet into W miles north of Copp

LOCKED IN ICE

Above is a picture of the Hudson's Bay company boat Baychimo, which has been locked in the ice of the Arctic regions,

October 18: A howling gale blowing all day, but we hope for a break tomorrow. Time is getting short.

A crowd of us went to church today, Quaker or Friends' Church they call it. It was rather queer. The preacher, a bright young American, was dressed in breeches, a sweater, and a bow tie. The congregation was mostly Eskimos and the sermon was interpreted as it went along. They stood up to pray and sat down to sing, and the music was provided by an organ and a fiddle. We had some hymn singing in the evening with the player piano.

October 19: The weather is beautiful and the airport was busy this morning. Pilot Victor Ross got back from the *Baychimo* at 4 p.m. with Skinner, Ware, Wood, the second engineer, and four sailors. One of the passengers nearly burned up Ross's plane by trying to light his gasoline stove, thinking this was the way the machine was to be heated. Flying *is* a dangerous business!

We sent our parkas north for the men to wear coming back. If they had been forced down some would have perished, I am sure, because they are awfully poorly clad.

Nome, Alaska; October 20: By 8:30 a.m. we were in the air. It was a lovely morning, and we were in Nome in two hours after a beautiful flight across the mountains and gold diggings of the Seward Peninsula. By 4 p.m. the planes had brought the balance of the men in and everyone was in residence at the Golden Gate Hotel, once no doubt a mecca for millionaires but now dilapidated, old-fashioned and poor.

Nome is a dilapidated place altogether and the many empty, falling-down buildings give it a queer effect. It is on an open coast with no shelter whatsoever. The *Victoria* is lying a couple of miles offshore discharging her cargo with lighters. There is no second-class accommodation, only steerage at $50 and first class at $115. For an extra $10 steerage passengers can eat with the others, so our men will take that. Patmore, Kimpton, and I will pay $115 each. I wired Winnipeg to find out if the government will pay the fares of the sailors, being Distressed British Seamen, and what class Mate Coe and the second engineer should travel.

When I went to the hotel I was immediately interviewed by the son of the proprietor of the local newspaper, the *Nome Nugget,* on behalf of the Associated Press. I hope I am not reported as saying anything the office can object to. I have bunked the crew two to a bed and given them $4 each sustenance money, to last until Thursday afternoon when we go on board the *Victoria.*

October 21: I had a fine sleep in my corner room, which in its heyday was no doubt occupied by some mining millionaire. Now the wallpaper is hanging from the walls, the doors are awry, and the carpets are faded.

I paid Polet, the merchant, for the goods he sent up to the *Baychimo* by the planes. Some of his prices seemed high, dried fruits at 30¢ and turkeys at 70¢, but he explained that the fruits were fancy quality so I had to pay him. I then called on Harry Lowen in the drugstore. The Lowen brothers are the big people around here—they own huge reindeer herds, a transportation business, several boats running from Seattle, and the drugstore. Harry Lowen is also in the photography business. He does some beautiful photography and tinting. Foolishly, I am afraid, I succumbed to the desire to buy a picture of Eskimos out sealing for $20. It is a nice picture with lovely colours in it, and very typical of the ice in spring.

There is bootlegging of all kinds going on here. The men tell me you can get good beer and hard liquor all over town, and there is an old saloon right on the main drag openly selling beer and moonshine. There are a lot of miners in town waiting for the *Victoria* but there is little sign of drunkenness.

I had a wire from the Winnipeg office approving my two weeks' leave to commence on November 21, and wired Mary the glad news that the wedding could be on that day. I can't realize we are really getting out at last. We seem to have been so long on the way.

October 22: The sailing of the *Victoria* has been postponed until tomorrow, as there are ten passengers to fly in from Deering as well as our men from the *Baychimo*. First word from the *Baychimo* this morning was that no planes had turned up and that visibility was poor. But at noon we heard that the planes had arrived about two hours apart; they must have become separated and spent the night on the ice in different places. If they can't get down tomorrow they'll miss the boat.

Went into the bank today and saw some gold bricks worth about $400,000. There has been just over $1 million in gold shipped out of here this year. In the boom years as much as $15 million was shipped. We had to give a bond for $2000 to the customs today to guarantee delivery of the *Baychimo*'s cargo to a Canadian port. The immigration officer took down a lot of particulars regarding everyone and then released us to go aboard. I got the tickets from the steamship company but they are to bill the British consul in Nome for the crew's fares as Distressed British Seamen.

I have purchased quite a few ivory curios to take out. It is awful how the money goes in a place like this. I mustn't spend any more, as I shall need every cent I can lay my hands on.

October 23: The first lighter left for the ship at 9 a.m., and I got all our people on it. Then began a day of much anxiety wondering if the planes would make it from the *Baychimo*. Shortly before noon we heard they had left the ship. At 2 p.m. we heard they had just left Kotzebue. At 4 p.m. I went to the aerodrome, and just before dark Vic Ross came in with Mate Coe and three sailors. By this time it was dark but two planes were reported 60 miles away, heading in. At the telegraph office I was informed the planes were in, but then I found that one had not got in and we were three men short. This could not be helped. I paid Northern Air Transport $3,643 in full, and at 9 p.m. we went on board the steamer.

The sailors got drunk, and I found one in the saloon selling the parkas we had sent north for their plane trip. One man was going away with a parka he had paid $7 for and I had to return his money to get it back. Of all the crooked dirty tricks that was the worst.

Great confusion on the ship. The steerage accommodation is very poor. Our men have insufficient blankets and are complaining. All my district men wanted to pay the difference in fare and get cabins, so I got them moved up at once with the help of the purser and second steward. I have quite a comfortable little room, small, but situated where I shall not feel the motion of the ship too much.

We sailed before midnight.

Happy Endings

5

On the eve of Bonnycastle's wedding—November 27, 1931—in the midst of a howling Arctic storm, the ice-bound *Baychimo* suddenly and mysteriously disappeared. Captain Cornwell and the four crew members wintering in the makeshift hut on shore radioed the news to the outside world, and the Winnipeg press carried this account on December 1, 1931:

> On the night of the 26th, after the five had settled down to wait through the long Arctic winter, a severe storm swept the coast. The next morning the weather moderated slightly and on looking out towards the ice pack, a huge pile of crushed and broken ice lay where the ship had been. The mound was estimated to be 80 feet high and increasing in size. During the afternoon the gale increased and the storm became more severe with the wind blowing 45 miles an hour. The gale raised the water along the shore several inches and the storm continued through the next night and day.
>
> At noon Monday the weather moderated and the men on shore went out to where the ship had been. A mound or pressure ridge was found in the ice at the spot but no trace was found of the vessel. The search was extended, with men going 10 miles out on the ice pack and north and south along the shore but no signs of the ship were seen. Whether the ship had been carried far out by the shifting ice, or ground to pieces and sunk, was not decided. Aboard the *Baychimo* was a valuable cargo of furs valued at many thousands of dollars.

For the Hudson's Bay Company, the loss of the *Baychimo* and her cargo was a fitting end to a disastrous year which had seen the collapse of the fur market and the forced resignation of the governor, C.V. Sale, in a conflict of interest scandal. For Dick Bonnycastle, the outlook seemed no brighter. When he sat down two weeks after his wedding to tally the accounts for his annual report, his worst fears were more than realized. Misled by his own optimism and aggressive business methods, he had embarked on an ambitious program of competition and expansion, but now the Depression had killed any hope that his investment would be repaid. In 1930 his loss in the Western Arctic had been $80,914.38; in 1931 this ballooned to a loss of $207,672.60.

Bonnycastle bravely took the blame on his own shoulders and offered no excuses.

"This disastrous outcome is the result during the past year of poor organization and great lack of foresight in not realizing in time the extent and meaning of changing business conditions. Thus the market declines and decreased hunts found us entirely unprepared, heavily stocked with expensive goods, and with large advances out, far larger than would be justified in any circumstances, so that loss has been added to loss to reach this high figure.

"It is no use attempting to evade our responsibilities. Circumstances beyond our control have contributed greatly to the results, but only the most exceptional collections realizing the highest prices would have excused, without justifying, the basis on which we operated last year. Too late for Outfit 261, steps have been taken to correct matters and put our trade on a profitable basis. All expenses have been carefully budgeted and limits set so as to leave a margin in favour of anticipated profits from sales. Merchandise purchases have been greatly reduced for Outfit 262, while requisitions for Outfit 263 are being confined to staples and necessities. All measures possible are being put into force for promoting sales and reducing existing overstocks. Credit advances have been restricted to amounts considered quite safe for collection, and then only given where deemed really desirable.

"The gravity of our situation has been driven home to the post managers and great pains taken to see that they are in no doubt as to what is expected of them. A clear-cut objective has been laid down for each post and the necessity clearly shown for achieving it. We all have our backs to the wall realizing that times have changed and that we must achieve results or make way for others, and we do not intend to do the latter."

Although he had fallen into exactly the same pit as his predecessors H.H. Hall and Gaston Herodier, Bonnycastle was kept on, the Company realizing perhaps that a district manager who had so contritely learned his lesson was a better risk than another greenhorn. Commissioner French's intuition had been right: Bonnycastle had been too confident, too lenient, and his post managers had let him down. Dick did not blame them, only his own "grievous error in judgement" in hiring them. It was, however, the end of the road for Bill Murray, who had bungled Aklavik, and for Pat Wyant, who, in a spectacular spree, had run up nearly $80,000 in bad debts at Baillie Island and blown over $12,000 in personal expenses. Bonnycastle's report contains an interesting footnote about Jack Parsons, former manager at Aklavik:

"A man who may be a source of trouble is J. Parsons, ex-post manager of ours, who has just set up in trade on his own account at Aklavik having bought an outfit from Captain Pedersen at Herschel Island. This man is quite a clever trader and built up a considerable trade for us while at Aklavik. However it was a very expensive trade and if he does not conduct his own business any better than he did ours he will not last long. Everything points to Mr. Parsons having a silent partner in Dr. Urquhart, the department [of the Interior]'s medical health officer there. The latter is beginning to interest himself quite openly in

Mr. Parson's business, even going so far as to transport his goods with the department's motor launch and actually influencing natives to trade with Parsons instead of the Company. It is very difficult to obtain definite proof of Dr. Urquhart's activities, which are not compatible with his official position, but if anything can be done to have him removed from his present office it would be greatly to our advantage to do so."

Although Bonnycastle's promised profits did not materialize, he justified the Company's faith by reducing the Western Arctic debt to $48,847 in 1932. When Captain Charlie Klengenberg died in 1931, his sons and daughters became subcontractors to the Hudson's Bay Company, removing one major rival, and Northern Traders went bankrupt in the same year, failing to pay the Company a cent on its $200,000 loan. But Bonnycastle's hopes of putting Captain Pedersen out of business remained unfulfilled until 1936, when the *Patterson* made its last trip to Herschel Island. It was the last summer too for another old friend:

August 11th, 1933, after she had been adrift for two years, [the Baychimo*] was again sighted, this time by three vessels—first by the schooner* Patterson. *The reports were conflicting and I was not at all clear about it until I read an account in* North to the Rime-ringed Sun *by Isobel Wylie Hutchinson. This daring Scot (who justified her adventurous wanderings by collecting plants and handicrafts) was on her way to Barrow and (she hoped) to Herschel Island as a passenger in the ten-ton schooner* Trader.... *When* Trader *reached Wainwright, a report was brought aboard that the* Baychimo *was then just twelve miles off-shore—returned again almost exactly to the position where she had been abandoned in 1931.*

Captain Palsson managed to force a passage through the twelve miles of pack ice and get alongside the derelict. This is how Miss Hutchinson describes it:

"At last, when success seemed about to desert us, Kari spied a lead turning towards the very cake upon which Baychimo *was poised, her giant hull, rust-stained and battered by the frozen seas, looming tower-like above the little* Trader.

"She was riding upon a pan of ice which looked already almost upon the verge of breaking up, though it might be that the winter freeze-up would set the stranded ship upon yet another year's wandering.

"It was no easy matter boarding the Baychimo, *when at last* Trader *triumphantly drove her anchor into the cake which she rode. But at last, up a broken wooden ladder and a precarious rope suspended from her tall hull, I was hauled on board by willing hands. (Eskimos had gone out in the umiaks.)*

"A strange spectacle the decks presented, calling up pictures of Robert Louis Stevenson, Captain Hook, and Long John Silver. The main hold was open to the winds, but its half-rifted depths still contained sacks of mineral ore, caribou skins, and a cargo of various descriptions. As if to lend colour to the piratical appearance of the ship, a pair of handcuffs lay upon the hatch. On a sack of sinew thread stood a rusted but unused typewriter. Parkas from the eastern Arctic were here, for a sack of curios had been in the hold, though I was too

late to retrieve any of its treasures for Cambridge save a couple of stone stoves and an attiga purchased next day from its native possessor.

"Writing paper, photographic films, ledgers of the Hudson's Bay Company, typewriter ribbons—all were here for the taking! In a wooden crate was an unsullied edition of the **Times History of the Great War** in many tomes. Charts of all seas of the world lay scattered upon the decks of the pilot-house. In the dining room natives were already busy wrenching the wire mattresses from the sofas and unfixing the pivot chairs from the floor. (They had filled their umiaks with cartons of Sunlight Soap, tins of Brasso, pickles and heaven knows what else.) A breakfast menu tossed in the doorway indicated that the crew of the unlucky ship were at least in no danger of starvation, for there was a choice of some six courses.

"Alas! **Trader** was far too small a vessel to undertake the salvage of the **Baychimo**. Neither was it possible, without a vessel of much greater power, to blast the derelict from her icy bed or attempt to tow her ashore.

"'If only we had more power I could get her engines going again in a short time' (said Kari, the engineer of the **Trader**) '—they are not damaged in the least. A new propeller is all she needs, and she has one on board. If only we had more power we could tow her to Teller or Seattle or Vancouver.'"

But the **Baychimo** remained, undamaged, unsinkable, defiant of the most destructive power in the world, the polar pack, to haunt the seas. On her way to Point Barrow the **Trader** again sighted her. I quote Miss Hutchinson:

"Next morning the wind blew strongly from the south-west, and looking southward, what should we see but the **Baychimo** travelling almost hurriedly northward on her pan of ice, well outside of the shoals (the Sea-horse Shoals), 'just as if a Master-Hand were directing her,' as Pete said.

"The scene next morning was glorious, the sun glittered upon the still water and the sparkling ice.... Far out over the ice-field, a little ahead of us now, rode the uncanny **Baychimo**, travelling with the current towards Barrow. Everything was still with the unearthly stillness of ice, which gives one the sensation of being in another world.

"Sometimes through the glasses we could see reflected the mirage of the ice-field and shore far to the northward, hanging upside down in the sky. Our last glimpse of the **Baychimo** was in this curious manner, standing on her head in a mirage. She...was travelling with the current steadily north, and a day later was no longer visible."

But that was not the last seen of her. She was sighted off and on for **five years**. She seems to have done her best to put herself where men could reach her as the tides took her over the same course. She appeared seven times, the last in 1936.

Of that occasion an extraordinary story is reported to have been told by Captain Parker, commander of the cutter **Northland**. He came upon her near the edge of the pack, sitting there to all appearances still waiting for her men to release her, a little more weather-worn and forlorn, but the same **Baychimo** with tall yellow funnel aft and white crow's nest and bridge—just as though ready to sail, if a hand could but ring the signals on her telegraph and another set that giant pulse beating. The Captain thought he might be able to get alongside, but before he could reach her a bank of fog drifted over and hid her. He waited for the fog to clear. When at last it rolled away there was no **Baychimo**.

Some men are convinced that in those few minutes she had gone down, her death-plunge *veiled from their sight just as though the shock of being found again was too much for her. They swear that it was no ghost they had seen! But I am not so sure. There may have been a mirage again, of the kind I had seen at Fort Hearne. The old whalers saw mirages—saw vessels below the horizon thirty miles away lifted in full upright image to their gaze. She could have been many miles away too, and thus lifted like a phantom. But of course I do not know the conditions prevailing, whereas Captain Parker knew all about mirages. It remains a mystery, and rightly so. She was never seen again.* —D.W. Gillingham, Umiak!

Bonnycastle made his last visit to the Arctic as a company man the following summer. In his new job as secretary to the Canadian Committee, he was the Hudson's Bay Company's official representative on a viceregal excursion down the Mackenzie River by the Governor-General, Lord Tweedsmuir. The trip was brilliantly documented by photographer Margaret Bourke-White in a cover story for *Life* magazine but Bonnycastle's own view—published in *The Canadian Alpine Journal*—was, as usual, personal and unique.

Lord Tweedsmuir, Canada's Governor-General from 1935 to 1940 and (as John Buchan) author of many novels, including *Sick Heart River* and *The Thirty-Nine Steps*

LORD TWEEDSMUIR'S TRIP DOWN THE MACKENZIE RIVER AND ASCENT OF BEAR MOUNTAIN
R. H. G. BONNYCASTLE

In July, 1937, I was assigned by my employers, the Hudson's Bay Company, to accompany Lord Tweedsmuir, then Governor-General of Canada, on the trip he proposed to make down the Mackenzie river to the Arctic on board the Company's steamers.

As I had made many previous journeys both up and down the Mackenzie, I did not at first appreciate my good fortune, and felt some uneasiness about the formality and ceremony which I imagined might be demanded by the occasion. My fears were soon set at rest, because it took only a few minutes after the arrival of the special train at Waterways, Alberta, where the river voyage was to begin, to discover that the Governor-General was a most natural, friendly and charming person, and the members of his party were also fine travelling companions.

I shall always value most highly, as one of the great privileges of my life, the few weeks' association with Lord Tweedsmuir on that trip.

At Waterways we boarded the S.S. Northland Echo, which carried us three hundred miles down the Athabasca and Slave rivers, past historic Fort Chipewyan, to Fort Fitzgerald. From here we traveled the sixteen-mile portage by automobile, past the rapids, across the boundary line between Alberta and the Northwest Territories, to Fort Smith. There we boarded the S.S. Distributor for the 1,300-mile journey down the Mackenzie. The weather was glorious, such as only fine and far northern summers, with their long hours of daylight, can be, and the Governor-General, lover of the world of nature and of new surroundings, revelled in everything he saw and did.

Our sternwheel steamer stopped a few hours at Fort Resolution, Hay river, Forts Providence, Simpson and Wrigley, and reached Fort Norman, at 7.00 a.m. on July 28. Here we were delayed for a day while the fires in the steamer's boilers were put out and the engineers washed the river mud out of the boilers.

Fort Norman is a more or less typical fur trade post, located on the right bank of the Mackenzie, just above the junction of the Bear river which drains from Great Bear lake. It boasts the trading posts of the Hudson's Bay Company and other traders, a Royal Canadian Mounted Police detachment, two missions, a government radio station, and several log cabins of trappers or Indians.

Looking south from the post across the mighty Mackenzie, here nearly a mile wide, one has a magnificent view of the snow-capped Mackenzie mountains in the distance. Down-stream, just below the mouth of the Bear river, Bear Rock rears itself up 1,300 feet from the river's edge, fairly sheer on the river side, but wooded and less steep on the other slope.

The Governor-General was always keen for physical exercise, and a mountain climber of repute, with experience in many parts of the world, and no sooner did he set eyes on Bear Rock than he wanted to climb it.

The enforced delay at Norman fitted in perfectly, and a party of a dozen or so was soon made up, comprising His Excellency, Mr. A. S. Redfern, Secretary to the Governor-General, Mrs. Redfern, Lieutenant Rivers-Smith, R.N., A.D.C., Dr. George A. Macdonald of Edmonton, Inspector Martin, R.C.M.P., the writer, and a number of others. A local half-breed lad, Fred Gaudet, and a young Indian boy, came along in the capacity of guides. A motor boat ran us down the few miles to the foot of the mountain.

It was a perfect morning for a climb. Each took a package of sandwiches in his pocket. I took two thermos bottles of tea, which I left in the boat and a small flask of whisky which I carried with me.

The guides were late in arriving and the Governor-General and I led the procession, first *through a strip of woods to the foot of the mountain, and then up the shale and rocky slopes. I had been up some years previously, and this time, avoiding the face of the mountain, which I knew was difficult, worked around to the wooded part of the slope. His Excellency insisted on going up the steep face while Lieutenant Rivers-Smith went up somewhere in the middle. The others followed in various places.*

I told Lieutenant Rivers-Smith that I did not like to see His Excellency going up the place he had chosen, but the reply was he was an experienced mountaineer and we were not. Fred Gaudet and the Indian boy overtook us about this time and said the best way was the route I was taking. However Lieutenant Rivers-Smith and Dr. Macdonald swung in behind Lord Tweedsmuir, who was making good progress, and the two guides followed them.

I made the best pace I could to the top by the easy route. I was uneasy about those climbing up the face because of its difficulty and danger. I recalled my experience of several years before when I thought I could neither go up nor down. Two companions above me were climbing painfully slowly and with great difficulty, and sent pieces of rock whizzing past me every time they made a move. They had got so far that they felt they could not retrace their steps, but advised me to do so and this I eventually managed. They finally crawled over the top and were thankful to get there. No one of us on that occasion was a climber in any sense of the word.

On the present occasion I reached the top by the back way, and then made my way down the first easy slope of the front, towards the top of the face, intending to look over and see how the others were doing. I arrived just in time to find the Governor-General crawling flat on his stomach over the crest assisted by Fred Gaudet from below. He had made the ascent with great difficulty, and was very pleased with the result, saying it was one of the nastiest climbs he had ever made and would make the blood of experienced Alpiners curdle. The rock was so insecure and crumbling that one could not depend on any of it.

His Excellency sat down for a rest while we considered the positions of Lieutenant Rivers-Smith and Dr. Macdonald who were at a standstill approximately 100 feet from the top with the most perilous part ahead of them. They shouted that they could neither come

up nor go down. The footholds Lord Tweedsmuir had found had either been dislodged or would not bear their heavier weight. They declared a rope was necessary to help them up or down. This meant some of us descending the Rock, going back to the ship and bringing ropes to the top again.

By this time one of the Fathers from the Mission reached the top by the route I followed, and I arranged that he should go down with a note instructing the motor-boat to return to the ship at Fort Norman to get men and ropes. I also sent Fred Gaudet and the Indian boy, who had now come up behind the Governor-General, back by the easy route to the foot, telling them to climb up to Lieutenant Rivers-Smith and Dr. Macdonald from the bottom and help them to hold on or to climb down.

His Excellency and I then went on up to the crest where we found two others of the party who had come up the easy way. We all had a sandwich and a dram from the flask which I carried, His Excellency saying I put him to shame as he had forgotten to bring his. After a good rest I went down to the brow of the hill again, quite a lengthy clamber in itself, to see how the others were below. I could not see Lieutenant Rivers-Smith, but by shouting to the Doctor I ascertained that Fred Gaudet and the Indian boy had helped the Lieutenant down to a place of safety by steering his feet into footholds he could not find himself. I watched them while they did the same for the Doctor and then I returned to the summit with the good news. We four then began the descent by the back way and reached the foot without further incident.

We got back to the beach just as the boat arrived with the rope, and found Mr. and Mrs. Redfern much worried about Lord Tweedsmuir's safety. We soon relieved their anxiety and were laughing over the adventure. Everyone, including the Governor-General, had torn his trousers, and it was accounted a first-rate day.

After seven years as secretary to the Canadian Committee and personnel manager for the Fur Trade, Dick Bonnycastle left the Hudson's Bay Company in February 1945 to take a job as managing director of Advocate Printers.

"I want to run something," he said, "and there's no way I'm ever going to run the Hudson's Bay Company."

In 1952 a group of Winnipeg businessmen led by Bonnycastle bought Advocate and another printing company, Stovel Press, and created Stovel Advocate Press, with Bonnycastle as president. One of Stovel Advocate's assets was Harlequin Books, a publisher of romantic fiction founded while Bonnycastle was at Advocate and owned jointly with him. Over the next ten years Bonnycastle built Harlequin into Canada's largest book publisher, acquiring the balance of the business when Stovel Advocate was sold in 1960.

He became a leading member of Winnipeg's business community, sitting on several corporate and charitable boards and serving as president of the Winnipeg Chamber of Commerce and Canadian president of Ducks Unlimited. In 1960 he was named the first chairman of Winnipeg's new Metropolitan Corporation. In 1967 he became the first chancellor of the new University of Winnipeg.

During the last week of August 1968, Dick Bonnycastle made a sentimental trip down the Mackenzie River at the controls of his own Cessna aircraft, camping out on the shore as he had done exactly forty years before. He found few familiar sights, and fewer familiar faces, but the ghosts were legion: Bishop Isaac Stringer, who as Archbishop of Rupertsland had performed his wedding ceremony in 1931; Philip Godsell, the dismissed HBC inspector who became a successful author of popular books about the Arctic; district manager Louis Romanet, hero of Lowell Thomas' *Kabluk of the Eskimo*; Hugh Conn, who had retired to Londonderry in 1934 and died, a mild and mellow man, at the age of 83; pilot Wop May, who had spotted the "mad trapper" Albert Johnson from his airplane; Alex Eames, the RCMP inspector Bonnycastle liked so much, head of security in Halifax during the Second World War and later Assistant Commissioner of the RCMP; Patsy Klengenberg, drowned when his schooner caught fire near Cambridge Bay, and Dick's own right-hand man, faithful Paddy Gibson—famous as the discoverer of the skeletons of four of Franklin's crew—burned to death in an aircraft over Great Bear Lake in 1942.

A month later, on September 29, 1968, Dick Bonnycastle was stricken by a heart attack while landing the Cessna on a lake north of Winnipeg. He died as the floats touched the water.

"He was a clever man, a wise man,
a reasonable man. He was a lovely man."
—L.A. Learmonth

BIBLIOGRAPHY

De Poncins, Gilbert. *Kabloona*, New York: Reynal, 1941

Fleming, Archibald Lang. *Archibald the Arctic*. New York: Appleton-Century-Crofts, 1956

Gillingham, D.W. *Umiak!* London, England: Museum Press, 1955

Godsell, Jean. *I Was No Lady*. Toronto: Ryerson Press, 1959

Godsell, Philip H. *Arctic Trader*. New York: Putnam's, 1934

Hearne, Samuel. *Journey from Prince of Wales Fort on Hudson's Bay to the Northern Ocean*. Reprinted Edmonton: Hurtig Publishers, 1971

Kemp, Vernon. *Without Fear, Favour, or Affection*. Toronto: Longmans, 1958

MacInnes, Tom (ed.) *Klengenberg of the Arctic*. London, England: Jonathan Cape, 1932

Molson, K.M. *Pioneering in Canadian Air Transport*. Winnipeg: James Richardson & Sons, 1974